Advance praise for
The Angel Investor's Handbook—
How to Profit from Early-Stage Investing
by Gerald A. Benjamin and Joel Margulis

"This is the first book that captures the essence of what an angel investor is and the underlying motivations that make angel investors tick.... Not only is *The Angel Investor's Handbook* invaluable for individuals wishing to become angels, but it is a must for any entrepreneur. **I wish this book had appeared about six years ago when I became a full-time professional angel. It would have prevented me from investing in several disasters and saved me several hundred of thousands of dollars.**"

> JOHN ASON
> Board Member, NJ Entrepreneurs Network
> Charter angel, NY New Media Association

"A comprehensive primer for an angel investor. **Regardless of investor experience, *The Angel Investor's Handbook* provides invaluable strategies,** tools, and insights."

> TIMOTHY E. MAHONEY
> Chairman and CEO, vFinance.com, Inc.

"Every investor must read Benjamin's chapter on due diligence!"

> CAROL SANDS
> Managing Member, The Angels' Forum

"Over the years, I've made a variety of angel investments—learning from my mistakes the hard way. I certainly wish I'd had this book along the way. **This is a must-read before signing a check to a start-up.**"

> TOM TAULLI
> Author of *Investing in IPOs Version 2.0* and
> *Stock Options—Getting Your Share of the Action*

"Benjamin and Margulis have done an excellent job in outlining the potential pitfalls and rewards in angel investing. **I applaud the sensible conclusions made in this handbook. I would encourage any angel investor to read this book.**"

> NEIL C. GOULD
> Angel investor and senior partner
> Gould & Company

"Learning from your mistakes is an expensive way to learn angel investing! You need to know what you are doing before you get out the checkbook. *The Angel Investor's Handbook* offers clear and hands-on advice on private equity investing. Gerald Benjamin and Joel Margulis's thorough work **covers the gamut: from generating deal flow to negotiating the sale of your private equity investment. It is a must-read for investors and entrepreneurs alike.**"

> MIKE POGUE
> President and CEO
> Angel Capital Network, Inc.

"Having launched the Springboard Women's Venture Forum Series, I know that **private investors, especially women angels who are newer to this arena, need to educate themselves** about the equity markets. **This book is a valuable tool** for understanding and navigating current angel investment opportunities."

> KAY KOPLOVITZ
> Chair, National Women's Business Council
> CEO, Working Woman Network

"Every angel will want a copy of this invaluable handbook."

> JOHN MAY
> Angel investor; founder and managing partner
> New Vantage Group

THE
Angel
Investor's
HANDBOOK

Also available from
Bloomberg Press

Zero Gravity 2.0:
Launching Technology Companies
in a Tougher Venture Capital World
by Steve Harmon

Investing in IPOs Version 2.0:
Revised and Updated Edition
by Tom Taulli

Stock Options—Getting Your Share of the Action:
Negotiating Shares and Terms in
Incentive and Nonqualified Plans
by Tom Taulli

A complete list of our titles is available at
www.Bloomberg.com/Books

Attention Corporations

BLOOMBERG PRESS BOOKS are available at quantity discounts with bulk purchase for sales promotional use and for corporate education or other business uses. Special editions or book excerpts can also be created. For information, please call 609-279-4670 or write to: Special Sales Dept., Bloomberg Press, P.O. Box 888, Princeton, NJ 08542.

BLOOMBERG PROFESSIONAL LIBRARY

GERALD A. BENJAMIN
AND JOEL MARGULIS

THE Angel Investor's HANDBOOK

HOW TO PROFIT FROM EARLY-STAGE INVESTING

BLOOMBERG PRESS

PRINCETON

First edition published 2001
1 3 5 7 9 10 8 6 4 2

Library of Congress Cataloging-in-Publication Data

Benjamin, Gerald A.
      The angel investor's handbook: how to profit from early stage investing / Gerald A. Benjamin and Joel Margulis.
            p. cm. – (Bloomberg professional library)
      Includes bibliographical references and index.
      ISBN 1-57660-076-9 (alk. paper)
            1. Venture capital—United States—Handbooks, manuals, etc. 2. Angels (Investors)—United States—Handbooks, manuals, etc. 3. Investments—United States—Handbooks, manuals, etc. I. Margulis, Joel, 1937- II. Title. III. Series.

HG4963 .B463 2001
332'.0415'0973—dc21   2001025209

Edited by Rhona Ferling
Design by Don Morris Design

To the teachers in my life who nurtured
my curiosity and inspired a joy of learning:
Jack Benjamin, Thomas Carey, Ralph Castro,
Robert Crowe, Richard Davis, Martin Moore-Ede,
David Spears, and Anthony Tasca
—Gerald Benjamin

To Dinah, more than ever

To Manuel Levin,
Mike Kovac
and to Angela Harris and Dick Friedrich
—Joel Margulis

CONTENTS

Understanding and Managing Risk 55

Types of Angel Investment Strategies 69

Negotiating and Structuring the Deal 197

CHAPTER 9

Valuation of the Early-Stage Company 219

Acknowledgments

WE HARDLY KNOW HOW TO THANK four astute experts in their fields for their generous help in putting together some critical areas of this book: John Cadle of Lafayette, California; William D. Evers of Foley & Lardner, San Francisco; Laird Q. Cagan of Cagan Capital, Woodside, California; and John MacPherson of MacPherson and MacPherson, San Francisco. As always, we appreciate the wonderful work of the best of literary agents, John T. Willig of Literary Services, Inc., Barnegat, New Jersey. And certainly our debt to Rhona Ferling of Bloomberg Press, Princeton, New Jersey, is enormous. She has had a truly positive effect on the book. Finally, we also wish to thank Tracy Tait of Bloomberg Press for her fine editorial work.

PREFACE

THE ANGEL INVESTOR'S HANDBOOK

PUDD'NHEAD WILSON, Mark Twain's indomitable protagonist, once scribbled on his calendar: "The holy passion of Friendship is of so sweet and steady and loyal and enduring a nature that it will last through a whole lifetime, if not asked to lend money."

We agree. But what strikes us is how different the circumstances become when people are asked not to lend but to invest. Far from being irritated, put-upon, or out-

and-out offended, they seem eager—perhaps too eager. In fact, the *New York Times* financial reporter Diana B. Henriques recently lamented "just how drunk with dreams of instant wealth Americans are these days."

Regardless of recent corrections in the public stock markets, interest continued to run high among early-stage, private-equity investors. In the late 1990s, the U.S. deal-making community was swirling amid unprecedented dollar amounts of capital. Confirming new levels of venture capital activity, the National Venture Capital Association reported that venture capital companies nationwide had invested $48 billion in more than 3,000 ventures in 1999, more than three times the amount invested during the previous three years combined, and, astonishingly, six times the amount invested in 1995, just four years before. Moreover, global sums put an exclamation point on the U.S. figures: Credit Suisse First Boston's technology group estimates that $120 billion has been raised worldwide for venture investments.

Our concern—and a major motivation for writing this book—is that with this much money pinballing around, it might not be handled judiciously. For example, in a recent International Capital Resources study of more than 1,200 investors, we found that 35 percent would invest in early-stage deals without seeing a business plan. Given the enormous risk associated with the failure of companies, or their failure to achieve projected revenues (and thus investor returns), a cavalier attitude breeds unnecessary risk. It's an attitude that radiates directly from huge amounts of wealth and from the rush to participate in the pre-IPO market.

Anecdotal evidence from our interviews with investors confirms that some make decisions using only executive summaries to determine whether to invest. They are making their decisions very quickly, ignoring the level of due diligence that this type of high-risk investing requires. This ill-advised haste is another motivation for writing this book.

Further, investors feel that if they don't move quickly, they might miss out on the next Netscape. Focusing on the home run leaves them vulnerable to the high level of risk and potential failure. The purpose of this book is to help investors avoid such failure.

Angel investing in the pre-IPO market, as we will discuss, is risky enough without the added dimension of rapid judgment and lack of due diligence. Discipline becomes the key; in fact, only discipline can offset the feeling that alchemy is at work. Successful investing does not involve some magical formula, concocted by a mysterious alchemist transmuting baser elements into gold, someone whom only the superstars of investing are privy to.

On the contrary, an underlying process does exist, a formula that the winners follow, allowing them to manage the risk. Although superficially they appear to nonchalantly hit the home run, what you don't see is the amount of due diligence, investigation, negotiation, valuation, deal structuring, and exit planning—all the things that have gone into their investment and protected them from the downside risk. Other elements you don't see are the hedging strategies and years of monitoring and intervention that ensure the success of the investment and the company and, by extension, a payoff for the investment.

This long-term approach demands constant discipline and vigilance. But we are now seeing an influx of newcomers to the venture capital arena. We have dubbed them "less-experienced angels." Corporations are starting capital funds every week—quite a change from five years ago, when few corporations bothered to indulge. Corporate investors are now setting up their own venture funds for direct investment, an area in which they traditionally had no experience. The same is true of self-made millionaires: individual entrepreneurs, presidents of companies who have taken their companies public—many in their late twenties and early thirties—who have the vision and the ability to take that company forward but do not yet necessarily have the skills to engage in long-term angel investing.

Angel investing takes time. And today, time is compressed in ways Einstein never imagined. Proper analysis and due diligence suddenly seem luxuries rather than necessities. To become competitive, to "get in first"—especially now, when individuals are taking deals to different people simultaneously—becomes the priority, and judgment runs a distant second.

Today's new crop of investors seem prematurely willing to discuss structure and to do deals before they engage in all the pre-liminary steps. They're not willing to "sweat the small stuff," unaware that in angel investing, no step in this interwoven process can be considered "small." These misperceptions leave them vul-nerable to risk. Time pressures turn focus into foolhardiness, bold-ness into bravado.

We have also observed a huge jump in the amount of money pri-vate investors are presently investing. From a range five years ago of $25,000 to $50,000, the average investment is now $100,000 per investor, or from $10,000 to $2 million per investment. So we are witnessing a double whammy: Investments are now being made faster and are also much larger than before—circumstances com-pounding the possibility of error.

The deals flowing through International Capital Resources are an excellent example. Just one of ICR's twelve offices reviewed nearly 5,000 business plans in 1999. Of those, only 250 possessed the basic elements to justify close and costly examination of the ventures; only about 100 of those reached the level of financeabil-ity for investors. So although many ventures look for capital, only a very small percentage deserve capital investment. Moreover, rarely do unsolicited investments seem attractive. These ventures simply lack the quality that characterizes the ones that ICR, for example, actively seeks for our investors.

Today, more than 1 million U.S. households have the capability through discretionary net worth to invest directly in early-stage companies or ventures, according to our proprietary research. And since 90 percent of all millionaires in the United States are self-made, not inheritors of wealth, they know firsthand that profits can be derived from successful start-up ventures. Yet, despite all this, the United States sports a significant capital gap in the early-stage market, a gap that represents a deficiency in mechanisms facilitat-ing communication between investors who might be willing to invest in early-stage ventures and those hungry ventures seeking capital.

Now, this capital gap has been adequately defined in our two earlier books, *Finding Your Wings* and *Angel Financing*, and many analysts blame the gap on inexperienced entrepreneurs who don't know how to raise money—or so dislike the process that they are ineffective at it.

We, however, disagree. The larger problem is the lack of understanding of this unique form of investing among individuals who potentially could invest on this scale. The highly inefficient angel capital market lacks mechanisms for bringing investors and entrepreneurs together, and highly constrictive securities regulations inhibit communication between promising ventures and savvy investors. Currently, no academic courses are taught on raising private-equity capital among the many entrepreneurial finance programs in the country; few seminars and books address this issue. (See the Suggested Reading List in Appendix G.) With only a few recognized experts in the country, we hope to accomplish four purposes in writing this book:

1 To demonstrate through comprehensive proprietary research the unique nature of the angel market, the skills required both to succeed and to avoid pitfalls, and the unsuitability of other models for investing in this market.

2 To provide angel investors with a reality check on how their most successful peers are managing their portfolios and maintaining high returns while reducing the downside risk. This information applies as well to the many families, friends, or colleagues of entrepreneurs who step up to support them through investment, and will help them underline this process more completely. Perhaps more importantly, this information will introduce angel investing to households with the discretionary net worth to enter this market. These households may have some interest in diversifying their equity portfolios through investment directly into private companies or fund structures that include private companies.

3 To provide an overview and assess the model used in managing the angel investing process in a highly inefficient market. This is directed to uninitiated investors contemplating an angel capital investment prospect; often, these investors have been enticed by the high returns that some well-publicized angel investors achieve.

4 To show that it's not just about how to invest successfully; it's about the issues investors need to be attentive to in avoiding critical mistakes.

So we address this book to the nearly 1 million high-net-worth investor households in the United States and to their advisers, securities attorneys, investment bankers, executive directors of investor-entrepreneur matching services, chairpersons of venture forums, securities brokers and dealers, fund managers, registered investment advisers, small business investment company directors, financial intermediaries, "finders," CPAs, venture capital club officers, and various financial consultants. In addition, we address this book to the academic community—graduate students and their professors, who are looking for alternative information sources to educate their students about the realities of this very private capital market.

INTRODUCTION

It's all about information.

—CHARLES SCHWAB

ANGEL INVESTORS NUMBER in the hundreds of thousands and are proliferating at a rapid rate. These affluent individuals provide entrepreneurs and new ventures with needed venture capital, especially when more traditional sources of capital, such as investment banks and larger money management venture capital firms, are not willing to get involved.

Angel investors have been major engines of the booming New Economy. Angel investors generate new ideas, contribute innovative technologies to the marketplace, and inject much-needed vitality into complacent industries. New ventures occasionally grow into major corporations, such as Microsoft, Dell, America Online, Netscape, and others.

We cannot underestimate how astute many of these investors are. They are self-made millionaires. Over and above their homes and cars, they typically have a net worth of $1 million to $10 million, having been extremely successful investors in the public as well as the private market. In most cases, they bank on their own judgment to once again select a venture like the one that made them wealthy.

Venture capital itself has been defined as the search for significantly above average long-term investment returns accomplished primarily through equity ownership of or involvement in risky start-up or emerging companies, companies typically managed by experienced executives. Such companies tend to focus on rapidly growing markets and to provide innovative products, technology, or services.

Venture investment can range from riskier *seed, R&D,* and *start-up* funding at the earlier stages through *bridge, acquisition, merger,* and *turnaround* investments at later stages in the development of the venture. Obviously, ventures at the riskier end of the spectrum offer potentially higher returns if they meet their projections.

Typically, *seed* defines a company in the idea stage, when its processes are being organized. *R&D* is typical of the financing of product development for early-stage but more developed companies. *Start-up* designates a venture completing its product development and initial marketing. At the less-risky end, *bridge* designates a venture requiring short-term capital to reach stability. *Acquisition* and *merger* refer to a company's need for capital to finance an acquisition. *Turnaround* denotes a venture that needs capital to change from an unprofitable to a more profitable circumstance.

Private investors are investing about $40 billion a year into as many as 140,000 of these early-stage companies, approximately 4 percent of the 3.5 million start-ups in the United States. When you add in "cradle investment" by family, friends, and associates, as well as by the founders themselves, the total investment may exceed $60 billion a year.

These investors form a pool, together with the richest families in the United States, of about $8.2 trillion in net worth, derived from approximately 3.4 million households. However, when we correct for those who make only these aggressive types of investments, the numbers drop to approximately 1 million possible households, with 400,000 angels investing each year. Still, the numbers represent the major pool of capital available to fill the capital gap in the United States, and this pool is growing at a rate of around 14 to 20 percent per year. When compared, for example, to pension fund growth, currently at 8 percent per year, we see an immense source of capital for hungry young companies.

This wealth was created by the thriving economy and the bull market of the late 1990s, the M&A boom, and stock options enriching executives, but a number of other trends are contributing to this source of capital. Laws have been relaxed in a few states—California, for example, has a recent 25102(n) law, making it easier for small companies to raise start-up and growth financing from the use of public advertising. Many investors view this as an opportunity to "get in on the ground floor" of emerging businesses and to "hit it big" as small businesses grow into large ones. Insiders also say that angel investing has become fashionable, and that being an angel investor or venture capitalist is the newest status symbol.

Small-business investments are among the most risky that investors can make, particularly into *illiquid* private companies. With an understanding of the concepts in this book, an individual will be better informed to decide whether this type of investing is something he or she wants to get involved in. Greater numbers of private investors are getting in on the ground floor by investing in small and emerging companies. When successful, these enterprises enhance the economy by creating jobs, expanding the tax base, and increasing technological innovation and development, all of which contribute to the U.S.'s global competitiveness. These enterprises can also provide new investment opportunities and handsome returns; however, these must be balanced against the inherently risky nature of small-business investments. When considering a small-business investment, investors should proceed with caution and, above all, never invest more than they can afford to lose.

This is a key point, because most investors have an unrealistic view of venture capital and its potential returns. They expect the highly publicized returns of successful new ventures but either do not want to take the attendant risk or remain ignorant of or blind to that risk. Consequently, such investors go into the highly *inefficient* private marketplace looking for opportunities to invest venture capital but never finding an investment that meets their *unrealistic* expectations. One of the objectives of our book is to help investors to temper their unreasonable expectations and transform them into manageable private equity investment strategies.

The Private Investor

IN THIS BOOK, WE FOCUS ON the private individual who invests first rounds of funding in earlier-stage, higher-risk, private-equity transactions, a more active form of investing that creates the opportunity for the investor to influence the investment's outcome. This influence is one of the unique attributes of this type of investment, compared to the public market, where the individual has no impact whatsoever. Angel investors perform the important role of plugging the gap between what the entrepreneur can raise to get the firm off the ground and the level at which institutional investors and creditors will invest.

This private investor market is, in fact, a principal source of capital contributing to the financial stability of smaller companies, which make up a sizable source of jobs in the United States. Successful investors deliver insight directly into the process of high-risk, high-return investing. The private investor market includes high-net-worth private investors who choose to target companies operating at particular stages of development, usually those with which they are familiar. Fund managers and managers of venture capital funds also participate in this market. These professionals must screen thousands of deals a year to identify which companies the firm will invest in, thereby guiding their clients to more informed decisions. In this market, fund managers as well as investment advisers must identify investment opportunities, conduct due diligence, and make worthwhile referrals to their clients.

A major portion of the book provides private investors with lessons learned from seasoned angels about how to avoid the big mistakes and ubiquitous pitfalls inherent in this high-risk investing arena. Private investors can avoid the traps that have ensnared other investors. This helps prospective angels learn what kinds of investments other successful investors are making, their investment approaches and strategies, and some of the critical aspects that they should pay attention to—especially evaluation, valuation, due diligence, deal structuring and negotiation, and exit routes. Investors also will benefit from knowing the right questions to ask to bring winning investment opportunities bubbling to the surface.

With that in mind, we have tried to solidify the discussion of the direct equity venture process and explore in great detail the essential components of angel investing.

As you can see from the suggested reading list and bibliography, very little information exists on this esoteric, idiosyncratic arena. Private investors are just that—*private.*

Today, private investors, or angels (a term that in more recent history described the well-heeled backers of Broadway shows), are typically wealthy individuals and families willing to invest in high-risk deals offered by entrepreneurs whom they admire and with whom they wish to be associated. One of the things we'll be discussing in this book is the wide range of motivations that inspire people to try this type of investing, over and above return on investment. It's not just about the money, though money is important. Angels are also looking for qualitative returns on their investments.

In essence, angel investors are private, informal venture capitalists. They typically possess the discretionary income needed for such risky ventures. In most cases, they set aside a portion of their equity portfolio capital for private investments. This discretionary net worth sets the angel investor apart. An affluent individual may have an annual income of $100,000 but annual expenses totaling $150,000. Large incomes, we know, can carry even larger debts. For this reason, we distinguish between those who are affluent and those who are wealthy.

Angel investors basically have a healthy appetite for self-arranged private deals. Such direct investment serves to maintain their high confidence and demonstrates their continuing ability to succeed and make money. These investors have amassed wealth precisely because they know how to invest. Further, we can reasonably assume that they will remain active investors. Typical angel investors include retired officers of corporations and private companies, windfall transfers, casualties of corporate downsizing, and the thirty-something and forty-something chief executive officers of small high-technology companies. Angels usually have saved money, have made money in the public market, are financially astute, and possess engaging and challenging intellects. They have the desire, energy, and time to diversify their portfolios with more active investments.

In addition, these investors are concerned with after-tax returns and returns after expenses, such as the costs of due diligence, intermediaries, and investment banking firms. Angel investors represent patient money, remaining comfortable with long-term buy/hold strategies, money that often won't be available in the near term. As one investor said, you must be able to lose the investment or lose access to it for an extended period of time. The returns can be phenomenal: $50,000 invested in Qualcomm a couple of years ago would have an estimated value today of $1.1 million. A $10,000 first-round investment in eBay would be valued today at $4 million. A $100,000 investment in Siena Corporation a few years ago is now worth $260 million.

But more realistic return possibilities are demonstrated by the case of the New York pediatrician who invested $50,000 in a medical instruments start-up: five years later, when the company went public, the doctor cashed out for $2 million. Likewise the investment of six New Jersey physicians, who with several other investors each put up $13,000 to start a facility to treat kidney stones. In ten years, the doctors earned seven times their outlay, and the venture still provides returns for those investors.

Angel investors also understand that by the time someone is reading about an IPO in the newspaper, the money has already been made, regardless of whether it is still possible to invest. The only way to position themselves, they realize, is to get involved at the very earliest stages. They know that if the investment is structured properly, they can receive excellent returns on their transaction.

Another aspect that helps to put this marketplace in perspective is that fewer than 1 percent of the companies in the United States are publicly traded. In the great majority of companies, then, lies great opportunity. Many of these operating companies are or will be profitable, so investors have a chance to find the gems. Of course, going public becomes an added benefit. Alternatively a merger, a buyout, or other exit route will provide returns to investors. We will describe other exit routes later in the book.

The primary objective of venture capital or angel investing is an active investment approach, and the successful active investor requires a complex set of technical and interpersonal skills. Venture capital investing is popularly referred to as the "business of building businesses." Implicit in this definition is the commitment to contribute more than money to the company. Venture investing involves building and financing successful self-sustaining companies, often from scratch. Many investors believe that a successful company by definition will become a rewarding investment. This form of investing also requires a disciplined, focused, long-term orientation plus a high tolerance for risk and its associated illiquidity; patience; and, of course, good luck.

From a historical perspective, venture capital is far from being new. Consider Queen Isabella's financing of Columbus's voyage to the New World, the financing of the Saugus Ironworks in 1645, or a Scottish law firm's pooling of local industrialists' surplus pounds in the late nineteenth century. Modern institutional venture capital began with American research and development in 1946 and its later investment into DEC (Digital Equipment Corporation). It continued with small-business investment companies starting in the late '50s, the individual and family funds of the '60s and '70s, the private pension funds of the '80s, the public venture capital funds of the '90s, and now the angel market in 2000 and beyond. Venture capital and private high-risk, early-stage investing have had a distinguished history and will be with us for years to come.

AN
OVERVIEW
OF THE
ANGEL CAPITAL MARKET

Defining Angel Capital and Pre-IPO Investments

WHAT IS ANGEL CAPITAL? What is pre-IPO capital? Based

on research by International Capital Resources and

according to PricewaterhouseCoopers; VentureOne, the

San Francisco research firm; and others, *angel capital* or

venture capital is money provided by private investors,

professional investors, and money managers to young,

rapidly growing companies that have the potential to develop into significant contributors to our economy. The money investors invest usually takes the form of equity investment. Venture capital is the main source of financing for start-up companies. It is supplemented by cash from the companies' founders, families, friends, colleagues, business associates, employees, suppliers, and distributors, plus bootstrapping from the earnings of companies.

These investors, whom we will discuss in detail in later chapters, focus on new and fast-growing companies because of the potential capital appreciation these companies embody. Typically, investor transactions with these companies involve equity securities. In addition, these investors add value beyond the money they invest by helping to develop products and/or services and by providing advice. In addition, as expected, they take significant risks with their capital early on, which affects the way they approach valuation, deal structuring, and expectations of returns.

Last, most of these investors are experienced enough to be willing to endure long-term horizons, long-term commitments (inherent in these investments), and long-term loss of access to their capital. This type of investment can be passive or active. Active investors may serve on a board of directors or advisory board, or act as a consultant or a monitor. Regardless of their various inclinations or roles, these investors will become actively involved in working with management as the company develops. It is this experience and knowledge that distinguishes these investors from, for example, passive investors in the public market.

In contrast to institutional investors—who are essentially institutional venture capitalists managing money supplied by pension funds, insurance companies, and endowments—angel investors are private-equity direct investors, *pre-IPO* investors who are investing their own money.

Trends Increasing Private Equity Investment

A NUMBER OF TRENDS HAVE INCREASED angel financing or pre-IPO investing. These include more ventures, more capital, and improved survival rates for start-ups. According to the Small Business Administration, Wells Fargo, and the NFIB Educational Foundation on Business Start-ups, in 1997 individuals started up more than 3.5 million new businesses. In addition, 900,000 owners have purchased businesses, and 68,000 others have inherited or otherwise acquired businesses. To place this astounding growth in perspective, the total of all small businesses in 1994 was just 5 million companies. According to the SBA's Office of Advocacy, "Under a broad definition—a definition that includes not only persons running a business full-time but also those doing so part-time—about 16 million Americans are engaged in some entrepreneurial activity. At least 16 million entrepreneurs represent about 13 percent of all non-agriculture workers." We see here a major trend in our society towards entrepreneurship.

Along with this growth, potential dream makers are growing in numbers and shifting their investment orientation. In 1990, United States consumer assets totaled $8.2 trillion, with baby boomers holding 20 percent. For the beginning of the new century, the United States Bureau of the Census projected that United States consumer assets would increase to $9.8 trillion; of that amount, baby boomers would hold 39 percent. By then baby boomers would be in their fifties, the typical age for private venture investing.

According to the Federal Reserve's survey of consumer finances in 1992, households with a net worth of $1 million to $10 million placed 66 percent of their discretionary net worth into equity investments and 31 percent into savings deposits. The Federal Reserve projected then that this amount would increase to 83 percent in equity investments by 2001. Clearly, we have no shortage of risk capital.

Public stock market fluctuations aside, the fundamentals underlying the U.S. economy remain sound. Wealth has been increasing in real dollars. Between 1983 and 1989, the assets of the richest 500 families rose from $2.5 trillion to $5 trillion. Meanwhile, corporations are downsizing, releasing experienced executives with substantial severance and cash-outs.

From 1995 to 1999 the United States economy grew at the rate of 3 percent per year. Although tempered by corrections in 2000 to 2001, the Internet economy did grow at the astounding rate of 175 percent per year! Today, 7.1 million households have a net worth of at least $1 million, double the number in 1994, according to Spectrum Research Group. While not everyone's income has risen equally—for example, those of African-Americans and unmarried female householders have not risen as much—many other United States households are approaching median incomes of $50,000 a year in constant 1997 dollars and are consistently earning more money, based on long-term trend analyses by the Census Bureau as reported in the 1999 Statistical Abstract of the United States.

Despite recent corrections to their portfolios, Americans also benefited economically from investments in a bull stock market. Total market capitalization of publicly traded Internet companies alone rose from $214 billion in 1998 to $1 trillion in 1999. According to research reported by Robertson Stephens Private Capital Market Group, "1999 was another strong year for the United States equity markets." The report confirmed that the major indices—Dow Jones (up 25.2 percent), Standard and Poor's 500 (up 19 percent), Nasdaq (up 85.6 percent), and Russell 200 and MidCap 400 (each up more than 13 percent)—closed at "all-time highs." Charles Schwab reported $10 billion invested into Schwab-offered mutual funds in the first quarter of 2000. During 1999, less than $10 billion had been invested into mutual funds during the entire year!

According to Dun & Bradstreet's longitudinal study of all small businesses started in 1985, by 1994 74 percent had survived and were still operating. In addition, many companies in the 25 to 26 percent group that were considered failures had, in fact, not declared bankruptcy but instead were voluntarily terminated by the owners because they had failed to meet projected returns—either income for the entrepreneurs or potential returns for the investors. They did not fail to *survive;* they failed *only* in achieving certain objectives—a big difference. In fact, many of those businesses still may have been protected by providing investors return *of* their investment or a small return *on* investment. So the failure rate for small start-up businesses is very low compared with rates in the '70s and the '80s.

Still, in spite of the ample numbers of promising ventures, available equity capital, and higher probability of a venture's success, we have a problem in the United States—a capital gap, and with it, a corresponding investment opportunity. According to Arthur Andersen's 1995 national study, 36 percent of small, fast-growing companies reported an inability to meet their capital needs. Using this data and information on the size of private transactions, Arthur Andersen calculated approximately a $61 billion nationwide capital shortfall. And if we add in slow-growth companies, the shortfall could increase to $100 billion. This shortfall, then, represents the investment opportunity in the pre-IPO market that we address in this book.

How Angel Capital Has Provided an Infrastructure for Today's Economy

WE CAN NO LONGER IGNORE the significance of the angel investor contribution. Investors understand that these new companies are the cornerstone of our economic success. They created 20 million new jobs—67 percent of the total—between 1979 and 1993, and 12 million more by 1997. Start-up businesses specifically create 27 percent of new jobs, according to Professor David Birch at MIT. Private investors finance many of these fast-growing companies, up to at least 30 percent above contributions from family and friends, especially during the all important first three years of development and growth.

Moreover, small companies represent 47 percent of all sales, 51 percent of the private gross domestic product, 52 percent of business net worth, and 99 percent of all companies in the United States. Small business employers increased to more than 5 million in 1994, a 6.5 percent increase over 1988. By 1996, new businesses established another record level. According to the Bureau of Labor Statistics, small firms are expected to contribute about 60 percent of the new jobs to be created between 1994 and the year 2005. In addition, 55 percent of all technological innovation comes through these small companies—twice the number of innovations per employee as that of larger corporations, an aspect that keeps the United States globally competitive. According to the National Venture Capital Association, start-up ventures that receive angel and VC money are investing three times as much as *Fortune* 500 companies in the same industries in annual R&D efforts.

Further, companies financed by private investors and institutional investors contribute to economic strength because these companies increase their sales much faster than more-established *Fortune* 500 companies. In studies by PricewaterhouseCoopers and others, the difference is significant, with early-stage companies that receive private and venture capital increasing their sales by as much as 66 percent per year, compared with growth rates of *Fortune* 500 companies in the same industries of only about 5 percent per year.

In addition, pre-IPO financing can have a significant impact on productivity, whether that financing came from angel investors, institutional investors, or a combination of the two at different stages of development. Using the productivity measure of sales per employee, studies by VentureOne suggest that companies backed by venture capital investment are growing twice as quickly as their *Fortune* 500 counterparts.

Inefficiencies in the Market for Early-Stage Company Equity

PART OF THE PROBLEM that angel investors face is the absence of an efficient private venture investor market, a problem that leads to underinvestment. This, in turn, contributes to the capital gap we mentioned earlier. The problem persists because no organized capital provider system targets these entrepreneurial, earlier-stage companies, whether seed, R&D, start-up, or expansion companies that fall within the criteria of a pre-IPO company. Information about sources of funds or venture opportunities is simply not readily available.

Another part of the problem is that no secondary market currently provides small-company investors with an exit route. Further, restrictive securities regulations limit the flow of information. Many securities industry professionals believe these companies are not worthy of investment because no standard, consistent deal structures exist. These structures, because of their unique nature, can raise transaction costs and, through legal vulnerability, create high liability costs.

What creates the inefficiency in the pre-IPO marketplace for early-stage company equity? First, we have no analysts in the pre-IPO market, except for a few periodicals like the *Private Equity Review*. Second, we have no significant analysts at work on the private equity market specifically for direct private investors. This scarcity adds to the severely limited market information. It is limited at both the micro level, regarding individual companies, and the macro level. Therefore, individual investors are precluded from performing comparative analyses on their deals against baselines of compiled statistics on groups of other deals.

So investors are left with no information readily available on valuations, deal structures, return rates, and liquidity options or alternatives. Without those baselines, investors face the difficult task of evaluating the risk/reward potential of the deal. Their analysis ends up depending a lot on their subjective natures and personal experiences. Both investors and entrepreneurs face inconvenience. The investor faces the additional challenge of finding promising investments.

Extensive studies by International Capital Resources suggest that more than 50 percent of private investors' deal flow comes through family, friends, associates, and colleagues—an extremely limited source of deal flow. Without looking at a large number of plans every year, investors are far less likely to find those few golden nuggets that have potential and that will meet all of the investors' criteria. Obviously, as noted in our earlier two books, the search is also extremely inconvenient for the seller, the entrepreneur, because angel investors prize their privacy. For good reason, they make themselves extremely difficult to find. The entrepreneur has a difficult time indeed locating investors with the discretionary net worth, the inclination to subject themselves to the high levels of risk associated with this type of investment, and the skills necessary to evaluate and add value to these ventures.

In addition, professional assistance and advisory counsel is extremely expensive. All of these factors can make assistance costs add up: legal counsel, accounting and financial analysis support, investment banking counsel on the structuring of transactions or analysis of valuation, technical support in evaluating prototypes of various technologies, management consulting support to evaluate business plans, and perhaps private investigator support to do background checks on entrepreneurs.

And there is no real-time liquidity in these transactions. ICR's research suggests an average hold time before liquidity of eight years. Clearly this is "patient" money, but there's a significant period of time during which investors lose access to their capital without any returns coming in through dividends, interest payments, and so on. It is difficult to evaluate these companies. They are all "blue sky"; they have no financial history, and often they won't be generating revenues or profit for many years, a common characteristic of e-commerce firms. So when the investor calculates the value of these companies, he faces a difficult task. Searching for, evaluating, and completing these transactions takes considerable time and energy. These elements alone form a barrier for many investors—all because of the inefficiency in this market and the lack of standardization in its transactions.

Government Attempts to Facilitate Pre-IPO Investments

DESPITE FEDERAL PROGRAMS that address the capital gap, none has succeeded in bolstering or providing capital for this hungry segment of our economy. We remain merrily astonished that angel capital investing occurs despite these obstacles:

◆ inadequate capital gains tax incentives, particularly when compared to incentives in other countries;

◆ a scarcity of legitimate, well-organized investment networks or mechanisms to facilitate bringing investors and ventures together;

◆ less bank lending, the result of stricter enforcement of banking regulations after the savings and loan debacle of the late '80s;

◆ educational institutions that have failed to provide investors and entrepreneurs with a full understanding of the unique pre-IPO investment transaction and of what is involved in planning for the investment process; and

◆ a climate of legal and regulatory constraints strangling the free flow of information between ethical, well-intentioned entrepreneurs and sophisticated, self-made, affluent private investors and institutional investors. These investors possess experience, analytical skills, and understanding of the risks, and they are clearly individuals capable of making their own informed investment decisions.

If we look at SBA programs, for example, we see that in addition to good character and management skills, applicants must demonstrate a history of earnings and a cash flow record. Moreover, applicants without collateral and generally without a one-third capital contribution to the total cost of the project are not likely to receive the loan. Further complications arise with SBA programs when small companies face state and federal requirements. These circumstances create a situation in which the government program is touted as a resource but has become, in reality, capitalism without the capital.

Although the government increased appropriations for SBA loans with the Small Business Guaranteed Credit Enhancement Act of 1993, permitted a capital gains exclusion for certain small-business stock investments with the Omnibus Budget Reconciliation Act of 1993, and eased the burden of financial institutions lending to small business with a capital availability program, it has not increased the availability of capital, which continues to shrink. Compounding this shrinkage are the financial institutions and managers who have increased their investments into government securities.

That said, the government has made an effort in its tax incentive bill, which contains provisions that can stimulate investment growth. Topping the marginal income tax increase at 39.6 percent, the government retained the ceiling on the capital gains rate on all asset classes at 28 percent. And while the tax benefits traditionally associated with R&D partnerships have largely been removed, debt vehicles for structuring transactions remain. If a loss occurs, the investor may still write off a substantial percentage of any loss.

Also, when the investor leaves money in an investment in risky start-ups for longer than five years, provisions in the Omnibus Budget Reconciliation Act of 1993 capped capital gains. The act drops the tax on capital gains from 28 percent to 14 percent when stock is liquidated in small-business stock holdings or when the company is sold. This decrease applies only to stock issued after August 10, 1993, the date of the bill's enactment. We don't dispute that here and there the government has been responsive to the problems of capital availability, but clearly, the market drives public policy; public policy does not drive the market.

For example, Ace-Net (the Access to Capital Electronic Network) is a government program that raised expectations but has failed. Ace-Net was the government's attempt to link entrepreneurs with angel investors, an initiative born out of suggestions from delegates to the 1995 White House Conference on Small Business. Ace-Net had hoped to attract entrepreneurs seeking $250,000 to $5 million in equity capital. It also had hoped to net accredited investors—who must certify that they satisfy the SEC's definition of accreditation: a net worth of more than $1 million or an annual income of more than $200,000.

Daunting registration requirements and related expenses slowed Ace-Net's start, failing to attract some of the more appealing ventures while burdening potential investors with requirements such as no first-cut review of deals, coupled with their having to cite their preferred industry, deal size, stage of development, and the like. And, of course, investor criteria must match exactly what the deal purports to offer. Ace-Net is not designed to support a custom search or tailored direct referral, eliminating those investors who have expressed interest in a certain type of investment and might welcome information on a deal that interests them.

In addition, investors have expressed confidentiality and privacy concerns with Ace-Net, concerns that seem to be inhibiting its growth. Problematic, too, is Ace-Net's inability to screen entrepreneurs beyond the minimal listing information and the listing fee. In a word, Ace-Net has failed to meet investor expectations. Thus, the Internet remains the most efficient means for researching companies once they've been identified, though it has yet to prove itself as a viable mechanism for finding attractive investment opportunities.

The Roles of Traditional Venture Capital and Angel Investors in the Early-Stage Capital Market

FOUNDERS, THEIR FAMILIES, and their friends continue to initially finance the majority of all small businesses, start-ups, and expansion ventures in North America. Following this initial funding, active business angel investors in the United States provide early-stage companies with 90 percent of all rounds of financing under $1 million and 80 percent of all dollars. Meanwhile, institutional venture capital resources provide later-stage financing in growing companies that were originally financed by the founders, family, friends, and angel investors.

PricewaterhouseCoopers in its *Money Tree Report* estimates that in 1998 institutional venture capital invested $14.3 billion into 1,824 deals. The majority of this capital was placed in California, which received $5.7 billion. Massachusetts received $1.6 billion; Texas, $816 million; New York, $562 million; and Colorado, $489 million. The primary industries receiving distributions, according to PricewaterhouseCoopers, were software, receiving $4.5 billion in approximately 950 deals; communications, receiving $3.9 billion for 587 deals; health care services, $1.1 billion in about 256 deals; medical devices, $686 million, distributed among 173 deals; biotechnology, $638 million in 140 deals; computers, $436 million for 87 deals; and electronics, $306 million in 96 deals.

Meanwhile, investment in the Internet fueled investment growth. In 1998, investment into Internet software and database companies—e-commerce ventures, companies providing infrastructure, ISPs, content and publisher providers, and business services—totaled about $5 billion. Again, start-up valuations reached a new high as venture capital firms and institutional investors competed for the same deals, with a median pre-money valuation in 1998 of $17 million. Median valuation for seed-stage companies hovered around $2.5 million, and valuations for first-round transactions came in at $6 million to $7 million. The median investment among institutional venture capitalists was approximately $5 million.

VentureOne reports that in 1999, 607 venture capital firms invested $37.4 billion in 3,083 companies, a figure that exceeded the total venture capital industry investment of the previous three years combined. Reports vary on the level of VC investment. For example, Venture Economics reports that in 1999, people invested $50 billion into 2,969 companies. However, both researchers agree that VCs are funding less than 0.5 percent of the deal flow they receive.

VC industry watchers generally agree that the smallest start-ups—early-stage firms—receive just $84.5 million, or 0.5 percent, of the total VC investment level per quarter. These early-stage investments average about $3 million; 90 percent of start-up, R&D, and first-round companies do not need this much, according to VentureOne.

Studies by International Capital Resources belie a popular belief in a shortage of pre-IPO risk capital from private investors. Compared with the institutional VCs, investors in the United States today who have the demographic profile and the financial resources (the discretionary net worth) to shrink the capital gap number approximately 2 million. Interestingly enough, and for reasons we will discuss, only about 400,000 of this group are active.

Studies by William Wetzel, Jr. and Jeffrey Sohl, International Capital Resources, Gaston, and others put the annual investment by this group at approximately $40 billion a year. We estimate that at any given time, approximately 700,000 companies are actively trying to raise capital. When looking specifically at deals completed at the seed, R&D, and start-up stages, we see sophisticated or accredited investors investing approximately $5 billion directly into such ventures. Of these deals, at least 54,000 are extremely early stage transactions. Ninety percent of the transactions are less than $1 million, with a mean investment of $100,000 per investor.

The mean investment share, or the amount of equity taken by these investors for the first round beyond family and friends, is typically about 25 percent. A study recently concluded by ICR of 1,200 investors in its proprietary database suggests that 20 percent are investing less than $25,000 per deal; 40 percent are investing between $25,000 and $99,999; 25 percent are investing $100,000 to $250,000; and 15 percent are investing more than $250,000. Reported investments ranged from $10,000 to $2 million per deal. These investments and amounts are per deal and per transaction.

To better understand the private-investor market, it is important to see it not as a monolithic capital market but as a number of affluent market segments, each of which represents a unique asset-harvesting opportunity. These affluent market segments are the product of an inheritance boom and unprecedented assets of a mature market. Together, they create the most tantalizing accumulation of wealth in fifty years.

In examining the various groups that constitute these different market segments, beginning with those with a net worth of less than $500,000, we find at the low end the young affluent and retired affluent. As net worth increases to $1 million to $1.5 million, the career-minded and business owners begin entering the group. At the $2 million to $4 million level of net worth are senior corporate executives and people who are wealthy through inheritance. And above the $5 million segment, we observe more active wealth, in both their business activities and investment activities.

In reviewing information from Department of Treasury surveys, we discover approximately 1.7 million United States households with a net worth of $500,000, or approximately 1.9 percent of all households. In addition, we find about .01 percent of U.S. households—approximately 9,330—with a net worth of more than $10 million. These two groups illustrate the extremes of the distribution—those with a net worth of less than $500,000 (excluding house and car) and those with a net worth of more than $10 million—groups not represented by those who engage in private equity pre-IPO direct investing. Those in the low-end group lack resources; those in the high-end group typically have a family office that handles fiduciary responsibility for the family and that obviates investments into these very high risk, illiquid transactions, unless the investor herself has retained control of a portion of her capital for higher-risk personal investing.

Two core groups of investors fill the angel ranks. Investors in the first core group active in the pre-IPO market sport a net worth of $1 million to $5 million, representing about 672,000 households, or approximately 0.7 percent of the total number of U.S. households. The second group is made up of those with a net worth of between $5 million and $10 million, or about 158,000 households. This group represents about 0.17 percent of U.S. households. If we look at these two core groups, at the structure of the high-net-worth private investor market in the United States, the most active group consists of those with a net worth of between $1 million and $10 million, approximately 830,000 households.

Obviously, many potential angels don't have the time, the discretionary net worth, the experience or interest in making these investments, the intestinal fortitude to take the risks, or the patience to get involved when access to the capital is, as we have pointed out, lost for an extended period. When we correct for these drawbacks, we understand why only 400,000 or so currently indulge in this market.

If we correlate the level of investment risk with the stage of entrepreneurial firm development, we discover that when the investment risk is very high and the development stage is early—as it is in seed and R&D—the founder, friends, and family are typically financing the deal. But as the deal moves closer to the start-up stage—reducing the risk associated with the pre-seed, seed, and R&D stages—business angels begin entering the picture, usually when the transactions begin to exceed approximately $450,000. However, these investors will still become involved in smaller transactions of, say, $250,000 when they have an affinity for, and an understanding and appreciation of, the technology.

A number of attributes of angel investors make them significantly different from money managers or traditional venture capitalists who might be investing money from institutions and pension funds. Angel investors are deeply concerned about a firm's success. They are, after all, investing their own money. These investors typically look for a smaller equity share, and they typically do not make more than four investments per year. They have extensive small business experience, and over 80 percent of them—based on ICR's proprietary research—have started a company of their own. They're characteristically part-time investors, genuinely involved in other companies, other investments, their own companies, or charitable and fund-raising work for causes that interest them.

They are entrepreneurial managers in that they are willing to take active roles and bring their expertise to bear, either by sitting as a director or—if they can't take the legal exposure of being a director or officer—by acting as an adviser or a consultant if the fledgling company requires a periodic review or needs monitoring or an intervention. These are value-adding, active investors, and they focus on the entrepreneur. Many times we have heard these investors say that they are most concerned with management— with the quality, experience, background, credibility, and character of that group.

For many business angels, location is important. ICR's research finds that 65 percent of angel investors like to invest in deals reasonably close to where they live, within 300 to 500 miles. This makes a visit to the firm a manageable trip, allowing for a feeling of security that comes from being closer to the deal and making it easier to monitor. But what that statistic overshadows is the 35 percent who do *not* have that need. These coinvestors will participate as long as a lead investor lives geographically close to the enterprise.

Although institutional investors will invest less often in industries they don't understand or don't have experience in, angel investors are more involved in industries they don't have direct experience in, 59 percent of the time investing in industries in which they have no direct experience. For example, we were startled to discover through our research the amount of investment that is made in e-commerce and various aspects of the Internet without a concomitant understanding and appreciation of the technology.

The return *of* investment and return *on* investment objective is usually a minimum of 30 percent. In addition, the due diligence cycle for angel investors and the time they take to make a decision, then finally go through the structuring and negotiation cycle, can be very quick. We have seen it completed in as little as three weeks.

The Pre-IPO Investment Opportunity Defined

A NUMBER OF EXPERTS and researchers in the private equity market claim that there are more than 300,000 operating private companies in the United States growing at annual double-digit rates, companies they contend are promising pre-IPO candidates. It is true that this is a substantially greater number than the 30,000 publicly traded companies, which represent less than 1 percent of the 22 million total operating companies in the United States.

But even if we narrowed down the 300,000 companies to those growing at faster rates, these companies are not the primary candidates for angel investment. In the more developed ventures, the size of the transactions is far beyond the scope of a small group of angel coinvestors, putting control of the financial round beyond their reach and further increasing risks. Multiple seed, R&D, start-up, and first-round investments in a diversified technology portfolio are a much better basis for achieving the kind of returns angels expect.

Another mistake less experienced angels make is overemphasizing the IPO as the primary exit route. For the informal market, comprised of high-net-worth individuals or angel investors, the IPO is the *exception,* not the rule. At the same time, less experienced angels continue to pour into the private equity arena. What was once the province of the ultrarich and superannuated CEO is now being expanded by people under thirty, who want to make early-stage investments their vocation rather than their avocation.

Offroad Capital's research demonstrates that traditional funding sources, such as investment banks, serve only about 2 percent of all small-business financing needs. In 1999 investment banks raised a total of $2.1 trillion, mainly for more developed companies, not earlier stage, undeveloped companies.

According to Thomson Financial Securities Data, there were 546 IPOs in 1999, raising a total of $69 billion. An equivalent amount of capital, almost $60 billion, comes from informal networks of angel investors, friends, family, and associates, according to recent studies by the Kauffman Center for Entrepreneurial Leadership Global Entrepreneurship Monitor.

While liquidity via IPO for venture-backed companies dried up, declining from 260 deals raising $11.8 billion in 1996 to just 77 deals in 1998 raising only $4.2 billion, the growing percentage of VC-backed IPOs of Internet companies helped to temper the decline in 1999. When you consider the small number of deals achieving liquidity through an IPO, compared with the number of angel- and VC-backed investee companies looking for liquidity for early-stage investors, this fixation on the IPO as the primary exit route for angels becomes glaringly ludicrous. Of the 3.5 million companies started up in 1999, approximately 140,000 are totally funded by nonrelated angel investors.

To some extent, a percentage of these same financing rounds were also beneficiaries of "cradle equity" from the entrepreneurs themselves and from family, friends, and associates. According to Jeffrey Sohl of the Center for Venture Research at the University of New Hampshire, 400,000 angels are investing $40 billion a year, with each investment ranging from $50,000 to $2 million. More than 500 IPOs are not cashing out the multitude of early-stage investors, while at the same time, the estimate is that as many as 2 million private companies have outside investors (10 percent of private firms).

How Angel Investors Add Value Beyond Capital

ANGEL CAPITAL IS NOT ONLY about money; it has more to do with the resources angels bring to fledgling ventures. Many investors are investing for more than just their return *of* investment and return *on* investment. Angel investors wish to be high-worth investors, not just high-net-worth investors. In many cases, they not only supply much-needed development capital but also contribute the business skills necessary to a start-up venture.

The monitoring and advisory counsel that investors provide to companies they invest in is a crucial element in early- and expansion-stage companies. Appreciating that these pre-IPO investors provide more than money to new firms is essential to understanding their importance in our economy. Many times, whether it's adding a skilled board member or an advisory board member at important points in a firm's development—someone who can provide informal advice or become more involved operationally if the firm has problems or changes in management—the private investors can help entrepreneurs through the trying tasks of monitoring, evaluation, and intervention.

Private investors offer their help through a number of specific mechanisms. They usually have a multidisciplinary external contact network, which may include functional resources to assist with various tasks if these skills are lacking in the management team. Or the investor may have extensive experience in the industry itself. In addition, they can provide technical and marketing guidance and other types of functional advice personally, depending upon their individual experience and background.

Commonly, in a director's role, investors contribute their judgments and suggestions, assisting in strategy development, financing decisions, and recruiting issues—with feedback on continuing employment or additions to the management team. These investors also provide contacts with potential customers, vendors, suppliers, distributors, and financing institutions they have worked with over the years. An investor who has made an investment and has a stake in the venture may well get involved in assisting the company with the equity offering. This may include contacting other investors in their own personal network or working with investors that the company identifies; assisting in the financing process or in joint ventures; or, at liquidity, advising on an acquisition or merger.

Usually, through their board involvement in other investments, these investors bring alliances with larger corporate partners. Or, through their connections in specific industries or in technological areas, they can arrange and facilitate technology exchanges. Having top-notch directors and investors can improve the process of recruiting top-notch management. The investors understand the industries they invest in and appreciate the market opportunities new companies can take advantage of.

Angels have an extensive network of contacts with which to evaluate markets for the company. We cannot underestimate the value of having the sounding board of an experienced investor to speak to about alternative strategies. These investors are skilled and understand different types of incentive and compensation systems, and if team-oriented, they can help the entrepreneurs design compensation packages that will attract talent. Finally, the investors' reputation and background can help recruit new customers for the company and provide a strong cultural or emotional foundation of patience, fortitude, and calmness in the face of the emotional roller-coaster ride inherent in many early-stage entrepreneurial ventures.

It is worth noting that investors add this value while incurring costs to themselves. It is only fair to recognize that high-risk, time-consuming angel investments place stress on the angels, their families, and their relationships. And as we have noted, add to that the loss of access to their money and the potential loss of the money itself. The process of adding value takes huge chunks of time. And even when a venture is ultimately successful, the stress and anxiety suffered over the average eight-year hold time can leave an indelible imprint, creating pressure and possibly resentment within the investor's family and circle of coinvestor friends.

Introduction to the Pre-IPO Investment Process

THE FOLLOWING CHAPTER offers a brief introduction to the pre-IPO investment process. Pre-IPO investing is not easy. It requires a high tolerance for risk and the unexpected, as well as an ability to tolerate lack of diversification and liquidity, higher mortality rates, and significant dissatisfaction with existing channels of communication with businesses seeking financing.

To be sure, the rate of return is significant on successful ventures. Angels and private investors soared with this past century's technology start-ups. Witness Siena Corporation: Angel investor Kevin Kimberland invested $100,000 in the company in 1994. Three years later, after Siena floated an IPO, his investment grew to a value of $285 million. The IPO share price quickly rose more than 200 times, achieving an 11,500 percent return over the first-round private-equity share price.

However, these investors also appreciate that more than 39 percent of the time, direct investors will suffer a partial or complete loss, and 19 percent of the time they will break even or experience nominal levels of return—in many cases even after holding the investment for as long as eight years. If it's true, as the saying goes, that there's a broken heart for every light on Broadway, the same is no doubt true forty blocks to the south, where Broad Street meets Wall Street.

Angel investing requires industry savvy to analyze deals and command the energy and personality to actively attract promising deals from the many who seek capital. Angel investing requires a significant time commitment to active investments. Accompanying their early- and expansion-stage investments are sophisticated mentors who offer assistance, even hand-holding—a precondition that becomes a rewarding responsibility integral to gaining knowledge and understanding of the management team and of oneself that serve as a hedge against the downside risk and potential problems.

This type of investing requires patience and long-term horizons. Investors need to take the time to learn the art of successful private investing from veterans who have made the most of their experience and have survived financially to pass their stories along. The readers of this book must determine whether they have the skills, or can learn them well enough, to be effective at the pre-IPO investing game.

CHAPTER 2

KEY FACTORS IN SUCCESSFUL ANGEL INVESTING

Why Angel Investing Is Attractive

ANGEL OR PRE-IPO INVESTING has a number of advantages that prompt high-net-worth individuals to explore its opportunities. Some unique advantages accrue to the early-stage and expansion-stage private equity market or to direct investment in such companies and ventures. One of the advantages is the absence of a middleman. It becomes an individual investor's solo ability that allows him to identify qualified, promising ventures; to conduct due diligence; and to properly value and structure deals. And, to a great extent, she needs the intuition, intelligence, and analytical skills—not to mention luck—to identify a winner.

Another attractive advantage is the possibility of hitting a home run, and we will provide examples of the high possible returns in the book. The upside potential in these investments is unlimited. These transactions are not debt that will return one's capital plus a percentage of interest over and above the investment. For example, if you own 30 percent of a company and it becomes an AOL, you stand to make millions. So every one of these investors has the incentive to hit it big. Why not?

Another draw for many executives late in their careers is the satisfying and exciting opportunity to be involved in a newly formed or emerging company. Bored with the businesses they own or manage, bored with jobs they are no longer challenged by or careers they no longer find fulfilling, they relish the opportunity to wear many hats or to be a part of the entrepreneurial experience. The idea of investing directly in a company, of being able to help the management team, of being able not only to provide capital but also to add value, can satisfy. By once again becoming involved, investors can craft a company's development, help when they are needed, and bring to bear their experience, intelligence, understanding, and wisdom.

So becoming involved in a number of constantly changing activities and confronting challenges that might be absent in more structured, older organizations whets the appetite of this investor. Moreover, the investor feels satisfied because the investment is a sort of hedging strategy that allows him to more closely monitor the investment and keep an eye on the downside risk. The investor manages some of the downside risk by identifying an issue or problem that might just be raising a venture-threatening calamity.

Not least among the tugs on the investor's heartstrings is the enticement of being able to influence the outcome of an investment. In this type of investment, the investor is not dependent on sales by a broker, nor on analytical reports by stock research analysts. Not at all. Here is an investment that speaks to the process component, to an individual being deeply involved in every aspect of the company by getting to know its operations and management, studying its strengths and weaknesses, determining the risks involved, calculating the valuation, developing a structure that makes sense with the company and its advisers, and closely monitoring the investment after writing the check. Here is the investor's opportunity to provide advice and counsel and to add value as she nurtures that company. The essence of angel investing is not "exit"; the essence of angel investing is to build successful companies and to relish the joy of creating something and manifesting oneself in the world.

Specifics on Private Equity Classes

PRIVATE EQUITY CLASSES comprise an array of investment opportunities representing direct investments into companies at varying stages of development. These stages range from the earliest levels of development, and obviously higher levels of risk, to much-later-stage investing. Private equity classes include pre-seed, seed, research and development, start-up, first stage, expansion stage, mezzanine, bridge, acquisitions and mergers, LBO, buy-out and spin-out, post venture, turnaround, and special investment situations and distressed security investing.

Angel investors are concerned with the following classes of primary private equity because these classes position them in the pre-IPO market: seed, R&D, start-up, first stage, expansion stage, mezzanine, bridge, acquisition and merger, and turnaround. In the relay to riches, in all other private equity classes, the baton is passed to the institutional investors.

Seed stage describes ventures in the idea phase or in the process of being organized. *Research and development stage* firms focus on financing product development for early-stage or more developed companies. A company in the *start-up stage* is completing product development and initial marketing and has been in business less than two years. A *first stage* investment opportunity is a venture with a working prototype that has gone through beta testing and is beginning commercialization. An *expansion stage* investment opportunity is a venture characterized by expanding commercialization and is typically in need of growth capital. *Mezzanine* investments involve ventures that have increasing sales volume and are possibly breaking even or becoming profitable. These investments usually provide funds for expansion, marketing, or working capital. A *bridge* investment opportunity is a venture that requires short-term capital to reach a clearly defined and stable position or to reach a liquidity event. *Acquisition* and *merger* denote ventures in need of capital to finance those events. And a *turnaround* is a venture in need of capital to effect a change from unprofitability to profitability.

Demographics of Angel Investors

PRIVATE VENTURE INVESTORS form a diverse population of wealthy individuals, many of whom have created their own successful ventures. By providing early-stage private equity financing for start-up firms and equity financing for established and expanding firms, they fill a void in the venture capital market.

In interviews with more than 1,200 investors during 1999 and 2000, the principals of International Capital Resources found that angel investors are usually men from 46 to 65 years of age. Age *does* seem to influence the proclivity of certain investors to be attracted to this type of investment. The principals also observed that within this age group, investors were inclined to deploy some of their income, particularly toward growth potential opportunities characterized by capital appreciation. In the 56-to-65-year-old bracket, ICR's principals noted much more active portfolio management, in which these investors tended to trust their own judgment rather than that of brokers or intermediaries, particularly in direct investments into private business ventures.

These investors are often technical individuals with postgraduate degrees. They may also be individuals with extensive professional executive careers. Their previous experience spans everything from starting companies to operating established companies to building and selling a successful business. Commonly, angel investors have owned and then sold their own companies. Having had to raise money for their businesses, they are experienced in dealing with investors who have sought significant discounts in valuation and price for early-stage, high-risk money. As a result, they now have a personal interest in and familiarity with the benefits of early-stage investing from the investors' side. They recognize the potential in these transactions for extremely high returns through capital appreciation based on a competitive initial purchase price.

Additional research by International Capital Resources indicates that investments range from less than $25,000 per investor per deal to more than $250,000 per investor. Of ICR's sample of 1,200 investors, 20 percent indicated they invest less than $25,000 per deal (one to four deals a year). Forty percent indicated investments between $25,000 and $99,999. Twenty-five percent invest $100,000 to $250,000 per deal. Fifteen percent invest more than $250,000 per deal. Nor is it uncommon for these investors to pool their money, or invest with a syndicate of coinvestors who ponder hedging strategies and seek to better manage risk. The more sophisticated angel investors do prefer to participate with other like-minded investors to share the financial risk and due diligence work.

The investors commonly show a preference for transactions that match their technical or industry expertise. In writing *Finding Your Wings,* we found among the investors an inclination for manufacturing ventures. That is not the case today, when many investors are interested in everything: e-commerce, business, business services, medical and health-care-related ventures, biotechnology, computer hardware and software—and an interest in manufacturing, of not only high-tech products but also industrial, commercial, and consumer products.

Active investors whom we surveyed tend to invest in one to four transactions per year, with the mean approximately three transactions. Based on discussions with investors, we found that the angel hold on investments ran from five to ten years.

Further, a misconception persists that all angel investors invest only close to home. As we pointed out in Chapter 1, while approximately two-thirds of angel investors do want to invest close to home, our most recent study found that for 35 percent of the angels, geographic proximity to the venture is not a major concern.

The qualifying issue here, however, was their need for the lead investor to be close by for the deal. Also, the lead investor had to be someone whom the rest of the angels knew and respected.

The majority of investors whom ICR interviewed—even those investing less than $25,000 a deal—sought to position themselves to invest in a multitude of deals they learned about from friends, family, trusted associates, and intermediaries, and to a much lesser extent through direct contact with entrepreneurs seeking investors. Almost all of the investors were interested in seeing more pre-screened investment opportunities that met their investment preferences. All of them were accredited investors, and 90 percent were self-made millionaires.

One interesting conclusion was that angel investors do not form a monolithic group. This is a market of splintered segments, composed of distinct individuals with different motivations. Their demographics reflect a highly idiosyncratic bunch. Although there is a generic demography, we vigorously emphasize their singularity, a trait that is also revealed in our other two books.

Required Skills for Successful Angel Investing

THE ANGEL INVESTMENT PROCESS requires a number of skills for each phase. Later chapters will explore each of these activities and their associated tasks and skills in much greater detail. Meanwhile, our purpose is to provide an overview.

We want to accentuate here that successful angel investing is a process. You can't complete just one phase and drink a toast to yourself for a job well done. On the contrary, it's better to perform all phases—to manage all of them—and to avoid mistakes rather than excelling at any single phase. This type of investing evokes a system. In other words, the absence of any one element will have a severe impact on the overall effectiveness of the entire system. It's the old saying about "the weakest link in the chain." In fact, each element is interdependent with the others, so if an earlier component was not well-managed, it will reduce or inhibit output.

The first set of skills relates to deal generation, or creating deal flow. The primary reason for this skill set is that few of the ventures you will discover in this market merit angel investment. Many ventures have not reached a viable stage of development yet, or the management team isn't solid or doesn't exist, or the business plan and target market have not yet been fleshed out, or the technology has not been developed. Sometimes management lacks an understanding of the competition or is not even clear about how much money to raise or what to do with it. Whatever the reason (and they are legion), different factors often reduce dramatically the number of investment opportunities. That's why you need to develop a large deal flow to find that 5 percent—only 5 percent, mind you—that can boast some merit, only 5 percent worthy of putting in the time and costs necessary.

So deal generation is the first step. Developing a deal flow, informing this market of your interest, encouraging entrepreneurs to get those deals to you in a timely manner and in a format that facilitates review, ensuring privacy and confidentiality—all of these issues need tending to. At the same time, you need to be free of legal entrapments, such as nondisclosure agreements, so that you can enter freely into different kinds of deals.

The second area that requires attention—and lots of it—is due diligence: the whole area of screening the deals that come in; reviewing the business plans; investigating management and individuals' temperaments, characters, records, and finance savvy; understanding the state of intellectual property protection; identifying and evaluating ventures of merit; and comparing them against your investment criteria as well as your own investment plan. Completing this process responsibly becomes urgent, so that costs and time commitments are reasonable.

Next is the process of ascribing value—valuing ventures of nonoperating companies, being involved in "blue sky" projections to determine value—which is far less a science than an art form. We will discuss this critical step in its own chapter.

The next set of skills has to do with structuring the deal and negotiating the terms of the investment agreement. A large component of structuring the deal is being familiar with the options in early-stage, private equity, direct investments. We will cover those in greater detail later.

Still another consideration is negotiating a constructive agreement between the parties that does not alienate anyone. Negotiations should promote a win/win strategy by which both parties understand the structure, terms, conditions, covenants, representations, warranties, and other clauses in the legal agreements. In the angel market, all parties to the agreement must capture its essence and spirit; otherwise, trouble follows quickly.

Another set of essential skills is assessing risk and developing risk-management strategies. These include coinvestment, diversification, monitoring, and hedging strategies. Investors have to follow commonsense guidelines, such as avoiding companies that have not taken the time to prepare a business plan and a cogent financial model. Investors benefit from understanding the downside risks in this type of investing.

All of these elements require the individual to evaluate the risk and think about risk management. A critical component is not only understanding your own skill set but also developing an advisory team to support you in due diligence, in valuation, in deal structuring, and in negotiation. If a potential investor lacks experience in any of these areas, she needs the help of an advisory team to counsel her.

The process throughout tests the investor's knack for interpersonal skills, the diplomatic and political dexterity associated with monitoring the investment. Active investors must understand how to interact with the entrepreneurial company, and they must understand the role of a director or officer of the company; of a board or advisory board member; or of someone who provides consulting, advice, and counsel.

The investor needs assurance during negotiations that terms and conditions leave open the door for her to glide in should the company not meet its projections or otherwise head for trouble. This close relationship between developing reasonable and enforceable structures, on the one hand, and conditions and terms with which to monitor the investment, on the other, should allow the investor to be involved when it *is* appropriate but let the management run the company when it is *not*.

The next set of skills has to do with identifying the various exit opportunities, opportunities that should have been negotiated into the terms and conditions of the investment agreement. But again, perhaps more important is the investor's ability to monitor the company, providing the kind of objective counsel that ensures the company will achieve its liquidity goals within the agreed-upon time frames. Investors can add value here as they assist with the process of moving toward exit.

Other issues that you should clarify early are your investment orientation, the skills you bring to the equation, your risk tolerance, and your realistic expectations of returns that might be possible.

Another important piece of the process lies in the investor's ability to understand direct private equity investing—that is, the angel investing process—in light of the overall equity portfolio. Thoughtful portfolio management demands a sense of what to commit to private equity investment; in other words, diversifying the equity portfolio to include perhaps 5 percent to 15 percent in the private market while leaving the balance in the public market. In addition, once the investor has diversified the private equity component, she must decide about diversifying it into varying stages of development, different industries and technologies, and even alternative regional economic areas.

And last, in considering portfolio management, the investor must decide how to balance the different types of available private equity investment. For example, should active investment come by direct investment into one company, or is passive investment better? In passive investment, one invests either into a public or private fund managed by a fund manager or into a fund in which the ventures are predefined. A passive investment, as the term indicates, allows the investor to take a more passive, or limited-partner-like, role in the transaction.

In conclusion, the requisite skills we have discussed in this section amount to a process of inextricable links—alone *and* together, side-by-side *and* intertwined, parallel *and* recursive—that the savvy investor needs to manage with great care.

Developing Angel Investment Criteria

PRIVATE INVESTORS INVESTING DIRECTLY into companies consider a range of criteria. To a great extent, they become steeped in the excitement and the fun of a unique form of investing, feelings that often figure as prominently as return on investment. We'll discuss more of this in the motivation section, but for now it's worth mentioning that private investors commonly search for investment opportunities with a proprietary advantage, whether that edge tenders a patented technology, a unique technology handled as a trade secret, a competitive strategy advantage, or a head start in the market that acts as a barrier to competition.

The reason for this is simple: having a technological advantage provides a significant benefit in terms of pricing the product or technology for the market, and it increases the potential for a faster return on investment. Essentially, leading technology and proprietary technology offer a price advantage. This technology can be as simple as new features that recognized competitors don't have, technology capable of erecting a barrier to competition.

Many successful investors that we have spoken to over the years want to understand the industry that they invest in, or at least have an underlying appreciation of the technology and the market. Sometimes they want to solve a major problem through their company and its technology. They will be acutely conscious of whether the company or venture and its technology, product, or service is something they can wrap their arms around, identify with, and become excited about.

Later on, when we discuss the "investability" of ventures—that is, whether a venture merits investment—we'll talk in much greater detail about investment criteria. But for now, let's say that investment decisions really do require a receptive market. If the company has to do extensive missionary selling to awaken or convert a sleeping market, it will not be attractive to investors, whose criteria match a more receptive and established market.

Private investors will scrutinize new markets, looking for a driving force with a significant potential for fast growth. The company must have a technology that can lead to a sizable share of the market before they will consider it. Ideally, substantially larger players have not become firmly entrenched or received a head start. Most investors realize that management can be changed, but the market cannot.

Private investors and their advisers will scrutinize financial projections and forecasts. Assumptions must be sufficient to support the investors' return on expectations. Later we will discuss investor expectations for return on investment. In the case of an operating company, it's common for more successful investors to want to see a history of profitability—that is, a track record that demonstrates financial success.

While researching the book, we often heard investors say, "What I'm interested in is not just an invention but a plan for profit." Investors want to invest in businesses, not just an idea. Seasoned investors realize that many technologies masquerade as companies and potential businesses. They want to be able to separate business plans from strategy, and differentiate among strategies based on noncost elements, such as product engineering or proprietary technological leadership.

Our research in 1999 and 2000 found that approximately 35 percent of investors would invest in a venture without a business plan. This cavalier attitude encourages unnecessary risk. Successful, experienced investors *do* require entrepreneurs to develop a business plan, one that thoroughly defines the business, business strategy, management team, costs of bringing the product to market, plan for developing the technology, and financial plan for company profitability.

The business plan does not have to be long, but the business concept should be encapsulated within a document that communicates the vision and the business and investment opportunity. The business plan demonstrates in writing management's hypothesis about elements in the business over which it claims it has or plans to have control. The plan's logic, strategy, and support reflect management's assumptions about cause and effect. If management does X, Y is likely to occur.

Without a business plan, the parties engaged in due diligence can still determine the feasibility of management's assumptions, but expectations will become even more subjective than they already are. The parties should see the business plan as essential in managing risk. Consequently, the absence of a business plan should be enough to send investors inquiring elsewhere. A business plan forces the persons seeking the investors' money and time to define their argument, opportunity, strategy, and resource requirements, and it makes them assess the risks in their plans. If the business plan does not impress the investor, she should not move forward with management-team meetings or due diligence on the product or the market, nor should she spend time on the financial analysis. Investors must know when to say "No!" And the absence of a proper business plan should set the "no" buzzer ringing in their ears.

A big part of investor criteria centers on the management team and its perseverance, decency, competence, track record, personal financial commitment, and desire to succeed. Likewise, investors should carry out extensive background checks on the team's character, ethics, and personal histories.

Successful investors are also clear about the level of active or passive involvement that particular investments will require and understand early on the level of activity they seek in investment opportunities. They want to take the time to appreciate how much they will be involved in an investment and whether that is consistent with their availability and expectations.

Another element in angels' investment criteria centers on how much they can afford to invest, how much they can afford to lose, and, most important, how long they can afford to lose access to the money. If an investment is successful, investors may want to invest more money into the venture, either to avail themselves of further profits or to protect their position. Also, if an investment is unsuccessful, the investor should not throw good money after bad. Follow-on investment to vindicate poor judgment earlier in a frantic attempt to possibly break even does not save the investor. Most often, it exacerbates the loss. It's important for investors to be sure they can afford their initial investment. This includes the ability to back it up if the venture merits it, as well as the ability to lose access to the money over an extended period, perhaps five to ten years.

Also, many successful investors want to include the opportunity to structure the transaction for incremental funding based on performance. While this does make the structuring and negotiating of the deal more complex, one way to manage the downside risk is to offer the entrepreneur the money she's requested in stages, based upon achieving projected results. In other words, instead of presenting the entrepreneur with all the capital at once and letting her run with it, together they set realistic milestones. The investment capital is then doled out to the entrepreneur as she achieves each benchmark. Often, as the entrepreneur meets each target, the investor is required by the investment agreement to come up with the next tranche of financing. If the entrepreneur fails to meet a milestone, the investor retains the option to invest but is not required to provide any additional capital. In fact, the investor may receive the right to negotiate a lower-priced deal.

The last criteria of private investors involves their insistence on due diligence on the venture, the plan, the financial model and earnings prospect, the claims of the management team regarding vulnerability to competition or to product obsolescence, the managers themselves, and the proposed exit strategy for the venture. Just stating that the company is going to go public is not adequate. Investors commonly require some assessment of how other companies in this industry with similar technologies have achieved liquidity for their investors. And integral to the due diligence process is research into exit strategies by similar companies.

Structuring an Angel Investment Plan

WHEN THEY DEVELOP an investment plan, angels should consider a number of things. The first is to define the industries they have experience with and understand. In addition, angels should be familiar with the markets, either through direct experience or study, and they should understand the underlying technologies the companies use. Defining the industries, markets, and technologies that they think are promising is the first step in clarifying the direction of their investment. Angels need to engage in this defining process *before* they begin to generate deal flow.

In the next phase of the investment process, the investor needs to decide the geographic region of interest. The implications of this decision are important. Not only will it have an impact on the plan that the investor develops to generate deal flow, but it will also delineate the cost and time to perform direct-contact due diligence, visit the companies, meet with management, and observe road-show presentations by the management team. Investors who need to be involved in these aspects obviously should invest in companies close to where they live. By contrast, investors who already have such local investments, who are trying to diversify their portfolio, and who have established some coinvestment contacts in other geographic regions may feel comfortable with a passive role and don't need to be close at hand.

The next step is for investors to be honest with themselves about their level of acceptable risk. The risk associated with direct investment for extended periods can create anxiety and pressure, conditions that can translate into discomfort and strain on them and their families.

So the question for them to answer is how much risk they can stomach. And if you look at the private equity classes we describe, the highest risks clearly are in the pre-seed, seed, R&D, and start-up stages. If this level of risk gives an investor significant pause, she should turn to first-round and expansion capital, bridge, and mezzanine transactions. Obviously, seed and pre-seed will entail greater risk than a start-up or first round. So investors must have a sense of the private equity classes they want to focus on, factoring in their personal experiences.

Later we'll supply some information on success and failure rates of early-stage investment, rates of return, and how to compute them. For now, we want to stress how important it is for an investor to enunciate her expectations and compare them to entrepreneurs' business projections. Establishing a targeted compound rate of return or a multiple is crucial. Investors need a sense of their expectations for return before they enter the due diligence and valuation stages. Levels of return significantly change as the risk associated with the venture rises. When we discuss our research, we will illustrate this.

Next, investors should spell out procedures to protect themselves from loss or to minimize some of the downside risks associated with early-stage investing. The risk management chapter covers this in detail. Let's mention now, however, that it's a good idea to bring aboard other investors as early as possible, to share the due diligence process and to develop structures within the negotiated agreement. This allows them to move immediately into investment situations when entrepreneurs are not measuring up to expectations. In addition, this allows investors to develop monitoring strategies and reports and make other arrangements so they can identify problems before they escalate into major issues.

Before completing the planning process, investors should get a sense of the preferred liquidity options. If the investor is looking exclusively for pre-IPO situations, the criteria a company must meet may differ widely from the criteria of a company that will provide returns through a buyback of the stock from investors, or perhaps through merger and acquisition. Understanding their preferred liquidity options will help investors to recognize the kind of financial criteria companies will have to meet when the investors first look at them, as well as their projections later on. And investors need to understand the financial requirements of going public, which we will clarify to identify whether an IPO realistically should be their preferred liquidity option.

Harmonizing Financial and Psychological Returns

THE PRIMARY MOTIVATION for a number of private investors is, of course, return on investment. But return on investment is only one of many considerations in the decision to invest in earlier, expansion-stage deals. Private investors, after all, do not *have* to invest and do not invest solely for monetary returns. Therefore, unlike an institutional investor or money manager, private investors have many incentives for deciding to invest.

When you understand the kinds of returns that investors receive, you will appreciate that high-risk investing is not for everyone. Our study of angel investors found that 39 percent of investors reported a total loss of investment, a partial loss, or only a write-off or tax benefit as a result of a negative return. Nineteen percent of angels surveyed reported break-even or nominal returns that were lower than projected. Thirty percent reported returns of 50 percent or more, and 12 percent reported returns greater than 100 percent. Internal rates of return were compounded annually over the term of the hold, and returns were cash on cash, plus capital gains. A number of highly successful investors reported multiples exceeding twenty times return on investment. The greatest returns occurred when the original investment was in firms at seed, R&D, or start-up stages of development. Last, the losers became apparent within three years after investment.

Again, these were cash-on-cash plus capital gains. Now, given those results, investors' returns on investment result from a combination of good judgment, skill, and luck. Investment plans that establish reasonable expectations for returns become critical. Obviously, investment at earlier stages must offer the investor an internal rate of return substantially higher than those at later, less-risky stages of development.

A major consideration in calculating rate of return is the amount of time that passes before harvesting the returns. For example, three times the investment over three years yields a 44 percent return on investment, whereas three times the investment in five years yields a 38 percent return on investment. As venture capitalist Lucien Ruby shrewdly observes, "Venture capital investors do not have to get their desired return. In fact, they usually do not. But they want to see the desired return as a possibility." Now, when we calculate the targeted rates of return for a typical direct investment, the multiple is a major consideration, but so is the time within which the investor wants to receive that multiple.

But angel investors seek a number of nonfinancial returns as well. At the macro level are the more obvious social benefits touted in the press. These include creating jobs in a region of high unemployment, developing socially useful technology, medicine, or energy, contributing to urban revitalization, encouraging women- or minority-owned ventures, and deriving personal satisfaction from assisting entrepreneurs in building successful ventures in a free enterprise economy.

At the micro level are a number of specific and, to some extent, idiosyncratic motivations that get investors involved in this highly risky area. One way these individuals (usually in their forties) can recapture their own successes is by using their acute analysis and intuition to invest in new and expanding companies. Scoring once again reinforces their self-image. They again prove the accuracy of their judgments, judgments that sustain their recognition in their investment and entrepreneurial communities and enhance their reputations within their social circles.

Another element is the desire of some investors to involve themselves in alleviating misfortune. One investor's story comes to mind: This individual had been a commodities trader for many years and received a substantial profit in a transaction. He went out and celebrated with his wife. Two or three months after that celebration, doctors diagnosed his wife with breast cancer, and shortly after that she died. He quit his job as a commodities trader and focused his wealth on financing early-stage cancer research. This wrenching story is a testament to the many investors whose incentives reach beyond the singular focus of return on investment. Here we have someone who wanted to use his wealth to relieve the pain of others.

For a number of investors who have inherited their wealth or have been extremely lucky in their careers, a sense of noblesse oblige often dwarfs milder incentives. Perhaps they suffer from survivor's guilt about how a particular fortune was made in the first place, or about the serendipitous nature of the luck and inheritance that came their way. Often, a compulsion is generated to contribute as previous generations have, through charitable giving. To give back what may have been gained darkly provides still another motive.

Truly, by the time the IPO occurs, the big money, for the most part, has been made. The question arises of how someone gets involved in the deal before the IPO. Getting the first crack at the next high-rise stock before the IPO means becoming involved in the process we outline in this book. What we mean by "getting the first crack" is being a part of the early stages of financing, whether it's seed, R&D, start-up, first round—all those rounds of financing in companies that have the potential to become an IPO.

Another motivation that investors need to be sensitive to is the potential to become addicted to high-risk investing, urges not unlike those of the compulsive gambler addicted to the rush of gambling. We have seen investors lose substantial amounts of money only to go back to similar ventures and once again fail to follow the procedures that more successful investors use, the procedures we prescribe here. They lose more money in future ventures, putting not only their own financial situation at risk but that of their families as well. This motivation is one that investors must be aware of. A great deal is at stake.

The investments generating interest among investors, particularly those in the new arena associated with the Web, e-commerce, and business-to-business, are for many investors fun and exciting. Operating in that kind of environment, and being called upon by young entrepreneurs, whose average age is around twenty-eight, provides the investor with a joy of contributing that's difficult to find elsewhere. One investor put it beautifully when he said, "You never know how much you know until a small company turns to you." In sum, when an investor can add to an early-stage, fledgling company's success, she reaps emotional rewards well beyond the financial returns associated with return on investment.

The last motivation we want to touch on is how dramatically the investing landscape is changing. More and more investors are taking control of their investments. Whether it's just a working Joe who's involved with a 401(k), or someone who trades stocks online, or an angel investor taking charge of the stock selection process, change is occurring.

Angel investing is one of the few investment arenas that allow the investor to directly influence the process. This has to do with the trend in the brokerage industry to discount brokers, and the stimulation of more active involvement using information available through various resources, such as the Internet, trade papers, and investment magazines. More investors are taking an active role in managing their own portfolios.

This type of investing allows investors to diversify their portfolios based on their past experience, a way to control the placement of a percentage of their portfolio in either public or private equity, a way to steer a portfolio percentage into private equity, and perhaps a way to increase the return or predictability in the portfolio. People today are thoroughly managing their retirement investments. For example, they are choosing mutual funds for their various retirement accounts. They want to increase their control using the technology and information that fuels this type of investing and the proactive attitude that gets the investor more directly involved in the deal itself.

However, in the same way that we can delineate motivations to invest, we can cite a number of *"de-*motivators," the reasons an angel rejects an investment or rejects the private equity process. These are things that investors assiduously avoid, for the ability to *avoid* a mistake in early-stage private equity investing is more important to many private investors than picking a runaway winner. Since these investors may make only one to four investments per year, picking a single poor investment can collapse heavily on the investor and have a significant impact on the overall return from all their investments.

Because the direct private equity investor makes so few investments, she must take greater care with each one. If a venture does not show enough potential to achieve the types of returns we've defined earlier, if the margins are not adequate to absorb the potential stalls, if delays and unexpected problems occur, if the risk/return ratio is not adequate, investors stray. In some instances, if chemistry or mutual respect is lacking between the key entrepreneurs and the investors, this disconnect undermines investors' motivation.

We cannot separate the people from the plan. Business plans don't get funded; people get funded. The private investor has the right to be turned off by the personalities and characteristics of the individuals regardless of how good the venture or plan may be. Finally, the investor has no one to report to about anything.

It's also important to remember, as mentioned earlier, that private investors want to have fun. It's fun to make money. They're looking for something different and engaging that enhances their sense of themselves and adds a new dimension to their lives. If they don't understand the business or if the venture is too technical, they may reject the proposal. Although many investors don't feel the need to completely understand the industry, many do not wish to invest in areas that they do not know, be it the technology, its application, the market, the industry, or the problem that the company's product or service solves.

For example, socially responsible investors are individuals whose values nudge them into investing that is either "inclusionary" (investment into companies whose values they share) or "exclusionary" (avoiding investing in companies whose values they don't share). So the socially responsible investor may feel justified in accepting or rejecting a deal if he perceives congruency—or a lack of it—in the venture's value system.

Private investors also are inclined to be demotivated when entrepreneurs overvalue their ventures or become unrealistic in their projections. Prospective investors may not share the entrepreneur's level of optimism for the venture's success. Successful, sophisticated venture investors are ultimately risk-averse; they attempt to manage risk through their familiarity with the dimensions of the venture. We see proof of this attitude in the angel hedging strategy that requires the prospective investee company to locate another angel not related to management or already involved enough to invest in the deal at the valuation proposed. They are quick to discount unrealistic projections.

Investors realize that always lurking in the background are needs for unforeseen follow-on financing. It's not that the entrepreneurs are intentionally deceptive; it's that perhaps in their enthusiasm, they haven't thoroughly analyzed the opportunity. The classic example occurs when the valuation of the proposed investment significantly deviates from published valuation information readily available from large accounting firms and venture capital associations on done deals in the industry. Sophisticated investors know that entrepreneurs become hypnotized by the omnipresent spreadsheet programs, which can be manipulated to predict exorbitant hockey-stick cash flow projections. These mesmerized entrepreneurs force many investors to use their own financial models when they value a venture and the potential return on investment. Poorly developed assumptions are a main reason that private investors reject financing proposals.

Earlier we provided an extensive list of investment criteria. This chapter outlined a wide range of private investor criteria and discussed the importance of congruence between a venture and management team, on the one hand, and an investor's criteria on the other. The failure to meet any one of those investor criteria may raise the red flag of rejection.

Successful angel investors like to build mountains with their money, not throw it down a hole. Investors are skeptical of early-stage and expansion-stage deals because they don't want their money used for large salaries, back salaries, old loan obligations, new loan obligations, other debts, or buyout of other early-stage investors or their founders. These are typical red flags that obstruct direct private investors who want not only to see their funding grow the company but also to see a substantial stake by the entrepreneurs in the firm's success.

A number of angel investors believe that the way for a company's founders to demonstrate their commitment is to invest their own money in the venture. When entrepreneurs are willing to invest their personal finances, angels see this as a positive sign, a sign that means more than the absolute amount of money the entrepreneur brings to the deal. Percentage counts here: If the entrepreneur's net worth is $10 million, $500,000 doesn't ring the confidence bell inside the chest of every investor, but an entrepreneur investing that same amount while worth a mere $2 million can really set the bell clanging.

Commonsense Guidelines for Successful Asset Allocation Decisions

TYPICALLY, PRIVATE EQUITY INVESTORS are investing a small portion of their equity portfolio into the private equity market. They are not investing their life savings in a single venture. Although angel investors are interested in investing in public equities, they also have become interested in diversifying their portfolios into private equity.

This diversification could include a range of possible investments from seed, R&D, and start-up through later-stage financings, depending upon the size of the investment capital available. Usually, these investors place amounts ranging from about 5 percent to 15 percent of their available equity portfolio. This represents discretionary net worth that is liquid and readily available to move into a new investment; that money becomes earmarked for higher-risk deals. Investors who are diversifying their portfolios can start by allocating a portion to private equity investment.

Angel investors can ask themselves a couple of questions to guide them in these decisions. Matching their private deal making with their investment strategy is very important. If they seek income, they can invest in a subordinated note providing interest, or perhaps preferred stock providing a dividend. If the capital strategy is to generate capital appreciation and capital gains, the investment could be in common or preferred equity transactions requiring the investor to hold that position for an extended period of time, thus losing access to the capital in the hope that the stock will appreciate in value.

In making allocation decisions, investors need to be honest with themselves about their stage of life and the kinds of investments suitable for them. Investors in their early thirties tend to be more concerned about buying real estate, perhaps investing to provide for their children's education, or spending money on other personal pursuits—on luxury items, vacations, jewelry, or art. These investors, in other words, are perhaps less likely to have the discretionary income after these types of expenditures to make the investments associated with pre-IPO opportunities.

Investors who have reached their late forties to late fifties face quite a different situation. At this stage of their lives, most of their children have finished school or are out of the house, and perhaps they have more discretionary income. With more discretionary income, investors can invest directly into companies. They also may have more time to get involved in their investments.

The investor must also assess her risk posture. Evaluation of her proclivity for risk and how much of the ambiguity of early-stage deals she can stomach is essential. An aggressive risk posture requires the ability to withstand the stresses, strains, and anxiety associated with pre-seed, seed, and start-up deals. Investors who do not have this ability would be better suited to later-stage private equity transactions, such as mezzanine or bridge financings, with payoffs scheduled within eighteen to twenty-four months.

Another area for investors to think about before making their allocation decision is the stages of corporate development with which they have the most professional experience. A private investor may catch the enthusiasm by hanging around entrepreneurs in early-stage companies. But if the investor has not had experience in that environment, perhaps having only worked in the government or in larger, more bureaucratic structures, her lack of understanding of the culture and environment makes her more vulnerable to buying into the deal. She is therefore less likely to understand the risk and less able to add value.

The investor who chooses to be more active has to understand the extent to which she can add value beyond the capital, because participatory investment by its very definition is time intensive. Investors need to assess their availability to ensure that they will be there not only to monitor the investment but also to make contributions should the situation merit it. For many private investors, looking for that participatory role is important, so they must be clear about the level of involvement they need to attain personal satisfaction.

But investors also must be clear with the entrepreneurs about their expectations so that conflicts don't develop with entrepreneurs who do not want that level of involvement. Clarifying commitment is a prominent component of the allocation decision.

Last, it is essential for investors to be clear, not only about their net worth but about their discretionary net worth, their income, their liquid financial assets, and their ability to put a portion of those assets at risk and to lose access to them for an extended period—or to lose them entirely. Part of the allocation decision requires investors to calculate how much they can play before entering this market.

Guiding Principles for
Prospective Angel Investors

TO CLOSE THIS CHAPTER, here are five basic principles of direct venture investing, principles to which most successful investors seem to adhere.

1 Know the business. Something Warren Buffett said can serve as food for thought: "I don't know what that world [technology] will look like in ten years. Technology is just something we don't understand, so we don't invest in it." It's simple: Know the business you're investing in. This provides a hedge against losing your investment while allowing you to intelligently monitor its performance.

2 Do your own due diligence on the management team, the market, and the technology.

3 Plan on having sufficient financial reserves for future rounds. This does not mean throwing good money after bad. If the venture has gone downhill and does not meet expectations, we hope you will have structured and negotiated the investment in such a way that an exit strategy is available. We are suggesting that when the company does meet projections and is performing well, investors have sufficient reserves to protect their position from dilution in future rounds. In negotiating terms and conditions, providing dilution protection is possible, although in certain instances it will not be.

4 Avoid unrealistically high valuations. Although the money managers in the venture-capital industry who are clawing for the same deal can afford valuation auctions—a luxury possible when they've raised $500-million-plus funds—this is not the case for the private or angel investor who is struggling to find one or two business plans among a hundred that are viable. At all costs, avoid getting involved in a business that is overvalued. The real opportunity in early-stage private equity investing is taking that high-level risk in order to receive discounts, premiums, and an appropriate percentage of equity.

5 Understand the liquidity risks and be clear about when to get out and when to stay in. Few companies really take the time in their business planning to think through an exit strategy. It is an unnecessary risk to get involved with a company that has not analyzed that aspect. The company should document a legitimate strategy and demonstrate that similar companies in the industry have successfully executed the plan. Particularly with the pre-IPO company, the company must have the potential to achieve financial results consistent with the stock exchange requirements for going public.

UNDERSTANDING
A N D
MANAGING RISK

CHAPTER 3

ONE OF THE PRIMARY motivations for getting involved in high-risk investing is, of course, the opportunity for the investor to hit it big. We believe that investors must manage the risk in all of the investments in their private equity portfolio. If they don't, when they finally do discover a prospective IPO—with its potentially stellar rate of return—they may also discover, to their great dismay, that they have already sacrificed the farm financially.

So they need to have the stamina, the momentum, and the acumen to proceed when they're not hitting home runs, and still invest in relatively risky situations.

The traditional approach to reducing risk in the private-equity market is by investing in less-risky situations. For example, instead of investing in seed, R&D, start-up, or first round, private investors would invest in second round, mezzanine, and bridge to IPO. In other words, move to later-stage situations with companies that have audited financials, have achieved break-even profitability, have an established market, and have a position in that market. Investors using this strategy gravitate toward and benefit from more traditional types of analysis.

In sophisticated angel investing, the situation is more complex. For the reasons mentioned above, while looking for a diamond in the rough investors must still have a chance for outstanding returns to justify the type of risk that they're dealing with in this market. The major risk is, of course, illiquidity. Based on our interviews with successful investors, we urge investors to manage the potential peril with risk and hedging strategies. The purpose of this chapter is to provide some insight into the approaches that savvy investors use in managing risk.

In understanding the risks associated with early-stage private equity investing, another key point is to never make a small business investment that you cannot afford to lose entirely or lose access to for an extended period, perhaps five to ten years. Never use funds that you might need for other purposes: retirement, loan repayment, child's college education, or medical expenses. Instead, use discretionary net worth that is liquid or set aside for luxury purposes. Other appropriate sources include funds earmarked for further investments into the public market or for diversification from the public market into other types of investments.

Investors should try to limit their risks by avoiding mistakes that can deprive them of the opportunity to invest in a stellar deal when it comes to their attention. Always remember that as security, guarantees, and recourse for the investor rise, the levels of return slide. And if those returns go down to the 20 percent or 25 percent level, the prospect of entering this time-consuming and anxiety-provoking area becomes much more dubious.

In later chapters—particularly those on valuation, negotiation, deal structuring, and monitoring—we will detail a number of approaches that have a direct impact on managing or containing risk.

All investors should keep in mind that to achieve attractive rates of return, they must avoid the bad deals—a significantly more important aspect of investing than hitting the home run. To avoid the bad ones, investors must rely on a sound investment plan.

Disadvantages of Angel Investing

WHILE VENTURE-CAPITAL INVESTMENTS involve high potential for return, they likewise involve high risk. Disadvantages of direct investment include illiquidity, higher mortality rates than when investing in more developed companies, a high anxiety factor, very little diversification, and a large time commitment. On this last issue, investors should always calculate not only the amount of return but also an acceptable time frame for realizing it. For example, a ten-times multiple may be possible, but it may require hanging in for an average of eight years or more. Investors must determine very early what time frame is acceptable to them, because getting into private investments is easy; getting out is not. Disadvantages may include severe restrictions on liquidity or transferability of registered securities in exempt offerings.

The SBA and independent research firms have overemphasized mortality rates, though rates are indeed higher for early-stage companies than for more developed companies. In fact, many of the companies do not necessarily fail, as defined by bankruptcy; rather, they fail to meet the investors' expectations or entrepreneur's pro forma financial projections. Therefore, the investments or the companies voluntarily close down. So we can't look at the kinds of studies the SBA has made available that suggest a 50 percent casualty rate for start-ups. That 50 percent of all start-ups are making or exceeding their projected performance does *not* mean that the other 50 percent are failing. In fact, if the deal is structured properly, investors will have ways of getting back at least a portion of their investment or of generating tax breaks.

Additional risks can occur anytime. Consider that most invest-ments fail to return their targeted multiples and their expected financial returns; consider, too, that financial projections are rarely met. Projected revenues might exceed actual revenues, and they often arrive later than projected; expenses might lag behind actu-al expenses, which often happens sooner than expected. Invari-ably, our experience tells us, the need for more capital, as well as larger and more frequent rounds, comes sooner than the parties originally anticipated. In their optimism, we have found, many entrepreneurs do not analyze conditions thoroughly enough; due diligence gets nudged aside. Worse, investors also fail to persevere in their analysis.

Investors should expect the unexpected and anticipate the worst. Build a healthy bit of caution into your financial modeling and into the analysis of the venture's viability. Pinpoint the expected poten-tial return you can reliably get for taking the risk on the deal.

Just because the state security organizations have registered an offering does not mean that the investment will succeed. The state does not evaluate or endorse the investment, and if anyone sug-gests otherwise to you, their suggestion is unlawful. Above all, never let a commission securities salesperson, financial intermediary or finder, or officer or director of the company convince you that these types of investments are not risky. Any such assurance is almost always inaccurate. Small business investments are generally highly illiquid even though the securities may technically be freely transferable. So if the company takes a turn for the worse, you will usually be unable to sell your securities.

Assessing Risk in a Potential Investment

RISK CAN VARY, DEPENDING UPON the different dimensions of an investment. It could be the category of the alternative private equi-ty class under consideration, such as the company's stage of devel-opment. Private equity classes, discussed earlier, make up different transactions from pre-seed, seed, start-up, growth, mezzanine, LBO, buy-out, spin-out, post-venture, turnaround, and special investment situations to distressed security investing. This life cycle of potential portfolio companies evolves from start-up through expansion to mezzanine. At the early stages, management is still struggling to pinpoint strategic advantages, develop a business plan, and begin to prove the viability of the venture.

In addition to considering stage of development risks inherent in early-stage transactions, you should study other types of risks as well. The first is management risk. Can the management personnel carry out the plan they so passionately present? Do they have the ability, the experience, the background, and the track record to accomplish the forecast and sales and to manage internal operations? More important, can they form a team within the ranks, or will they succumb to resentment because they must negotiate founders' stock shares? Has a note of discord been struck among the members of the management team?

Another type of risk you have to evaluate is product and technology risk. When a product is in development, the investors are being asked to put up money before a prototype has been unveiled. All of the following become critical calculations of risk: whether this product can be made to work, whether the machines actually exist, and whether other elements are available to actually manufacture the product once it has been developed. Additionally, if this technology has not yet been developed, significant risks surface. But if it is an existing technology that has been well tested and molded into a new one, the risk becomes substantially less.

A third type of risk has to do with the market. Will extensive missionary selling be necessary to drag the product into the market's awareness? This aspect involves the push/pull calculation of market forces. Having to push a product onto the market makes missionary selling necessary, which is an expensive proposition. However, a product pulled into the market by demand or by a severe problem that needs to be solved entails less risk. If the market has not demonstrated a desire to purchase the product, the company will run substantial risk in marketing it.

Another risk, operations, depends on a company's ability to meet its sales projections. Can the company actually produce, with quality, the projected volume to meet customer expectations and maintain their loyalty as well as the company's reputation? When evaluating operations risk, the company needs to anticipate problems, such as those experienced by Intel with the Pentium chip in 1995. If such a problem arises, can the company deliver the product in such a way that it will achieve its projections?

Financial risk also looms if the company needs more money than it originally forecast or if the angels' investment is a very small percentage of the amount the company claimed it needed. If a venture needs $10 million in the next round but the investor's contribution amounts to only $50,000, then the investor faces a major financial risk. Can the company raise that sum? Financial risk involves being able to raise money for not only the balance of the present round but also future rounds. When a company cannot raise the money it seeks, it must adjust its growth plans accordingly. At the same time, however, an investor's small investment shrinks. Investors face another financial risk because they can quantify and estimate possible returns only through pro forma financial statements.

Ask yourself about the kind of risks you are willing to take. Know your tolerance! This measurement is crucial to you as an angel investor and can provide you and your financial advisers with an important guidepost. If you have a high tolerance for risk, you may want to consider investing more than just 5 percent or 10 percent of your equity portfolio into these types of ventures.

Differentiating between Indirect and Direct Venture Investment

THERE HAVE ALWAYS BEEN indirect ways to get involved in angel investing. You can put money into mutual funds that include new ventures, for example, or into private venture-capital firms whose managers bankroll several enterprises with minimum investment, say around $100,000. You can also buy stock in publicly held venture investment companies, such as Internet Capital Group, CMGI, or Angel Investors, L.P.

We are talking here about investing directly into a new or an expanding company. In return, the angel typically takes equity in the business. How much money you want to invest; how active you intend to be in the investment decision; and your personal needs, goals, and tolerance for risk—are all issues you need to resolve before embarking on direct investing. Over time, your circumstances may change, so even seasoned angel investors will benefit from occasionally reassessing their position.

The private placement is essentially the issuance of treasury securities of a company to a small number of private investors. This investment can be an offering of debt or stock, warrants, or various combinations of these securities. The private placement has a number of definitions in the deal-making arena. At its most basic, it involves cash for equity and all types of offerings that are not publicly sold. Such transactions allow the company in many cases to circumvent onerous public offering requirements while accessing nonaffiliated market investors without a full registration compliance task.

Perhaps a more practical, realistic definition of the private placement is any deal you can legally negotiate and then have an attorney write up. The private placement is a record of the agreement between the angel investor and the entrepreneur. Therefore, we urge angels to avoid indulging prematurely in an overly structured security transaction—transactions many entrepreneurs, under the advice of expensive investment banking counsel, might be inclined to negotiate. Rather, we favor strategies in which the angel can promote a more open-minded, more negotiation-oriented, flexible posture. It's in the investor's interest to do so.

The angel investors can circle the deal and provide further legal, accounting, investment banking, and other types of support that the entrepreneur might need in structuring an agreement acceptable to all of the parties. In effect, the entrepreneur is selling the investor a story—perhaps a compelling and believable story, but a story nonetheless. It becomes the investors' task, then, to determine the objective circumstances, a notion we'll talk more about when we take up due diligence.

If the investor does decide to invest directly, he must determine at which stage of development he wants to get involved. Investors must consider their tolerance for risk here because the risk levels vary so widely. It pays investors to differentiate their preferred stages of development and to target only ventures *within* those stages.

The private placement affords the angel investor extensive benefits. Because angels prize their privacy, confidentiality is a very important aspect of the private placement investment process. If word gets out about his investment orientation, the angel is inundated with requests that rarely match his investment criteria. From a legal point of view, fewer and less onerous disclosure requirements attend a private placement, an especially attractive feature because complying with federal and state disclosure requirements raises the ante.

Further, in the private placement investment or exempt offering, the investor can protect his privacy and preserve his money. The investor can also be flexible, because the private placement can accommodate preferred stock transactions, common stock transactions, and debt or subordinated debt transactions. For example, from an investor's point of view, subordinated debt commonly has convertibility when the terms and conditions are negotiated. Convertible subordinated debt, or a convertible debenture, offers some protection on the downside of a failed company. If a proprietary technology in the venture is resalable at a later date, for instance, or if the company folds and the technology is liquidated, subordinated note holders can recover some of their money, once the company takes care of senior note holders. This provides some downside insurance for the investors.

Also, convertibility combined with subordinated debt permits sharing on the upside if the company succeeds; investors can convert the principal note into stock. With success, the investors will be able to convert the stock and share in the capital appreciation with a previously negotiated purchase price. Since the company is successful, the price of the stock is higher, allowing investors to purchase the stock at a lower price and eventually liquidate for appreciation and a return on the investment. If the company is not successful, does not go public, or is not acquired, but achieves some reasonable levels of success, the investors' debt can be repaid from cash flows. Hence, investors will get their principal back and their coupon or interest return on principal. And if the company fails, the investors are in line to get some of their money back when the company's assets are liquidated. All of these are examples of how the private placement can be structured to provide flexibility.

Private placements are also much less costly than other types of offerings, in terms of both time and money. Research suggests that entrepreneurial teams can expend up to 900 hours completing an IPO, whereas a private placement can be completed in far less time, enabling the principals more time for running the business. In addition, angels can deflect significant percentages of their investment from going sideways into front fees and back-end fees.

Last, private placements tend to accommodate smaller transactions. Since 90 percent of angel investments are under $1 million, the angel investing $100,000 can become a significant player in the transaction. Thus, the private placement accommodates smaller transactions that are, in fact, the hardest transactions to finance in the venture capital industry.

Assessing Your Own Risk Tolerance Level

FROM SURVEYS AND INTERVIEWS with more than 9,000 investors since 1989, we have drawn some conclusions about the underlying psychological characteristics of active angel investors and their tolerance for risk. The investors who prevail and have stamina to stay the course in this market seem to possess these characteristics. When assessing your own risk tolerance level, consider whether you are cautious, systematic, suspicious, patient, direct, decisive, focused, optimistic, inner-directed, diligent, or resilient. Let's discuss each of these character traits as they relate to angel investors.

The *cautious* are alert to hazards, perhaps because of their experience and their prudent due diligence and negotiation. They seem to have the ability to sense the dangers in the deal and ask the right questions. Because of that they usually come to a wiser decision.

The *systematic* angel investor organizes and plans the integration of the parts of the angel investment process. He excels at each phase and effectively intertwines them, an effort that efficiently improves synergy among the parts.

Investors who are *suspicious* tend to doubt the entrepreneur's claims. Without ever accusing the entrepreneur personally, this investor can intuitively sense that the entrepreneur's timelines or pro formas are unreliable. The investor who becomes infected by an entrepreneur's enthusiasm and who casts off a healthy skepticism often does something he later deeply regrets.

Successful angels possess *patience*. They bear the angel process with all its annoyances and provocations without loss of temper or displays of irritability. This quality helps to build solid relationships with entrepreneurs, and such perseverance avoids rash decisions.

They are also *direct* and straightforward, and they proceed with their goals clearly in mind. Angels tend to be candid and forthright, particularly with their questions.

They are *decisive* because they know they have the power in the situation. Likewise they are resolute and determined. Successful investors know when to stop the analysis, make a decision, and swing into action.

Successful angels are *focused*. Even in the fractured time frames of the typical interrupted business day, they can zero in on the strengths and weaknesses of the venture and those of the managers themselves.

Invariably, successful angels are also *optimists*. Surprised? They usually anticipate the most favorable result. However, this disposition is grounded by a trust in their own analysis, not a blind belief in the entrepreneur's projections, proposition, or presentation.

Angels are also *inner-directed* in that they possess their own set of values. They have their personal experience and unique set of motivations for entering into angel investing in general and in the deal under scrutiny in particular. Rarely do successful angels succumb to external pressures from entrepreneurs or third parties and their advisers.

Angel investors are *diligent* in their effort to learn and succeed at angel investing. They pursue their goal of finding that successful deal in a painstaking fashion. Most important, they learn from their mistakes. No pachyderm has a thicker skin. Despite their failures, they return untiringly to the fray.

This last characteristic emphasizes their *resilience*. They spring back, rebounding after working long and hard on a deal that was never consummated or a failed investment that embroiled them in board responsibilities. Though far from quixotic, they return to the process, not to be deceived by windmills but to search for that next possible star.

Managing Risk with Proven Hedging Strategies

IN DIRECT INVESTING, there invariably comes the intricate decision about managing risk, the consideration that involves hedging strategies. Foremost, the investor can begin to manage the risk by requiring a written business plan. Recent research by International Capital Resources reveals that 35 percent of investors said they would invest in a deal without a business plan.

In these hectic times, someone might feel the need to make a fast decision using *only* an extended executive summary. Don't! Work only with those companies whose management has taken the time to flesh out the business concept and strategy and can present it cogently. This is especially important in the context of the post-dot-com shakeout.

Again, investors should consider how much they can afford to invest. Investors should not let the portion of their capital earmarked for high-stakes, higher-risk investments burn a hole in their pockets. They need to answer the following critical questions:

◆ How much can I make?
◆ How much can I lose?
◆ How much can I invest?

Answering these questions involves calculating your own net worth, beginning with your assets, cash or equivalents, cash and checking accounts, certificates of deposit, receivable loans, and rental income. Also, calculate your retirement funds, IRA or Keogh, pension, profit sharing plan, treasury bills or notes, and money market funds. In addition, tally your investments—your stocks, bonds, and mutual funds, as well as equities you hold in other businesses. Add any life insurance policies and annuities and real estate holdings, including residence and income property. Don't forget about your personal property, including household furnishings, automobiles, art, jewelry, and so forth.

Part of this calculation obviously involves looking at liabilities: fixed expenses and credit-card payments; rent or mortgage; utilities and medical premiums; auto loans and auto insurance; life and medical insurance; property, personal, mortgage, or student expenses; and any state and federal taxes at the individual property and business levels. Compare these two parts and get a sense of your net worth *before* you make the final decision to enter the angel market.

We advocate allocating assets to different elements in the private equity class, or at the very least, differentiating one's investments by region, industry, technology, or stages of development. Obviously, managing venture investment risk involves high selectivity, discipline, and personal responsibility, such as allocating the assets to different elements in the private equity class or the various options that we have just described. If you plan to invest a large sum in a small business, you might consider investing smaller amounts in several smaller businesses. A few successful investments can offset the unsuccessful ones.

Moreover, you must audit and monitor the financial performance of your investments against expectations, pro formas, and financial projections. You can accomplish this through tight controls and strict financial reporting requirements that you have designed and integrated into the negotiations and deal structure. Also, rather than waiting until the venture "goes south" or discovering that milestones have been missed, emulate successful investors by hedging the risk. You can do this by taking a seat on the board and looking for increased involvement. Whether as an informal consultant, counselor, or adviser or as a part-time or full-time manager in the firm, you can keep close to the action and monitor the status of the investment.

Also, it's essential for the angel investor to aggressively structure terms and conditions early in the negotiations to protect against loss. Structuring transactions with available security or collateral, preferably using cash or cash equivalents, makes sense. Don't underestimate the value of good legal counsel in developing a strong set of conditions while negotiating before investing. The angel investor should not be afraid to negotiate steep discounts in security price, particularly at the earliest stage of investment. Many experienced investors say that it is never appropriate to invest at the price or valuation the entrepreneur suggests.

And think about controlling risk through a staged infusion of capital based upon the entrepreneur's or management's financial performance. Remember what we have said about investors releasing additional investment tranches only as the company achieves its goals.

As important as anything else that has been discussed is the assertive attitude angels must adopt in their responsibility for due diligence. Hedging strategies begin by conducting thorough due diligence. Better—much better—to say "NO" to a bad investment than to lose it all trying to hit it big. If you make only one to four investments per year, your ability to diversify the risk in your portfolio is limited. And since your time also is limited, you can manage and monitor only so many value-added deals.

Another strategy involves using other people's money as soon as possible in the transaction. For example, rather than directly investing in the venture, an individual may provide a guaranteed line of credit as part of the transaction. This saves the investor from touching current cash flow but guarantees his participation while using other financial capabilities that he possesses.

Along the same line, it pays to syndicate early. From the beginning, search for coinvestors to share not only due diligence but financial risk. Use other people's money as soon as possible in the transaction. Bring other investors into the deal, backing off from what you might have planned as your investment amount. Suppose, for example, an investor might plan to put in $250,000. The investor backs off to $125,000 and attracts other investors to make up the remaining portion. This strategy accomplishes a couple of things: Coinvestors can perform due diligence, and they can confirm or reject the original investor's opinion. If the additional investors do confirm, they can also help to bear the financial risk. This strategy positions the investor with reserves to back up his investment at a later date, if necessary.

CHAPTER 4

TYPES OF ANGEL INVESTMENT STRATEGIES

Defining Angel Investment Strategy

ARMED WITH AN UNDERSTANDING of their own motivations, allocation strategy, investment plan, and objectives, informed angel investors can make intelligent decisions about their approach to investing in private equity and specifically in the pre-IPO market. For angel investors, nothing approximates the experience of seeing a business evolve from an idea or a concept. It thrills them to participate in such growth. Michael Linnert, general partner of Technology Crossover Ventures, a Palo Alto, California, venture capital group that invested in Dunk.net, an Internet sporting goods retailer, happily admits that star power drives the traffic to its site. "Ultimately," he confessed, "that is how we will build an online business when there is so much noise out there." Mike Piazza, the star New York Mets catcher, declares, "I never thought I would be part of an Internet start-up. When you have a personal stake in a company, there is incentive for you to do everything possible for it to do well." Private equity investing serves as an opportunity to teach others what investors already know and allows them to share the excitement that growing a company generates.

Since 1989, International Capital Resources has conducted interviews, questionnaires, and surveys, and it has facilitated small-group discussions with more than 9,000 investors who make up its database, providing the authors with a unique perspective on the angel orientation to investing in early-stage companies and to the kinds of strategies they depend on to orchestrate their investments.

This brings us to the question of strategy. Strategy is a plan, method, or series of adroit moves for obtaining a specific goal or result. If you defined your investment plan and objectives using the guidelines we set forth in earlier chapters, your next step is to select and assemble the most appropriate mix of active and/or passive investment strategies to realize your objectives. Just remember the recursive nature of the beast; the process becomes simultaneously progressive and spotty. The process resembles working on a crossword puzzle: instead of operating in a strictly linear fashion, you soon find yourself focusing on more than a single aspect, filling in a word here, a word there.

How Demographics Affect the Choice of Active or Passive Angel Investment Strategies

DURING A RECENT INTERVIEW for Canadian television, one of us was asked, "How would you characterize the typical angel investment strategy?" The answer is simple: There is no typical strategy.

Investors vary in their approach and what they want from an investment strategy.

With approximately 400,000 active and passive angel investors and a potential pool of approximately 1 million households possessing the discretionary net worth to make angel investments, the strategies of successful investors, as one would expect, diverge significantly.

A number of demographic factors can influence strategy selection. Most of the angels we have come in contact with have some level of postgraduate education and extensive prior management experience. Many have owned their own companies. Given high levels of experience in specific industries and at the corporate level, different individuals might be inclined toward lead investment positions rather than to follow-on, more passive, investment strategies. Many angel investors are early-stage investors since they are interested in deals they can aggressively negotiate into strong discounts or premiums, and so find potential for high returns through capital appreciation. If an investor is not experienced in negotiating and structuring such equity transactions, she might not be inclined to active strategies.

From our research, we observe a bimodal distribution in the amount being invested, with a significant percentage of investments ranging from $25,000 to $100,000 and an equally significant percentage from $100,000 to $250,000. Depending on the amount of money available for investments, some investors might be inclined to invest in a single company, while others might be interested in spreading their investments over a larger, more diversified pool of candidates. Also, investors with limited amounts of discretionary net worth might be more inclined to pool their money and thus seek follow-on investors or coinvestment to reduce financial risk.

We have consistently identified a strong preference for technology-related ventures, particularly those that overlap with the investors' previous industry experience and expertise. So depending on the extent of the investor's deal flow, she might be inclined to invest in deals regardless of structure in industries with which she has the most familiarity.

Obviously, some segments of the high-net-worth private equity investor market are more inclined than others to the earliest stage of investing. Because of their age, need for income, need for security or collateral, and time remaining to garner capital appreciation, the retired affluent may find the highest-risk early-stage investing (with its longer-term horizons, longer hold times, and higher risk) less attractive than other affluent market segments do.

The age of investors can influence their selection of active or passive strategies. The age of private investors typically ranges from forty-six to sixty-five years old. Younger investors may seek strategies that will lead to capital appreciation. The young affluent include those whose wealth derives from inheritance; successful technological entrepreneurs; and, through career loyalty, cash in stock. The young affluent—deeply involved as they are in earlier stages of acquiring homes and material goods, of preparing for future security and their children's education, of time-consuming careers—will probably be less inclined to engage in the more active forms of early-stage investing, with their inherent risk and time requirements. They become much less available to provide the time-intensive dimension of added value needed in active early-stage investment. These economic elements and time elements make more active types of strategies less appealing to this market segment. Older investors, meanwhile, may be more inclined to income-based structures that will provide income from the investment and offer higher levels of security.

Individuals who are actively placing money back into the economy may be attracted to more active strategies. Likewise, senior corporate executives investing in industries they are familiar with and thoroughly understand, and business owners seeking to invest, diversify, and grow beyond their businesses through involvement in companies with similar technologies, may opt for more active strategies. This is also true of the career affluent seeking to broaden their retirement portfolio through capital appreciation over time. Career affluent investors are middle-aged individuals earning very high incomes from their professions and diversifying their investments beyond real estate, savings, and investments into the stock and bond market.

Variations in Angel Investment Strategies

DIFFERENT INVESTORS PREFER different levels of involvement in their ventures. These levels range along a spectrum from less active to more active involvement. Since the private venture investor helps to build value—that is, to build companies—most direct investments will require some additional work beyond just pouring money into the deal. This additional work often translates into being involved in some aspects of growing the business.

Also, the level of involvement can range dramatically in either direction, depending upon management's performance and the risk to the angel's investment. Less active angels may settle for a seat on a working board of directors, or they may require periodic detailed financial reports that they can review and analyze to assess company performance against objectives. Even this level of activity is far from being passive, although these persons are not looking for operating management responsibility. Meanwhile, consultants/investors may link their desire to invest with the development of their professional-services consulting practice. This investor will also look for remuneration and other perks from ongoing involvement in the company.

A number of factors influence where you choose to place yourself along the spectrum. For the more active investor, the primary concerns involve a focus on capital appreciation, higher-risk equity, a desire to take over lead investor activities, and some level of corporate involvement. This investor commits a great deal of time to the company and makes a minimum number of investments. And with regard to portfolio allocation strategies, her focus is on direct investment.

Active investors are seeking equity structures, whether preferred stock, preferred convertible stock, or common stock involvements, so they can participate in the increased value of ownership in the company. They make long-term commitments to grow the company into a successful venture, and then they participate in the increased value that derives from that successful growth. Since these investments by nature are truly equity investments, they tend to carry higher risks.

In addition, active investors tend to want to be lead investors, which means they possess the interest and the skills for taking on a much more active role in the company. Whether that means becoming a manager in the company, acting as a consultant when issues develop, or taking a board seat, all of these activities represent significant obligation.

Investors should consider becoming a member of a board of directors—an active role, to be sure. The primary responsibilities of directors are to follow SEC regulations, FASB considerations, and various stock market rules and regulations, as well as to stay current on the best practices in governance—in short, to reduce the frequency and severity of shareholder complaints and their resulting litigation against the directors and their firms. The directors and officers are motivated to maximize shareholder value. These duties typically require aggressive, bright people who "get" the business and "get" its strategy.

A recent study of thirty-nine technology companies by the Investor Responsibility Research Center—a nonprofit, corporate governance group—found that these boards are far smaller in start-up and early-stage companies than in typical S&P 500 companies (an average of 7.3 directors per board versus 11.9). They have a smaller percentage of independent directors (about half, versus two-thirds for larger companies), and average only two or three directors on their audit and compensation committees. Many new technology companies have small boards. Amazon has only six directors, with two inside directors. Yahoo! has six directors, including three company executives. A typical early-stage technology company board lineup consists of two or three insiders, two representatives of venture capital firms or the angel investors who helped launch the company, and a couple of independent directors.

Small boards can also have a difficult time adequately staffing committees. With the minimum resources associated with boards in early-stage companies, then, directors face greater responsibility and demands on their time. Still, some investors in early-stage companies decide to tackle director responsibilities because they wish to better follow the ventures or because they invested a significant amount. Even though a director's position is less active than, say, taking an operational role, these investors are still signing on for a considerable amount of time. This is why more active investors tend to make fewer investments per year. Even just a few investments represent a span of control that a single individual must manage. Don't forget: An angel investor is an individual, not a firm.

The active angel investment strategy also means monitoring the companies after the investments are made; generating the deal flow; reading the business plans; identifying the companies worth investing in; dealing with attorneys, accountants, and other advisers to ensure thorough due diligence; and negotiating the deal. All this takes *time*.

Last, the active investors differentiate themselves from passive investors in that they are direct investors. That is, they are more inclined to invest directly into a small number of companies with a significant amount of money in each, as opposed to diversifying across a large number of investments with smaller amounts of money or into fundlike structures.

Not all angel investors, however, are active. In comparing the active to the passive investor, the question really becomes what kind of investor you want to be, given your resources, inclination, background, and experience. More-passive investors are better suited to income-based structures. These might take the form of loans or of a return from cash flows until some multiple is achieved—one that was prearranged and structured during the negotiations. Risk of equity investment may be too much for them. They are inclined still to make investments in start-up and expanding ventures, but they're looking for income/return—and they're looking for that return sooner.

Another aspect of passive investors' makeup is their decision to manage risk by investing in a less chancy stage of development. So rather than investing in pre-seed, seed, or R&D situations, they will gravitate to expansion financing—for example, first round or second round, particularly of companies that show evidence of having generated some customers or revenues, even if they have not yet reached the break-even point.

The passive investors or the more passive strategies are typically associated with coinvestment, called *follow-on investments.* The more passive investment strategies follow on the heels of lead investors, providing their money to support the research, deal flow, development, and identification of promising ventures. This type of investing resembles a shareholder strategy. In other words, the individuals may be involved in monitoring the company and staying abreast of its financial performance and monitoring financial reports or other information on how the company is progressing toward its financial and strategic objectives. However, it is a relatively passive role compared to a board, operations, management, or consulting role.

Obviously these less-active roles do not require the amount of time to investigate deal-flow development, due diligence, or the pursuit of negotiations essential to the process. In addition, these investors often will spread their resources over a larger number of companies to create diversification. In some ways, this is a carry-over of the shareholders' strategy, as they diversify their portfolio among a number of different industries or companies in varying stages of development or in different localities. Commonly, we see more passive investment strategies manifesting themselves in indirect investment and diversification through investments in funds or in private placements that brokerages or investment banks might bring to the investor's attention.

Whether an investor selects a more active or more passive investment strategy, she makes a choice based on a number of additional considerations—secondary elements, if you will.

For example, if you know an industry well, if you have built or sold your own company and can empathize with the entrepreneur, you're going to be more inclined to take a lead investor position. But if you have never started your own company, if you have worked only for others and have never been an entrepreneur, if you don't understand the industry but are attracted to it nonetheless, then being a follow-on investor makes sense because you want to participate in a booming investment arena. Knowing the limits of your knowledge—that is, knowing what you don't know—becomes an important exercise worth walking through before selecting active or passive strategies.

Another thing to think about is your ability to find and qualify deals. In a later chapter we will touch on a proprietary deal-flow development strategy from International Capital Resources. But not everyone is up to developing an infrastructure to generate a large magnitude of deal flow, or to handle it once it begins to pour in. Many simply don't want to be bothered, or view it as an invasion of their privacy. So the ability to find and qualify deals becomes another mitigating issue in determining their strategic direction.

Another is the need for personal recognition. Ego plays its part. Over the years, we've met humble and endearing multimillionaires who have built and sold their own companies and learned how to be successful investors. We have also met megalomaniacs you couldn't stand to be in the same room with. You know the type: They make those giants of hubris—Sophocles' Oedipus and Shakespeare's Coriolanus—seem like self-effacing nondescripts. The idea here is to have a sense of your own need for recognition. Obviously, if you have a great need for recognition, you will find more active strategies to your liking, but if you're not quite so ego-driven, you will find passive strategies thoroughly acceptable.

Also on the investor's checklist is her need for control, a need that emanates from two areas. One, an executive who has labored through ubiquitous political sand traps brings to the table the political savvy necessary to get things done. Someone this persuasive may not feel the need for structural control. On the flip side, however, investors confess their war stories of having lost their shirt the one time they loosened their grips. It doesn't happen a second time to the shrewd investor; it's an error she commits only once. If your experience has led you to believe in the need for control to manage the risk, you will be disposed toward active strategies. If you feel you can handle things with diplomacy, or, when necessary, with a hint or two from Machiavelli, perhaps passive strategies will work for you.

And last, to get actively involved, you will need time. If you don't have it, opt for passive strategies.

Active Angel Investment Strategies

LEAD ANGEL INVESTMENT STRATEGY

EXPERIENCED ANGEL INVESTORS engineer lead investment; they prefer focus, agreement on the investment in the venture, simple equity-based structures, coinvesting, geographic proximity, intensive control and involvement, and clearly defined return expectations.

Lead angel investors talk from experience, not from theory. These individuals have built and sold their own companies or have been involved in taking a company public. And if they have not been part of the IPO team, they have invested in IPOs. They have been in the role of the entrepreneur, and consequently they can empathize with the start-up. They are viscerally linked to the entrepreneurial perspective. They have been deal makers; perhaps they have worked in investment banking, or at least have been on the investor's side of the table during negotiations. Or they have experience in intermediary capacities, possess a law or accounting degree, or augment their income through successful consulting.

In many cases, those inclined toward the lead angel investor strategy were successful executives with major publicly traded companies. They typically came from nontechnical backgrounds, focusing on corporate work, not on technical or engineering work. Many of them have obtained securities licenses or are familiar with the securities business, or in some way have worked with or invested in venture capital funds.

Our research shows that approximately 35 percent of angel investors surveyed indicated they would invest in industries that they didn't know anything about. This is not the case with lead angel investors as a group. Angel investors who select the lead investment strategy invest only in industries they know. They do so not only to hedge against the downside risks but to shorten the due diligence cycle through their familiarity with the research to support the market and financial forecasts. Though they may have sets of advisers, they rely on their own investigation and trust in their own judgment and intuition.

Another aspect of lead angel investment strategy is their understanding of the possible span of control or the number of investments they can legitimately control, and the rate of investment. These investors are the most active. Besides their one to four investments a year (typically worth $50,000 to $250,000 per deal), they add value. But most important, they are usually first in. These are not investors who suggest to an entrepreneur that they should go elsewhere to raise money and then come back and the investor will reconsider the deal. These investors seize the opportunity and make the commitment first, hence the name "lead" investor.

Lead angel investment strategy is predisposed toward equity investments. While lead investors periodically engage in debt transactions with sweeteners such as warrants, they emphasize deal structure and the inherent legal agreements associated with that structure to contain the risk. But their accent falls on conducting due diligence, selecting deals, and analyzing management. These investors require a business plan and a top management team. They're interested not in running the company but in working with senior executives who can run it. Their eye is focused on liquidity, not necessarily income during the term of the hold.

One investor told us, "I believe that we attract people to us because of our interests." This is true of lead investors, who learn early to leverage their own money by working with other people who have a passive investment strategy. The lead investors are out there generating the deal flow, identifying the opportunities, doing the preliminary due diligence, and laying the groundwork by negotiating the deal to make sure it is doable.

Yet they also have a strong network of coinvestors who trust in the lead investor's judgment and to whom they can take the deals they identify as promising. They put their own money into the deal first because they have the financial resources to make the deal happen with impressive velocity. This type of investor is consistently referring to others the deals in which they themselves are investing.

Among lead investors there's definitely a proximity preference. They want deals close to home, so they can monitor their progress and act before trouble erupts.

Lead investors focus more than anything else on people because they know that plans don't get funded, people get funded. As one investor said, "A good CEO without an exit strategy is better than a poor CEO *with* an exit strategy." These investors want to work with entrepreneurs they like. However, this does not preclude their desire for control, especially if the downside occurs and the entrepreneur does not meet the established milestones. An outside board can accomplish this control, though not necessarily through complete ownership of the company. The essence of lead investment strategy is involvement. Investors do this by providing input to management, making a contribution, holding a board seat, and, if interested in being extremely active for a short period of time, by assisting in problem solving as a consultant or adviser to the company. Operating here is the investor's shared desire with the entrepreneurs to build the company and, above all, have fun in doing it.

This investor will not concentrate solely on getting a return, though targets of 50 percent internal rate of return, compounded annually over the term of the hold of the investment, is a common objective. And while they might not always achieve that exact target, our research shows that about a third of the time they're reasonably successful. It is important for them to obtain such returns because there's a general belief among lead angel investors that this is the only way to subsequently attract institutional venture capital.

MANAGER INVESTMENT STRATEGY

THE MANAGER/INVESTOR STRATEGY is for those who seek to invest but who are also looking for a job. They may have been a casualty of corporate downsizing, sold their company, or received a golden parachute early, but found retirement unfulfilling. Now they want to get back in the fray, but in their late forties to late fifties have too much dignity to push a résumé across the table or are too affluent to have to make such a move.

In effect, manager/investors will buy their next job through their investment. And they will be linked to that investment for a long time. They want to be part of the team and are determined not to take a hit on the one deal they're investing in. Because they're looking for a longer-term, job-related commitment, these investors are less inclined to stomach high risk.

These manager/investors are concerned about playing a role in a company's business activities. They are not necessarily interested in control but wish to be active in the company. Their due diligence cycles are long-term. Some have even been accused by entrepreneurs on the receiving end of their evaluation of making a career out of due diligence. In any case, manager/investors typically are not interested in an idea or a seed-stage concept. They don't want to just invest but to participate in the formation, management, and direction of the company. They want "in" through an active operations position, or at least an ongoing consulting or board role.

Such individuals range in age from early forties to mid fifties and are often mid-to-late-career managers or former business owners, very seasoned executives with strong business analysis skills. The size of the investments can be substantial, ranging from $100,000 to $200,000. However, these investors typically are not a resource for subsequent rounds.

Obviously, in choosing this strategy, the investors will seek candidate companies with demonstrated viability and will be less likely to choose turnarounds. They are concerned about seeing a complete operational business plan, not just an investment-oriented business plan; they require clear pro forma statements and strong, clear, and realistic assumptions. Those who use this investment strategy are aggressive in private negotiations, seeking steep discounts and the benefit of significant appreciation on their equity investment. The investment opportunity must whet the investor's appetite with above-average returns. Most important, however, the chemistry has to be there between the manager/investor and the current management team and founders.

CORPORATE INVESTMENT STRATEGY

IN THE WORLD OF HIGH TECHNOLOGY, insightful corporate investors and angels who own their own companies have developed highly profitable returns and beneficial synergistic relationships by putting their cash reserves to work on funding promising higher-risk technology start-ups. Companies as diverse as advertising agencies and trucking companies are racing to set up venture capital funds of their own. More corporations are setting up venture capital arms, mostly to invest in enterprises whose work may affect their core business. Twenty percent of *Fortune* 1000 corporations have started their own venture funds. According to *The Corporate Venturing Report,* "corporate venturing exploded in 1999. Driven by the need to ensure long-term competitiveness, corporations last year announced the formation of venture capital programs totaling $6.3 billion," a figure up from 1998's $1.7 billion and 1997's $1.3 billion. Of twenty-eight firms that disclosed their fund size, this study informs us, nineteen committed at least $100 million to their corporate venturing programs. Companies active in corporate venture funding that have invested (with varying degrees of success) in hundreds of start-ups in the past few years include Intel, Nokia, Lucent Technologies, Artisan Entertainment, and United Parcel Service.

Intel began investing in start-ups in 1990. Its corporate business development unit completed more than 130 investments in 1998 with a value of $330 million. Intel has made more than 275 direct investments valued at approximately $3.5 billion, according to Asset Alternatives. Early-stage investments include Red Hat, Inktomi, and iVillage. Many of these investments focus on technology for the small-business customer. Nokia Ventures is a $100 million fund founded in 1998 to invest in early-stage, high-growth information technology companies. Nokia's motive for creating the fund was to learn about new markets, business models, and technologies. Its investments included Informative.com, SoftCoin, and NetSanity. According to Private Equity Alternatives, more than 160 U.S. corporations have corporate business development units investing directly into entrepreneurial-stage companies, creating a significant alternative source of start-up funding and, consequently, acting the part of angels for early-age companies.

Blake Modersitzki, the managing director of Novell Ventures, suggested in a recent article in *American Venture* that leading technology companies increasingly invest in start-ups to create valuable product synergies. In-house corporate venture capital divisions are taking the initiative with the goal of extending the market presence of both the investor company and the start-up, while enabling the exploration and creation of new markets. Novell employs a holistic investment approach, emphasizing long-term partnership and strategy direction instead of quick profits or the largest return on investment. Other major industry players include Intel, Microsoft, Oracle, Lycos, MCI WorldCom, and Comcast.

Lycos, Inc., the large Internet search engine service, started Lycos Labs, a business that invests in and fosters Internet start-ups in exchange for 20 percent equity in the companies. Lycos Labs has earmarked $100 million for investment and incubator development purposes. Corporations are motivated to invest in order to gain access to new technology, obtain strategic benefits, position themselves to promote their own services and products, leverage their own technological expertise, and—acting like a "lead investor"—convince other corporations to pool capital with them. For example, Intel convinced Dell, Ford Company, and GE to join Intel in the Intel 64 Fund, LLC. Foremost, however, corporate investing groups seek a strategic fit through which they can link their own R&D and corporate development with investee companies.

Since 1999, corporate venturing has come into vogue, with successful high-tech companies establishing organized, focused corporate venturing policies. Basically, these companies create a separate group inside the corporate development department dedicated solely to venture investing. When these groups grab a bite of the venture-capital-world apple, along with angel investors and syndicating investment opportunities among peer corporations, they ensure not only survival but also long-term success in the competitive high-tech world.

This strategy increases the quality of deal flow to the company and appeals to venture firms looking to validate technological and market opportunities. Whether the fear of missing the next big technological discovery is the driving force behind corporate venturing, or whether it's survival, companies like Novell and Intel and others invest in technology start-ups to help keep the company in sync with market changes.

The realities of corporate venturing have an interesting manifestation in the angel market. As we mentioned in our introduction, a lot of executives of well-known technology companies have managed to get rich in recent years on stock option grants. Now, academic research has identified how they are mining this particular vein of gold: they are using nonpublic information about their company's products and development to obtain returns.

Two respected accounting professors studied 324,000 stock trades made by officers at more than 10,000 public companies from January 1985 to November 1997. They concluded that insiders at technology companies profited greatly by trading (and treading) on nonpublic information. The study, by David Aboody, an assistant professor of accounting at the Anderson School of the University of California at Los Angeles, and Baruch Lev, the Philip Bardes Professor of Accounting and Finance at New York University Stern School of Business, split the companies into those that were heavy users of research and development (basically technology concerns) and those that weren't. They then compared the returns of the insiders.

In the March 12, 2000, edition of the *New York Times*'s Market Watch column, Gretchen Morgenson reported that company stock purchased by insiders at roughly 3,800 technology companies outperformed their counterparts at 6,200 or so other concerns by three to one. Sales by insiders at research-oriented companies also performed better, but by a narrower margin. In other words, technology insiders made 3 percent on their buys within twenty-five days; after six months, these insiders had gains of 9.6 percent. Insiders in ordinary companies earned 0.9 percent on their purchases within twenty-five days and 3.6 percent after six months.

Professor Lev noted that technology is poorly disclosed to investors. While some technology-related information should be kept secret from competitors, insiders and well-connected investors have an advantage. Those well-connected investors are the corporate investor funds and angel investors who become privy to such information. Not surprising is the exact parallel in the private market, an important indication of the kinds of returns possible through extensive deal-flow development and extensive due diligence.

It becomes important to focus on information or advantages held by technology-company insiders because research programs are unique to the developing company and hard for an outsider to assess. Capital investments share common characteristics across an industry. Plus, it is well known that investors react more strongly to news of technology-insider stock trades than they do to trades involving other companies. No suggestion of illegality here. Instead, corporate venturing—whether it's a large corporate investor like Intel and Novell or a corporation established mainly to invest in other corporate entities—is meant to gather research-based inside technology information and to position the investor for significantly higher levels of return.

The allure of a windfall has not escaped the big banks, which are less concerned with the inside track on innovation and are more concerned with grabbing a portion of the VC action. Banks, while not pure corporate investors, can be categorized as part of the corporate investment phenomenon. Banks have spotted the huge payoffs generated by venture capital and corporate investors in recent years. Chase Manhattan invested $289 million during the first quarter of 2000, according to the PricewaterhouseCoopers' *Money Tree Report*. Chase spread seed money to forty-five investments, earmarking 63 percent of its $6.8 billion private equity portfolio for the "new economy." In 1999 private investments accounted for about $2.08 billion of the bank's pretax income. Norwest Equity Partners, part of Wells Fargo, invested $119 million in the first quarter of 2000, and BancBoston Capital placed $115 million during the same period, according to PricewaterhouseCoopers.

ACQUISITION INVESTMENT STRATEGY

THIS NEXT ACTIVE angel investment strategy is called the acquisition investment strategy. Investors who choose this strategy have a strong need for control. In fact, this strategy has evolved partly as a response to prospective buyers' frustration with the inadequate business brokerage market. The business brokerage market is a mess because of the lack of professionalism and effectiveness of business brokerages in helping interested individuals buy companies appropriate to their desires, skill sets, and strategies. Hence, investors are funneling money into the private equity market, hoping to find a company worth owning.

In effect, the business brokerage market is being run like a multiple listing service adopted in real estate deals. A business brokerage outfit introduces the prospective buyer to what is on the books at the moment. No attempt is made to actively search for a company or to help a company get ready for sale, and no investment banking logic prevails. Many who want to buy their own business leave exasperated.

International Capital Resources had a client who had been using brokers to locate a company to buy for two years. Ultimately he settled on a company that he really didn't want—only because he got fed up with the search. This failure of the business brokerage market to accommodate investors and, secondarily, to reduce unrealistically high valuations of companies forces out many prospective buyers. They don't have the resources to keep searching in the face of such obstacles. And for those reasons, investors are now being funneled into the angel investor market, bringing with them their buyer's orientation to private investing.

Such individuals are using an acquisition approach to their investments. They have that need for control we discussed earlier. Therefore, they have built an extensive network of coinvestors to gain the leverage that large amounts of money give them, the leverage to have all the capital they need to buy a company. And while they would prefer to buy a more established company, perhaps at higher levels of development, they cannot close the deal because of the high valuations or because the business brokerage community did not serve them well.

As a result, they are actively functioning in lead investment capacities and searching out opportunities that will allow them to take control of the company through the investment process. The acquisition investment strategy represents some of the largest investments being made by individuals. We see investments of $1 million to $2 million or more by private individuals. These individuals, while they are approaching the investment within the context of angel investing and perhaps equity and stock purchase, are negotiating structures that belie what they're really doing: buying the company.

And in many cases, entrepreneurs accept this, especially those who are tired of trying to raise money. Perhaps they don't have the management background to grow the company; or the product is underdeveloped, and they need the money to get it into shape so the company can move forward. They may be trying to apply the technology to an inappropriate commercialization. Perhaps they have decided to attempt to conquer a market that will require "engineering" the public into recognizing the value of the product and the problem it solves. Perhaps weaknesses abound in the overall business model. The astute investor who identifies such problems will use any such information to negotiate the acquisition of the company. And a number of legal structures permit such collaboration between the investor and the entrepreneur.

One investor in ICR's network said, "Somebody once defined the survival of the fittest to me as not being the strongest, but finding the niche where you can exist and make things happen." In other words, it's not being the fittest that counts; it's finding the fit! And investors who really were buyers for an extended period of time, who were unable to find an acquisition, have decided to buy into a business but haven't relinquished the buyer's orientation. But what's important is recognizing that that's OK—that, in fact, many "companies" are not companies at all, but technologies in disguise or technologies masquerading as companies that would benefit from just such a buyer's leadership.

Sometimes an astute investor can identify that inconsistency. And when she does, her acquisition of that technology is thoroughly appropriate. And it becomes irrelevant whether she acquires it through a purchase of the assets or through some more involved structure, such as buying 100 percent of the equity and allowing the entrepreneur to earn back that equity over time. For what we're looking at is an acquisition transaction that was entered into through the pre-IPO investment door.

Obviously someone who has opted for the acquisition investment strategy is among the most active of all investors, someone who must conform to all of the criteria outlined for carrying out an active strategy.

PROFESSIONAL SERVICES BUSINESS DEVELOPMENT INVESTMENT STRATEGY

A NUMBER OF INTERMEDIARIES and professional service providers want to participate in the pre-IPO investment market and leverage that participation for business development purposes. Such professionals include financial intermediaries; management consultants assisting with business plan pro forma development; consultants, CPAs, and accountants assisting with the development of financial reports or responding to due diligence inquiries; investment bankers helping the company with deal structuring or valuation; or even securities attorneys assisting the company with their investment documentation. Whether attorneys, accountants, financial advisers, corporate finance specialists, management consultants, or whatever, these individuals are making relatively small investments—$25,000 or less. They then provide various services to the company in exchange for stock and/or defer their professional fees until funding is complete. Others frequently view them as having a stake in the company's survival, growth, and development.

In one survey we conducted, angel investors voiced their concern that prospective coinvestors who use this strategy may create a conflict of interest. In spite of these reservations, some professional service providers persist in leveraging their experience and skills to participate in the early-stage private-equity market.

Passive, Indirect Angel Investment Strategies

IN THIS SECTION we'll review four different types of angel investment strategies: angel consortium coinvestment strategy, barter investment strategy, socially responsible investment strategy, and fund-based investment strategy. Rest assured that "passive" carries no pejorative connotation; by passive, we simply mean "less active"—nothing more, nothing less. Engaging in less active investment strategies is every bit as appropriate as engaging in more active ones. It all depends on the investor. It's not unlike the physician who (we hope) makes a diagnosis before deciding on the remedy—maybe rest, maybe exercise, maybe both. The doctor diagnoses your condition; you agree to a strategy you can live with. What could be more appropriate?

ANGEL CONSORTIUM COINVESTMENT STRATEGY

IN A RECENT INTERVIEW, one investor observed, "I am a follow-on investor. I have been involved in a number of situations in which other investors have contributed substantial money in companies that I eventually got into as a follow-on investor. That's the kind of situation I like to see. If there's a major investor in the company, it's important for me to know that she has more invested in the company than I do, that she is committed to carrying on the company despite the blips."

In fact, follow-on investors can add value and be important to the transaction. Individuals who bring more than money to the table, however, are inclined to seek partnership and coinvestment with an active lead investor. The same investor mentioned earlier also said, "In experiences I've had with a few companies I've invested in, there was a lead private investor, a major investor who had invested close to a million dollars in the company. I felt secure because I knew that he had deep pockets. He had a vested interest in and a history with the company, so I knew if problems arose—they did, they always do—he would keep that company afloat."

Among your circle of private investors, getting one who can bring added value along with a significant amount of money can make the difference. If you are compatible and you know your lead investor, you will bring something of real value to the company as a passive coinvestor.

Follow-on or coinvestors are essentially contributing to the formation of a loose confederation. Typically the confederation members are not related by blood but are related through legal structures, such as an investment partnership. These individuals will also like having a lead investor who has experience in starting, running, or selling a company. Coinvestors want to have financial reports sent to them during the monitoring process, and they may be willing to function as a sounding board, but they will not formalize that role by taking a board seat, agreeing to do consulting, or, to be sure, accepting an operational job role or description.

One way to expand your coinvestor group is to draw on your collegial ties. Your alma mater directory, combined with a little networking, can go a long way toward creating your own informal network of coinvestors. Focus on alumni with a net worth of more than $1 million. Such coinvestment networking has already begun at Princeton, Stanford, Harvard, Yale, MIT, and Northwestern universities, so alumni of these schools need to identify the right contact person if they are interested in exploring these contacts. A sense of community exists among alumni, and perhaps you will feel more confident getting involved with a graduate of your college or university. Less-experienced angels who live in rural areas away from pockets of entrepreneurial activity may find this resource particularly valuable.

Follow-on investors are often closely connected with the active lead angel investors we discussed earlier, and they will consistently coinvest with those investors they believe in to both identify and monitor deals. These investors will invest from $50,000 to $500,000.

BARTER INVESTMENT STRATEGY

WE ONCE OVERHEARD an investor ask an entrepreneur, "Do you need the money that you're requesting with the business plan investment proposal, or do you need the items you were going to purchase with the money?"

This question captures the essence of the barter-investor strategy. Barter investors want to participate in a company by providing the assets (in exchange for equity) that the company sought to purchase with the proceeds of its financing. In effect, the investors are dovetailing assets they possess with the company they seek to invest in and trying to obtain equity by providing those assets. The strategy of barter investors is to provide the products or services slated for purchase in the company's use-of-funds statement. They identify what the company would acquire with the capital it is trying to raise. The investor supplies these assets directly in exchange for equity in the company. While the provision of the assets is partly participative, the investor's role in most cases is much more passive. He is offering infrastructure in exchange for equity.

One barter investor we interviewed explained, "My partner and I are very flexible in terms of how we go into a venture, but we want a significant equity position in the company. Common stock or convertible preferred, purchase options, licensing agreements, and joint ventures—we would consider all of these things.

"But let me back up a minute," he continued. "We have an active business today that might dovetail with what the entrepreneur seeking capital would do. We have an infrastructure in place. We advertise for customers, process customer orders, warehouse, ship, build computers, service computers in the field, and do all sorts of other things: bill, invoice, and collect. All of these things we might be able to add to your business if you think of us as an incubator in exchange for equity as well."

Barter investors, instead of using cash for investment, leverage the infrastructure of their existing entity—use what they already have. They might participate in the business or sit on the board, and if problems arise, they may assist management; but for the most part, the transaction is about the exchange of an asset for equity. As you can see, this is different from the kind of role that the active investor is looking for.

SOCIALLY RESPONSIBLE INVESTMENT STRATEGY

WHILE 90 PERCENT of the investors in ICR's proprietary database are self-made millionaires—individuals who have become wealthy by building their own companies—10 percent of the investors in the database possess inherited wealth.

For a number of self-made millionaires with a conscience and those who have inherited wealth, socially responsible investment of either an "inclusionary" or "exclusionary" nature is part of their portfolio strategy. A number of investors among the top percentile of the richest households in the United States are diversifying their portfolios into private equity but doing so with a social conscience. Recall that "inclusionary" investing means investing in companies whose values match those of the investor, while "exclusionary" investment strategies for the very wealthy preclude investing in areas anathema to their beliefs.

Those who choose the socially responsible investment find their counterpart in angel investing, albeit using a more passive strategy. Typically we call these investors "nurture" capitalists, those searching for opportunities with persons who share their values. These individuals may be less able to provide savvy business support; hence, we will not find them pursuing active investment strategies. Investing in ventures that address major social issues or solve social problems is one way these investors can give back to the community. For this reason, and to augment their deal flow, they diversify their portfolios with socially responsible investments, usually received through trusted advisers.

FUND-BASED INVESTMENT STRATEGY

ALTHOUGH ANGEL INVESTING is open only to the very wealthy, private-equity investing is more available now than ever, even if it's still not for the masses. The burgeoning interest in private equity is partly because of the press that IPOs receive, but the real money is in pre-IPO investment. When we compare it with public market returns, we see more upside potential.

Because of the high risk, minimal information for due diligence purposes, and need for monitoring ongoing performance, investing directly into a single company is not for everyone. If you lack deal flow or an invitation to participate from a lead investor with connections, perhaps you'll grasp the alternative of a more passive approach by investing in funds or through an investment broker or adviser. The danger, of course, in relying upon investment brokers is that some of the less scrupulous can be dumping low-grade companies or offering shares at much higher valuations and prices than they're worth.

If you don't know how to aggressively bargain over valuation and pricing of equity in negotiations, then rely on the investment brokers, advisers, and bankers to get into this market. We advise selecting an investment firm that invests its own money in the deal and invites customers to join them. Also, select firms that report investment performance to shareholders on a regular schedule. And whenever possible, obtain the names of other investors in the deal so that you can communicate with them during the term of the hold. If you don't have the time for the homework or the research associated with this type of investing, try publicly traded private equity funds.

Some investment banks to consider are Offroad Capital, Cagan

Capital, WR Hambrecht, e-Offering (owned by e-Trade), and even Charles Schwab. If funds are your option, consider investing in mutual funds or publicly traded companies that hold stakes in private firms. Publicly traded companies that invest in private businesses include CMGI, Internet Capital Group, and Angel Investors, LP. CMGI of Andover, Massachusetts, is an Internet venture fund that cut its teeth in 1995 when it formed Lycos, Inc., by buying the rights to search technology created by scientists at Carnegie Mellon University in 1994. Internet Capital Group of Wayne, Pennsylvania, is a venture fund for small investors. Angel Investors, LP, of Redwood City, California, has formed two funds totaling $180 million from wealthy individual investors investing in Northern California start-ups. Angel Investors, LP, counts Dana Carvey, Shaquille O'Neal, and Henry Kissinger among its investors.

Commonsense advice for any of these options is to avoid putting all of your eggs into one basket. Imitate the venture capital pros, who prefer a lot of small investments in many companies to big bets on just a few. Also, don't bet the ranch. Private equity is among the most aggressive investments and should form only a small portion of your equity portfolio, perhaps 5 percent to 15 percent at most.

The fund-based indirect investment strategy may be the only way for less experienced and less affluent private investors to get a share of the pre-IPO market. Obviously these are passive investment opportunities, and the individuals will not take a role in the company. In addition, the investors need to learn patience, because even with funds or investments into private placements through investment banks, the holds can range from five to ten years. Obviously, for individuals who select this type of investment strategy, the location of the companies will be less relevant, because they won't be visiting or monitoring them. Also, it does open up the door for investment in much smaller amounts, ranging from as little as $5,000 to $25,000.

Perhaps some insight into an individual who selected this route, as described in *Angel Investor* magazine in October 1999, would be worthwhile. Between 85 percent and 90 percent of Larry Warner's investment holdings are in blue-chip stocks. The other 10 to 15 percent is in venture capital. He says that the larger portfolio is boring but essential for his long-term financial well-being. The venture portfolio is fun. He explains that angel investing provides him with the excitement of watching a new venture evolve, as well as the opportunity for higher returns.

He attempts to keep his venture portfolio relatively small so that if the investments don't meet his expectations, he won't have to change his lifestyle. He is in a time-intensive service profession and simply doesn't have the hours to determine whether an entrepreneur has a good track record or whether the business idea has merit. Therefore, he relies upon venture firms to identify promising new companies and to perform extensive due diligence. While this doesn't eliminate all of the risk, the research they conduct enables this particular angel investor to make a more informed decision.

Through this mechanism, he has been able to invest in a series of deals across the high-tech, software, and medical research industries, thereby providing his portfolio with industry diversification. "I'm not truly knowledgeable regarding any of these industries that I've invested in," he says, "but I believe the types of companies in my portfolio represent the wave of the future. I could easily have invested the same amount of money in public companies and generated a return of 10 to 20 percent, but it wouldn't have been as exciting. My venture capital portfolio provides me with opportunities for an outsized win." Warner reveals that he used to race motorcycles and was a hard-driving athlete. "I've gotten to the age where I can't do some of the exciting athletic things that came naturally a decade ago. At this stage of my life I consider angel investing a way to capture that same sense of excitement."

DEAL-FLOW DEVELOPMENT: SURFACING ANGEL INVESTMENT OPPORTUNITIES

How Angels Historically Have Located Deals

HISTORICALLY, ANGELS FOUND their deals in three ways.

Research by International Capital Resources finds that

approximately 57 percent of more than 9,000 angel

investors uncovered deals through personal contacts.

Primary resources include acquaintances who have rela-

tionships with the principals of companies; friends, family members, or coworkers who believe in a venture's products or services; or relatives or colleagues who are themselves principals in a venture or investors in the deal.

Around 31 percent of the investors in our database have come across pre-IPO venture opportunities through referrals from attorneys, accountants, investment bankers, brokers, or other professional-service providers, such as formal or informal angel clubs. Typically, these professionals have had encounters or relationships with founders or principals of companies seeking capital.

Approximately 12 percent of the investors in our database suggest that they have received an unsolicited contact from a non-family representative of the firm seeking financing. In some cases, someone has made a telephone cold call or boldly approached them at a venture forum where entrepreneurs looking for capital may seize an opportunity to network with investors.

Satisfaction with Traditional Deal-Flow Development Techniques

BUT THESE TRADITIONAL METHODS—the cold call, the approach at a forum—have left angel investors with skimpy deal flows. The number of promising ventures that turn up in this manner generally has been dismal. Research by Harrison and Mason in 1996 found that approximately 33 percent of investors felt dissatisfied, and an additional 10 percent very dissatisfied, with these existing channels of communication. Such statistics reflect the cry from investors for more formal deal-flow development strategies. In any small group of investors, each person will go about developing his own deal flow, with a regional focus and a propensity for privacy—circumstances that account for the limited number of deals the investor finds worthy of review.

One of the reasons that these groups—whether individual investors or coinvestor groups—have traditionally remained small is that individual investors *do* prize their privacy. As soon as entrepreneurs spot angels, the angels become inundated with deals, few of which meet their investment criteria. They suddenly forfeit their privacy. At a party, a meeting, a professional event—it doesn't matter; someone will approach them, slide out the old guitar, and start singing the song. In short, the investor who surfaces has to be ready for what follows. However, as the research makes clear, although investors are concerned about their privacy, they are also dissatisfied with the existing mechanisms they are forced to rely on for finding investment opportunities.

To some extent investors can buffer themselves against intrusion by following our suggestions for properly organizing themselves with a deal-flow development process. This may mean making sure that home telephone numbers and addresses are never used for the receipt of business plans, establishing a different set of phone numbers and e-mail addresses, or even setting up a more formal office from which all of this business can be directed. In addition, as we will discuss, mechanisms for communicating your interest in this type of investing do provide levels of confidentiality and buffering.

Developing Your Angel Investment Goals and Objectives

DEVELOPING GOALS IS an individual creative step in the deal-flow development process. Establishing goals reflects key decisions in the investor's marketing process and significantly affects his investment of time, money, and energy to find deals. Clearly stated, goals can contribute meaning and structure to an investor's vision. Goals or general statements of direction are established in a hierarchy. The number of goals you set should be limited. Too many diffuse resources weakens the focus on deal-flow development. Better to concentrate resources and successfully attain goals than spread too thinly the scarce resources of the individual investor. In contrast, an objective needs to be a more specific and quantifiable statement. Attaining an objective should lead to accomplishing a goal. The more effort invested in specifying an objective, the easier it will be later to measure progress toward accomplishing it. Each goal is usually supported by one or more objectives.

Goals must be feasible. They should be challenging but realistic. Investment plans with unattainable goals create an atmosphere of failure. Those who create such lofty goals fail to recognize the human element in gaining acceptance for the deal-flow development program and the need to engender enthusiasm for implementing it.

Goal setting is not an easy process. Goals often masquerade as dreams and hopes, soon becoming unrealistic and impossible to measure. Pie-in-the-sky hardly makes for constructive planning. It is much more feasible to set goals with a thorough understanding of market size and opportunity and with knowledge grounded in experience with the target market.

Since angel investing is such a personal activity, it's impossible to separate personal goals from investment objectives. Therefore, the solo investor must take personal goals into account when establishing deal-flow development objectives. The trap is to allow investing to direct his life rather than the other way around. He must set his own priorities and then factor them into his investment objectives.

Most of the investors we have worked with have a deal-flow development strategy in mind. Some have taken the time to put these ideas into writing. For others, the plan is more intuitive. In other words, the deal-flow development strategy becomes a set of hunches, something implicit rather than explicit.

It is neither right nor wrong to have a written plan. Rather, the prime consideration is how well the investor has planned. But we believe the process of writing down and working through a deal-flow development plan is invaluable. Writing helps to assemble the data and organize the investor's thinking. We're reminded of novelist E. M. Forster's comment on this point: "How do I know what I think 'til I see what I've said?" The planning process clarifies assumptions and reveals the level of agreement when more than one investor is involved. Also, when you read through the written goals, much more becomes accessible: objectives, timing of activities, responsibilities and budgets, and errors in judgment or failure to think through deal-flow development assumptions.

In order to get the most out of creating a deal-flow development strategy, the investor must first think through a number of critical objectives. In the following paragraphs, we illuminate some of those elements.

◆ **First, define your purpose for investing in early-stage companies.** The earlier chapters have already introduced the concept of angel investor motivation and characteristics. This information will be valuable in helping to pinpoint the type of investors you want to build relations with, ensuring that you get involved only with investors who share a comparable orientation.

Specify your equity portfolio and determine what percentage of it you will diversify into the private area. Most investors we interviewed diversify between 5 percent and 15 percent of their equity portfolio into private or direct investment deals. Even the most aggressive money manager will allow a high-net-worth client a certain amount to invest at his discretion.

◆ **Second, define the size of the investment per company.** This is different from the portfolio amount that's committed to private investment. This calculation will help you determine whether you can diversify the capital appropriated for private investment into a single company or a small number of companies, or whether you should more appropriately forge an indirect coinvestment strategy because of the amount of money available.

◆ **Next, define your acceptable level of risk.** This involves a number of different things. One of the best ways to measure your risk tolerance is to pinpoint the development stage of the companies in which you're willing to invest. We have already defined different stages of development. Obviously the earlier the stage, the higher the risk; the later the stage, the lower the risk. Another condition to consider is liquidity timing. This does have an impact on your risk orientation. For example, our research indicates an eight-year average hold before liquidity in successful investments. However, this can range from as little as five years to as long as ten years. Is this an acceptable amount of time for you to lose access to your capital?

◆ **Think about the timing of the exit.** For pre-IPO investors who are focusing on the IPO as the primary means of exit, this liquidity option is obviously tied to the status of the public and IPO markets. If these markets are fluctuating negatively or you cannot predict such fluctuation in that market four to five years out, you need to understand the inherent risk in focusing solely on companies that will achieve liquidity through IPO. At the same time, you need to keep in mind that structured investments will provide liquidity and exit through buyback from the entrepreneurial team or through sale of the company.

◆ **Next, define your geographic preference.** The bottom line is how far you want to travel for meetings to keep tabs on the venture, follow up with the entrepreneurial or management team, board of directors' meetings, or getting involved if problems occur. It's simple. How many hours are you willing to drive or fly? Chart that radius, because it can influence which deal-flow development strategy is appropriate for you.

◆ **How active or passive do you want to be in the venture?** It's important to be up-front with entrepreneurs about expectation of involvement. In the development of individual identity materials, you must be straightforward about the level of activity you're looking for.

◆ **Finally, narrow down your preferred industries.** Successful angels invest in what they know. However, a number of investors who consider themselves "quick studies" choose unfamiliar areas that they can learn quickly. Specialize in what you know or what you can learn rapidly. This familiarity will reap significant benefits. For example, it will help you read business plans and perform due diligence more rapidly since you're more informed about market statistics and legitimate expectations for pro formas and valuations.

Shifting from Informal to More Formal Deal-Flow Development

EXTENSIVE INTERVIEWS WITH successful angel investors by International Capital Resources principals over an eleven-year period strongly suggest that savvy angel investors are taking a more structured approach to deal-flow development. Based on interviews and surveys with more than 9,000 investors since 1989, we have developed a model of deal-flow development that is being used by these investors as a group. In this chapter, we will introduce this strategic model.

Angel investors have turned from more haphazard historical

approaches to a more formal structured approach because of the dawning realization that they are a capital resource that is critical to our economy. Therefore, they can no longer leave to chance the important task of deal origination. These investors are good not only at investing but also at helping to build companies. Their service matters. They make a difference. And we think they have realized they have an obligation to let the world know about their capabilities.

Angels must create and maintain their presence in the mind of their target market. Angels need to communicate the benefits beyond capital that they bring to an investment, a process that means having to sell their value as individuals worthy of relationships and of capital. Investors must make these benefits tangible, for the greater the intangibility of the value added, the greater the need to etch themselves in the mind of the entrepreneurs.

Clearly, investors must hunt successfully in order to survive in the angel market. It's not just about money. Angels can't rest on the laurels of having previously contributed cash, because entrepreneurs now expect more. They want added value, and they're discriminating in the investors they associate with, knowing that the investors they choose will affect the caliber of institutional investors willing to buy at a later date. Here's the point: If you are an investor, the best deals will not beat a path to your door. *You have to go out and find them.*

This chapter defines deal-flow development in a bold yet simple way. Generating deal flow is much like professional-services business development and marketing. In other words, it encompasses all the activities principals or investors select to present themselves, their services, and in this case, their capital and added value components. The latter both yield a profit and have an impact on a potential investee's perception of the service value. As one of our colleagues has said, "Marketing is everything you do to promote your business from the first moment of conception to the point at which clients patronize your business on a regular basis." Deal-flow development meets these challenges to the degree that entrepreneurs are willing to spend money answering your due diligence inquiries instead of responding to another capital source or spending money on some other pressing issue. Only one other definition, from author and consultant Herman Holtz, would we trade for ours: "Anyone can sell cold drinks to thirsty people. Marketing is the art of finding or inventing ways to make people thirsty."

In this chapter we describe the elements needed for successful deal-flow development. The techniques we list are the blocking, tackling, passing, running, and kicking—all the fundamentals—of our chosen game. To underestimate the power of basics is a big mistake. By using a deal-flow development mix comprised of only basic deal-flow development techniques, investors can achieve their investment goals and objectives.

The Essential Elements in a Formal Deal-Flow Development Strategy

OVER THE YEARS, we have discovered that almost all angel investors, whether solo investors or a loosely knit collaborative group, have a deal-flow development strategy. Most have developed it intuitively but have not taken the time to make it explicit. Our research shows that all of these successful techniques can be organized into a comprehensive strategic model for deal-flow development. This model can guide angel investors, especially less-experienced investors or seasoned investors interested in expanding their investment activity by examining the critical decisions underlying the strategic deal-flow development. In this way, investors can identify ways to accelerate the deal-flow development process, increase the rate and number of deals that they see, improve their personal visibility in the angel market at less cost, and focus their deal-flow development effort, thereby leveraging deal-flow activity for multiple uses. In short, investors can obtain a better yield on their deal-flow development investments.

In the next sections, we review tactical options available to the angel investor. Investors have at their disposal multiple means for communicating to their target market the benefits that entrepreneurs can enjoy from the angel investor.

Solo investors face a unique situation. They require a special model of deal-flow development with realistic applications that will increase the likelihood of implementation. When compared with larger institutional venture capital counterparts, the solo investor encounters some of the following restraints:

1 Lack of resources, such as time, money, and support staff. The solo investor, for example, must still work a job, deliver services, administer his own business if he's still working, and invest in and develop deal flow. In most cases, the individual investor lacks the financial resources to use all of the proven techniques associated with traditional deal-flow development. Also, capital restrictions can lead to emphasis on short-term marketing programs at the expense of long-term deal-flow development strategies.

2 Many small investors lag behind in leveraging MIS technology. We recommend becoming familiar with the use of relational database systems to manage information about venture prospects and spreadsheet software to track data on past investment and referral contacts. We also suggest use of online systems for research, some of which are listed in the directory in the Appendices.

3 Surprisingly, many private investors are terribly unorganized when it comes to their own deal-flow development. Being a skilled technician or a skilled investor in their field is no guarantee of their ability to efficiently run the deal-flow development process. Simple logs and recordkeeping systems to track the deal flow resulting from different development programs are particularly helpful in identifying which programs generated quality deals.

Given these disadvantages, the investor must appreciate the importance of a well-designed deal-flow development plan, one that mandates that the theoretical framework for planning and the procedures for forming and applying the plan be uncomplicated and quickly accessible. Also, the investor needs a planning system that includes real-time methods for measuring results. So he needs a fail-safe mechanism to ensure program corrections, designed to prevent a major loss from a poorly performing deal-flow development program.

In the following sections we will discuss deal-flow development planning, including targeting the investee market, positioning, and clarifying investment size. We will also discuss organizing for the deal-flow development process, which includes the creation of individual investor identity materials and in-house support systems. We will also discuss three different types of deal-flow development communications by which to reach your targeted markets, including advertising, public relations, and referral-based networking.

Targeting, Positioning, and Defining Investment Size

DEAL-FLOW DEVELOPMENT PLANNING encompasses the market research components of segmenting the market that you're going after as an investor and targeting specific subsets. We also include positioning, a strategy based on competitive analyses of what other investors are doing. Also, we discuss here the importance of defining your investment size and its implications for your deal-flow development.

The foundation of any success in generating and originating promising ventures is deal-flow development planning. This includes the general activities of market research, positioning, and establishing the size of investments to which you are committed.

Market research is not just for the large investment firms. Many solo investors believe that market research is a luxury beyond their budget. But determining the potential size of your market or the universe of entrepreneur prospects is the first step in any deal-flow development program. A thorough market research study can help confirm whether the market has the potential to merit serious investment consideration.

The technique of market segmentation is a powerful market research procedure with successful application to the small investor. This activity entails analyzing your universe of prospects and determining whether you can group them by similar characteristics. A reliable method of developing criteria for segmenting the market is to review the deals from the past year or two that have interested you most, or those in which you invested. Using demographics, analyze these deals to develop categories or profiles of their common characteristics, for example, size of the company, geographic locale, stage of development, SIC code, and so on. By focusing business deal-flow development upon specific market segments, you can penetrate the market faster and at less cost. These outcomes in turn help you sustain deal-flow development programs longer, do a more thorough job of maintaining visibility in that market, and better position yourself for referral.

For example, let's take the investor interested in process industry firms. A close examination reveals that the process industry market can be grouped into petrochemical, mining, nuclear energy utilities, and specific process manufacturing industries. By refocusing the deal-flow development effort on these segments, we can improve returns from investment in communication programs to reach out to that market. This focus will help the investor frame suitable communications and language, become more familiar with industry-specific communication channels used by keen decision makers and promising companies, build reputation and references within the industry, and develop specific war stories that show how knowledgeable he is about the unique problems the industry's managers face.

The second activity in deal-flow development planning is positioning. Increased competition among investment resources for deals permeates the angel market. While you are out there hunting and fishing, other money sources are hunting and fishing, too. Since competition is present, growing, and inevitable, it becomes too dangerous for the investor to leave to chance decisions on deal-flow development design. Careful decisions about positioning yourself are made possible not only by the market research we discussed earlier but by competitive analyses. You don't have to be a major venture capital company or ace detective firm to practice and profit from competitive business intelligence. You can easily collect pertinent, timely, and accurate competitive information. With a little research and some help from a resourceful associate, colleague, or family member, you will realize the astounding amount of information competitors will disclose.

By actively participating in the communication programs outlined in this chapter and by using the resources listed in the appendices, you will garner information about what other investors are looking at; what their approach is; how they analyze, value, and structure deals; which liquidity options they prefer; how investors are hedging to manage risk; and so on. You will be pleasantly surprised at how open many investors become once you inform them that you share this unique investment interest.

After you carefully examine your competitors, you need to assess your own resources and capabilities. Compare your approaches to those of your competitors. In order to position yourself relative to the competition, you must analyze your own strengths and weaknesses. To do this, answer two questions: What is it about your approach to angel investing—or whatever type of investing you prefer—that sets you apart from the competitors interested in the same deals? And second, what is your "soft underbelly"? (Remember General Eisenhower's decision during World War II to invade Italy first because he felt it was the "soft underbelly" of the Axis powers, the point of greatest vulnerability in the fascist hold on Europe.) Every investor has an area of weakness that he must acknowledge and protect.

For example, the new investor without any past or current investees has no track record of successfully investing or helping companies. That's the investor's "underbelly." Few managers looking for added-value investors will align themselves with such an investor, who would lack an understanding of the long-term implications of carrying that weight and how it might affect the deal itself, not to mention institutional investors who might be a major source for liquidity down the line. Understanding the underbelly is central to developing a successful, defensive deal-flow development strategy and preparing potent rebuttals to objections that will arise during the deal-flow development and prospecting process.

The final element to be considered in deal-flow development planning is investment size. This is not unlike the task of setting the price of a product or service as one is entering a market. The objective here is to set a price, or establish an investment size, that will allow you to move *into*, not *out of*, the market. You accomplish this by establishing a competitive investment amount. Our investor base shows four investment size segments: under $25,000; $25,000 to $100,000; $100,000 to $250,000; and more than $250,000 per investment into each company. You must determine where you fall within that distribution so you can position yourself to execute your strategy, whether it's multiple investment, several diversified investments into different companies, or a highly focused strategy with larger investments into a smaller number of companies.

As an analogy, consider the larger firm that regularly conducts wage and salary surveys. The firm does so for two reasons: (1) to maintain internal equity among different positions within the firm, and (2) to offer skilled job candidates remuneration competitive with wages and salaries offered by other companies competing for the same skilled personnel. In the same way, investors have to make a decision on internal equity about what portion of their equity portfolio they diversify into the private equity market.

Second, regardless of that percentage, the individual investor now needs to make some decisions about the size of investment per company so that he can compete with other investors who are looking at the same deals. Entrepreneurs are not interested in having huge numbers of investors with whom they must communicate and hold hands. So it's important to understand the size of investment per company to determine the size of the transactions to target for generating deal-flow.

Maintaining competitiveness in investment size compared with other capital resources has never been more important than it is now. Today, investors must prepare to deal with entrepreneurs who will challenge an investor's investment size and/or pricing strategy. This is because entrepreneurs are learning that having a large number of investors in a deal creates an investor relations nightmare. Maintaining the competitive edge requires that investors have available more accurate and current information on how much they can invest and are willing to put at risk. This is important not only now but also later, when they may have to back up that investment to protect themselves from dilution should the company become successful. Clarifying your investment size early on is inexpensive and takes little effort. You can obtain research from industry insiders who publish independent surveys, such as International Capital Resources, Asset Alternatives, or Spencer-Trask, in the form of reports and newsletters that include annual surveys of investment amounts in completed transactions.

Organizing Investor Identity Materials and Deal-Flow Tracking Systems

THE NEXT STEP in the deal-flow development model focuses on organizing the process. The structural elements discussed here, which serve the solo investor and small multiperson informal investment group, are limited to individual investor identity materials and in-house deal-flow tracking systems.

If you have done a thorough job in deal-flow development planning, you have appropriately selected and designed an array of individual investor identity materials. A number of options are available to the angel investor in this area. The key is to avoid costly mistakes in the selection process, since the design and production of individual investor identity materials represent commitments that are usually expensive to change.

Investor identity materials are essential in marketing the investor. As noted, these materials help make tangible the intangible aspects of angel investment in the mind of the prospective investee. Properly created, individual investor identity materials engender an image of the investor as being concerned about more than money, increasing the entrepreneur's desire for your involvement in the venture. Don't underestimate the value of demystifying the benefits you bring to the table.

Some examples of individual investor identity materials include a Web site, stationery, business cards, perhaps a logo, and a set of readable past investment descriptions. Also useful is a media file of any articles in which the investor has been mentioned, quoted, or featured. In addition, use reprints of any articles that prominently feature the investor's opinions and ideas about investing and that may include suggestions for entrepreneurs to raise money. It might also serve the socially responsible investor to include a definition of a code of ethics on "inclusionary" or "exclusionary" investing approaches. Of further use are any audio or video programs that have captured presentations by the investor at a conference or comparable event.

Also included in individual investor identity materials might be a brochure if it's a more formal situation, or if less formal, a detailed curriculum vitae describing the investor's professional and academic background and any other relevant components, such as military background. Identity materials can include testimonials from entrepreneurs of companies that the investor has invested in, as well as an extensive set of references—including the investor's banker, attorney, accountant, and entrepreneurs, both from companies he has invested in and even those he is still looking at. Along with this last suggestion, the investor can include a comprehensive description of past investments or perhaps the investments that she is most proud of.

Finally, investors' decisions to invest in identity materials might afford them the buffer their privacy demands. For this reason, they may decide on an executive suite rather than a home office as a location for receiving calls and business plans, or decide simply on a separate address and phone number. They may even decide on a part-time office, perhaps an executive suite or a shared office in another business locale.

Many individual investors may view in-house support systems as an exorbitant administrative expense. In the case of deal-flow development database systems, nothing could be further from the truth. The reality is that you don't need a big budget to design and install support systems for use in tracking deal-flow development. In our experience, establishing in-house support systems leads to improvements in deal prospecting (before exposing yourself to time-consuming in-person visits), tracking venture leads, logging business plans, and generally positioning yourself to be much more responsive to inquiring entrepreneurs.

Quality information such as this will help the investor make profitable decisions on investments and contribute to the perception that the investor is responsive to entrepreneurs who send their business plan for his review. One investor asset is his list of entrepreneurs who have sent him business plans. This includes the business plan receipt log, current investments, prospective investments, future prospects, detailed term sheets used in transactions, pending investment agreements, referral sources, references, media contacts, and the like. Included in the database would be contact data of professional due diligence advisers, coinvestors, referral sources, and media resources.

To help you manage your list of contacts, we recommend a relational database system. A number of easy-to-use and relatively inexpensive database software packages are now available. Set up files for all the different groups mentioned above. Critical fields to use for identifying information include name, company, address, phones, fax, e-mail, and "field" identifiers: a *source field* detailing how the person came to you; a *status field* on the current situation; a *pending-action field* about the next step to take; and a *notes field* giving historical information about phone calls and meetings. Perhaps some kind of ranking system is useful on whether the prospective investment is "hot" or has been filed.

Taking the time to collect and input all the names will be the biggest hurdle to overcome in establishing an in-house database system. Next, create an update form and discipline yourself to use it after every contact into the firm. A system designed with these considerations lends itself to marketing research and monitoring the results of your deal-flow development program.

Criteria for Selecting the Most Appropriate Communication Channels to Attract Deal Flow

A STRONG FOUNDATION of deal-flow development planning and the establishment of in-house support systems form the basis for making informed choices about how to communicate your personal investment preferences and approach and how to bring to your target investee market your unique added-value capabilities. Advertising, public relations, or referral-based networking communications can battle anonymity, trumpet your benefits as an investor over competitive sources of capital, and overcome entrepreneur inertia.

Investors can select from among an array of tactical options for creating their personal deal-flow development mix. The question is no longer whether it is professional to develop your deal flow. Seeking investments is the only alternative to historical and serendipitous approaches or sitting around hoping a diamond in the rough will drop into your lap. An investor once said to us, "Good investments come to those who are looking for them." Today's challenge is how to select from among the many deal-flow development alternatives. The objective is to avoid costly mistakes and select communication channels that will give a positive return on investment. The three approaches most successful investors advocate for deal-flow development are advertising, public relations, and referral-based networking.

You need to consider certain criteria in selecting communication channels appropriate to your strengths and weaknesses. First, consider your personal style and skills. What are you most comfortable with? Seek communications methods that meet with your personal preferences. Whether you feel comfortable in using a specific technique or not can bear significantly on how well a technique will work for your deal-flow development. For example, if you are an accomplished public speaker, participating in investment conferences or on panels at venture forums might be comfortable venues where you can be effective at communicating the kind of deals you're interested in.

Next, consider your time limitations. Obviously, do not focus on long-term strategies like publishing articles or referral development if you need deal flow now. Initially, focus on short-term direct-advertising-based communications.

The extent to which the investor enjoys name recognition is another important consideration. It is no accident that research indicates among doctors, for example, that younger practitioners feel more positive toward advertising than their more established older colleagues. Of course, if one has an extensive number of past patients, peer contacts, referral sources, and community and media contacts, public relations and referral-based networking promotional techniques will be more cost-effective than advertising. In fact, there is the risk that investee companies might view direct approaches less favorably. However, to build deal flow promptly, the less-experienced investor should gravitate toward aggressive marketing strategies involving more direct advertising approaches.

Finally, you will need to consider your time, money, and energy in selecting communication channels. For example, consider speech making. Regardless of the number of prospects generated through such an event, soliciting, preparing, and delivering a speech and following up on the leads generated can be time consuming and physically draining. You must be honest with yourself about establishing a deal-flow development budget and determine the kind of commitment you can realistically make to the development effort.

Advertising

IN THIS SECTION, we provide an overview of six different advertising deal-flow development strategies. These include listing in printed directories and in private equity databases, participating in venture forums, joining computer matching networks, participating in Internet electronic networks, subscribing to angel and private equity newsletters, and joining venture capital clubs.

LISTING IN PRINTED DIRECTORIES AND PRIVATE EQUITY DATABASES

FOR YEARS ENTREPRENEURS and inventors have turned to a number of directories: *Pratt's Guide to Venture Capital, VanKirk's Venture Capital Directory,* and *Galante's Equity Guide.* There are also a number of other specific types of directories, such as *Private Fortunes* and other private equity directories published by Gale's Research. The requirements for listing in these directories are basic, and selecting a directory as a resource does not require you to disclose extensive information. Through directories, you can garner significant deal flow.

The fact is that many of these directories list what are called smaller storefront venture capital firms as well as individuals who have established themselves in more formal structures but are really just individual investors. Usually, these reference books will list about 500 to 600 resources and, in some cases, up to 1,000 resources. Although many of them include mainly institutional resources, they also list individual and less formal groups. If you've done a good job of defining and clearly stating your investment niche, directories can be a valuable resource for leads.

In addition to listing yourself in the well-known venture capital directories, you can also obtain membership in a number of association directories that would also be resources for referral. These are usually free to members of the association, with only a minimal fee to join. Again, there is no requirement for extensive personal information; in fact, there is more of a focus on investment interests. Some examples of associations that make available such directories are the Northern California Venture Capital Association, the Western New York Venture Association, the Toronto Venture Group, the New England Venture Capital Association, and the Houston Venture Capital Association.

A number of firms have moved their directories into software databases. These software databases are often designed with easy-to-use, interactive menus, permitting users to query the database using various criteria that describe the essential parameters of their deal: how much capital they're looking for, what industry they're in, the location of the firm, and so on. Using this relational database software, the user—usually an investee company—will generate a list of prospect firms and individuals possibly interested in investing in their particular area.

Normally, institutional investors and, to some extent, lenders form the primary listings in these databases, since their information is usually in the public domain already. But there is an opportunity for private investors or informal small groups of investors (those who structure themselves as an investment company, a limited liability company, or a corporation for investment purposes) to use these vehicles to announce themselves as a resource for capital. These individuals are basically publicizing themselves as resources and describing the kinds of investment opportunities they are most interested in reviewing. While angel investors do not have to invest as institutional investors do, angel investors must develop deal flow, and these mechanisms warrant their efforts. One need only contact the database developer, complete the necessary forms, and then submit them. The big players in database technology currently are Datamerge and Dataquest. While Datamerge primarily concentrates on lending resources, Dataquest focuses on equity-oriented investors.

PARTICIPATING IN VENTURE FORUMS

THE CONCEPT OF NETWORKING through forums, an activity that became popular in the late '80s, operates on the premise that principal players must be brought together, linking those who need money with those who have it. Typically, the original thrust of venture forums and of the venture forum movement was primarily educational, beginning as community service seminars and business development educational opportunities. Today, venture forums are set up by nonprofit agencies and for-profit companies that specialize in these types of events.

These conferences have quickly evolved into a way for investors to augment deal flow, to network with their peers, both private and institutional, and to provide an efficient way to gain exposure to a wider range of deals. Usually, companies will make restricted presentations, allowing the investors to compare many investment possibilities and also to meet the entrepreneurs and coinvestors face-to-face. Forums serve two functions: (1) providing information on investment prospects and the money-raising process, and (2) providing a vehicle for investors and entrepreneurs to meet face-to-face. Institutional investors initially delivered the primary thrust on venture forums; however, private investors today have begun to get deeply involved, especially the more sophisticated and wealthy private investors.

Forums take a number of different forms. Open forums feature keynote speakers or entrepreneurs, highlighting their ventures during, say, an extended breakfast, lunch, or dinner gathering. Besides offering question-and-answer exchanges, open forums enable the entrepreneurs to meet directly with investors. Panel forums are opportunities for investors to participate as a group, usually as a panel with a moderator, with similar networking opportunities after the presentation.

Another type of forum is the deal-mart meeting. Here investors use business plan submissions to screen entrepreneurs and businesspeople seeking financing. A mere handful of entrepreneurs meet with the investors and/or the venture capitalists, giving short, formal presentations. Entrepreneurs and investors usually have time to meet. Venture fairs offer opportunities for prescreened entrepreneurs and businesses seeking funding to set up booths and exhibits. Often involving large numbers of people and lasting more than a day, these fairs feature keynote speakers, presentations, special events, and evening social gatherings.

Attending meetings of these private investor networking organizations has become an ideal way to augment deal-flow development, not only because you see the business plan but also because you meet the management teams themselves. A wide range of formal investor forums are renowned for their accomplishments. They include the Mid-Atlantic Venture Fair, Investor's Choice California Venture Capital Conference, International Capital Resources Northern California Venture Forum, the Oklahoma Investment Forum, and the Arizona Venture Capital Conference. To give you a sense of how successful these groups are, our analysis of the top twenty formal investor conferences, including the ones mentioned above, indicates that those organizations raised more than $2.5 billion over a three-year period.

JOINING COMPUTER MATCHING NETWORKS

THE COMPUTERIZED MATCHING networks, the oldest of which is the MIT Venture Capital Network, have contributed greatly to the process of bringing investors and entrepreneurs together. In the computerized matching networks, computer technology is used to match the parameters of an investment with the criteria of the investor; when there is a match, the network sends the investor an executive summary describing the venture. This process preserves confidentiality while creating an added value: Investors receive only those deals that meet their criteria. These networks supply a valuable service, and studies echo the refrain of participating investors; they appreciate the screening and the privacy these organizations furnish.

These networks provide entrepreneurs and inventors an inexpensive mechanism by which they can expose their deals. From the investors' point of view, one of the benefits is to avoid conflicts with securities laws. Moreover, these networks also charge no finder's fees, so deals that investors get involved with through such networks would not be burdened in this way. In addition, companies must qualify at some level before they are permitted to list, although this varies by network.

These networks are driven by recent developments in database and personal computer technology, spurring many investors to band together. The desire for an increase in deal flow has motivated these organizations and individuals to invest in their communities or in their regions, a motivation traditionally reserved by universities, nonprofit organizations, and government agencies in their commitment to regional economic development and job creation. The interest in community investment and the desire of small informal networks of investors to increase their deal flow has nurtured this growing industry since the early '90s. The investor network is a more formal effort to ease the process of linking ventures and capital while safeguarding the investor's privacy. Many of these networks are nonprofit; some are for profit.

Computer networking relies on database linking of investors and entrepreneurs seeking financing. Specific information about both parties offers the possibility of matchups. In our earlier books we developed extensive directories of the most respected matching networks in the United States and Canada, and we have studied a number of them, including the following:

◆ The Capital Network
◆ Environmental Capital Network
◆ Georgia Capital Network
◆ Investors Circle
◆ Kentucky Investment Capital Network
◆ LA Venture Network
◆ Mid-Atlantic Investment Network
◆ North-West Capital Network
◆ Pacific Venture Capital Network
◆ Private Investor Network
◆ Seed Capital Network
◆ Technology Capital Network
◆ Tennessee Venture Capital Network
◆ Venture Capital Network of Minnesota
◆ Washington Investment Network

PARTICIPATING IN INTERNET NETWORKS

ONE OF THE RESOURCES currently receiving a lot of attention from entrepreneurs and investors alike are Internet networks and investment resources. We have listed a number of the relevant Web sites in Appendix A.

While the proprietary research by International Capital Resources indicates that the amount of money being invested by angel investors through these mechanisms is a small percentage of the total angel capital market, the activity on these sites is increasing. Entrepreneurs will take these mechanisms more seriously as more qualified investors get involved in them.

Some investors are resisting participating in Internet networks, and they do have legitimate concerns: about privacy; about listing their names, addresses, and contact information; and about the security of that information. No one wants to be exposed to crank deals and wacky characters. However, these Internet networks are wonderful research and educational clearinghouses for various services essential to investors.

These electronic resources are more important today than they were five years ago, and while they may not live up to their hype, they offer promising mechanisms for investors to augment their deal flow or to do research. The Internet may not be the best area on which to focus your deal-flow development resources, but clearly it is emerging and promises to become an excellent tool in the immediate future. We urge the reader to peruse the list of Web resources in Appendix A.

SUBSCRIBING TO ANGEL AND PRIVATE EQUITY NEWSLETTERS

MORE THAN 3,000 financial subscription newsletters in the United States cover a wide range of financial topics. Of these, approximately 10 percent to 20 percent relate to equity investment, and of these, a very small number of select publications focus on early-stage private equity investment. These newsletters include the *Private Equity Review, American Venture, Environmental Investors Newsletter,* and *Angel Investor,* among others.

These newsletters provide information about important events where investors can meet with coinvestors and entrepreneurs. They also provide articles about investing; letters from investors; descriptions of completed deals, structures, and evaluations; profiles of promising ventures; case histories of transactions; analysis of successful funding; reviews of various venture forums and conferences; reviews of books on angel investing and early-stage private equity investing; and information about key groups involved in this unique market.

For example, the *Private Equity Review* describes early-stage venture capital transactions occurring throughout the United States and Canada. The *Private Equity Review* is read by more than 9,000 accredited investors interested in angel investing. Its circulation has been increasing steadily since its inception in 1989. Newsletters read by investors provide a superb resource for getting in touch with potential coinvestors, finding promising deals, and providing baselines for comparing various ventures when conducting due diligence. In addition, some publications have moved beyond providing research and analysis and are now using the newsletter format to facilitate the matching and introduction process.

Newsletters convey information promptly, presenting it in the way investors have been trained to get information about the stock and bond markets. Newsletters also let investors study information at their leisure, exposing them to an assortment of deals, not just those, for example, that a computer matching software program "thinks" they should receive. Since many newsletter networks provide introductions, they develop proprietary databases on the investors and their investment preferences—information gathered from the investors' responses to various issues. This information is protected in ways that online systems may not be.

In addition, because the investors can interact with the newsletter publishers and editors, they can significantly influence the deals that these publishers and editors select, profile, and distribute through the various newsletters to the investment audience. This ability to interact and influence can expand the investors' deal flow. The newsletter concept of profiling ventures for investors is, after all, not new. Public companies have used this vehicle for years.

Two popular publications are *Sound Money Investor* and *Stock Deck Select*. These publications describe public companies and provide means for sophisticated investors to get in touch with companies that meet their investment criteria. The main benefit lies in the investors' being able to review summaries that describe the companies before requesting further information and committing themselves to read in-depth documentation.

JOINING VENTURE CAPITAL CLUBS

VENTURE CAPITAL CLUBS are a specialized spin-off, not unlike the small investment groups that make up such associations as the American Association of Individual Investors. These clubs bring together a number of novice and experienced investors, supply them with materials, and assist them in building a portfolio. In some instances, investors will pool their money, although they're not required to do so. But in most cases, any alliances and coinvestments that are established are not very formal; they're much more casual.

In effect, the venture capital club operates as an informal angel network of its own. Exchanges among investors can help the individual improve his understanding and appreciation of this unique form of investing, as well as share the tasks of deal finding and conducting due diligence. This also allows them to share the financial risk with coinvestors, and, in fact, the camaraderie and the preference to coinvest figures prominently into the mix. Interestingly, the traditional investment clubs emphasized publicly traded stocks that strongly influenced the creation of venture capital clubs. Those individuals interested in private equity and early-stage investing, feeling unwelcome in the traditional clubs, gradually migrated, using similar models to form their own groups. The result was this spin-off into today's brisk activity.

Approximately 150 venture capital clubs operate across the country, with typically twelve to fifty members in a group. Members tend to be geographically focused, smaller investors, and although the clubs include a few more affluent, seasoned angel investors, they serve mostly as mentors and as participants or leads in transactions.

Within the angel investor community, we find diverse segments inclined to participate in venture capital clubs: At one end of the spectrum are angels investing typically either less than $25,000 or $25,000 to $50,000 per transaction. Clubs also exist for investors investing much larger amounts; this group represents a different caliber of investor, those who join venture capital clubs to affiliate with other sophisticated, high-net-worth investors. Although individuals in a venture capital club can maintain their privacy, the venture capital club publicizes its endeavors, which facilitates deal flow to it and to the individual investors involved. This allows individuals to share not only in the deal flow, which increases the flow geometrically, but also in the responsibility of due diligence and financial investment, thereby hedging some of the risk in the investment.

In summary, individual investors join investor clubs primarily to attract more ventures to review than each investor would find on his own. Club members can also share due diligence and pool capital. Clubs like the New York New Media Angel Investor Program, founded in 1997, can increase an investor's deal flow and increase connections with other investors and entrepreneurs. Other groups are the Tri-State Investors Group in North Carolina and Capital Investors, LLC, in northern Virginia. Capital Investors counts among its twenty-three investor members the founder of Netscape, the CEO of America Online, the CEO of Teligent, the vice-chairman of MCI WorldCom, and the president of the Washington Post Company.

These clubs provide an ideal venue for investors to share knowledge and experience. Members may invest individually in deals or pool capital. More structured clubs, such as John May's the Dinner Club, form a limited liability corporation and put their money into a pledge fund. Explains May, "We try to do a round of financing one stage below professional VCs, $500,000 to $3 million." The Dinner Club requires its members to contribute at least $80,000 over three years and also to commit to attending meetings.

Public Relations

IN THIS SECTION we present a number of public relations strategies: they include sponsoring and/or speaking at venture-related seminars, workshops, clinics, and conferences; volunteering for advisory boards of incubators; publishing articles; joining target market trade/industry associations; and participating in research studies.

SPONSORING OR SPEAKING AT VENTURE-RELATED
SEMINARS, WORKSHOPS, CLINICS, AND CONFERENCES

SEMINARS CAREFULLY TARGET their audiences. The subjects can focus on raising capital, joint ventures, building partnerships with investors, business planning, and the like. Clinics and workshops are much more specialized and in-depth than seminars. Clinics and workshops focus on a special audience, a narrow group with specific interests. Central to the clinic is interaction. In this interaction between, for example, the investor and the entrepreneur, the investor can provide advice targeted to the interest of the participants.

In comparison with seminars, most clinics, workshops, and conferences aim at special industries or larger groups. Organizations characteristically will set up booths and exhibits in convention halls, and conferences can also involve large numbers of people attending various events and seminars held within the context of the conference. Presentations form an important part of these conferences, which can last two or three days, with individual sessions running from forty-five minutes to one-and-a-half hours. An example of a highly respected conference is the Great Mid-West Venture Capital Conference. (See Appendix B for an extensive directory of educational and other resources for investors to learn more about other conferences appropriate for sponsorship or speaking.)

Whether to sponsor or speak is an issue for the investor. The investor holds power at these events. When investors speak, entrepreneurs listen, all of them hungry for information from a person they might be approaching for capital. The investor can speak to any aspect of the investment process. They can talk about their investment preferences and history; they can share case stories or anecdotes about investments that went well or poorly; they can provide mentoring and counsel on what they look for in a deal. Or they can make suggestions to entrepreneurs on how best to write their business plan or present their venture, or they can talk about technical matters like due diligence, valuation, pro forma development, business plan writing, deal structuring, negotiating, preparation of the road show, and/or discussing liquidity options and exit events.

We urge investors to consider sponsoring events by identifying respected organizations that do the footwork to put them on, providing some modest capital infusion to assist the event, and then being prominently featured at the event, either in its literature or as a moderator, speaker, or panelist. If you do go the route of making presentations, we urge you to put together a PowerPoint presentation that captures your investment orientation and educational information, complemented by color slides. In addition, we also urge investors to have their presentations either recorded or videotaped. This technology positions them to transcribe the event, making it easier to write articles for publication, a task we discuss below.

Further, with the online revolution, speaking at events is no longer limited to bricks and mortar at major hotels or banquet halls. Departing from a tradition of relying on other companies to create content for its Internet portal, Yahoo! launched its own Web finance show, permitting users to see live interviews and news reports about business. The programming mimics cable television financial news, with company profiles and on-air hosts conducting live interviews of corporate executives, analysts, and investors. The show emanates primarily from studios in New York City, at the major stock exchanges, and from a studio near the company headquarters in Santa Clara, California. We urge the investor to keep an open mind about forums or events to sponsor, or venues and media in which to share their ideas.

VOLUNTEERING FOR ADVISORY BOARDS OF INCUBATORS

VOLUNTEERING TO PARTICIPATE on advisory boards with incubators is a magnificent mentoring opportunity for the angel investor. A major component of incubators is to provide not only services to help fledgling companies grow but also referrals, both formal and informal, to professionals qualified to assist the companies at various stages of development. So incubators are charged in part with the responsibility to facilitate introductions. Therefore, participating in the advisory board is a splendid way to gain access to the deal flow generated through an incubator. Another important feature of incubators is their industry focus, and with more than 650 different incubators in the United States, the investor can focus on incubators not only geographically close but industry-centered.

It's impossible to overemphasize the importance of this new generation of vehicles to incubate fledgling company growth. Volunteering as a mentor, adviser, or technical or advisory board member is an ideal way—and a prestigious way—to bond with that environment. As investors become immersed in the interlocking network of boards of directors and advisory boards of incubators, they will accrue deal flow. Developing relationships with other individuals looking for investments or making investments in the endeavors of incubators becomes a powerful tool for cracking the deal market.

Incubators are primarily not-for-profit concepts, growing out of community development efforts and spin-offs from university entrepreneurial programs. They foster the growth of early-stage companies and provide a range of business support services. People who direct incubators have realized that those early-stage companies coming to them for guidance also need to raise capital. To get launched, incubators have had to develop connections with venture capital sources and in some cases have raised their own venture funds.

Incubator directors realize that to serve their clients they have to set up liaisons with the financial community to help investment in these companies so that they, in turn, can grow their own incubators. Incubators have a vested interest in developing more formal mechanisms for investor involvement. So incubators have stimulated the movement toward matching networks and other resources for effecting introductions.

We urge the investor interested in this approach to contact the National Business Incubation Association at 740-593-4331. The NBIA will provide to interested investors a free sampling of incubators in three states.

PUBLISHING ARTICLES

ONE STRATEGY FOR BUILDING your reputation and increasing the awareness of your desire to participate as an investor in the angel market is to publish articles about investing with the entrepreneur in mind. This effort will stimulate and garner deal flow. The concept is simple: Entrepreneurs are hungry for information about how to raise capital. Most of them have no experience in it, do not like the process, and have no training—academic or otherwise—in it. So they need not only theoretical information but also practical, real-life experience coming directly from people they will be approaching in the course of raising money.

While at first the task of writing an article may seem burdensome, it isn't. If you use one of the other mechanisms we have discussed—giving presentations, participating in a panel, delivering speeches—you can, as we have suggested, record them on audio- or videocassette, have them transcribed, edit them to conform to the publication's editorial guidelines, and submit them. Professional administrative support can provide the basis for writing articles, articles that can be put together and edited fairly easily.

We suggest that you speak with some of the entrepreneurs in companies that you're considering investing in and ask them what publications they read. Once you've identified a few, contact the editors for their editorial guidelines, which will help you submit your piece in a format acceptable to the magazine. Once the article is published, you can make reprints for your investor identity package.

JOINING TARGET-MARKET TRADE AND INDUSTRY ASSOCIATIONS

ALMOST ALL INDUSTRY and trade associations offer inexpensive associate-level memberships. Getting involved in the associations allows you to develop a reputation and some contacts among more established firms in your target industry, firms that could well serve as a primary source of entrepreneurial talent that will ultimately set up their own businesses. Almost all trade and industry associations are chartered with helping their membership address critical issues, and one of the most critical issues facing companies is raising capital.

Any investor who can offer assistance can develop liaisons by speaking at industry conferences, participating in panels, contributing articles for the newsletter, or mentoring association members on the task of raising capital. The investor can form liaisons with more established companies that might be looking for alternatives to the more traditional financing mechanisms, such as bank loans. Associations can also help the investor quickly gain a reputation in a target industry among individuals who will break away from established companies to start their own firms. Clearly, this is a long-term strategy.

One of the most rewarding aspects of letting the membership of trade and industrial associations know about your interest in providing capital and investing is the mentoring opportunities that will surface. Here is a golden opportunity to mentor, to volunteer, and to help companies grow.

PARTICIPATING IN RESEARCH STUDIES

IN THE COURSE OF THE past year, one of us has been approached by three major research studies—one sponsored by Harvard, one by Oxford University, and another by the University of New Hampshire—to provide information on angel investing. These studies are submitted by respected academic researchers to angel investors and financing resources in the United States and Europe to gain a better understanding of the market, to analyze investment trends, and to provide information useful to investors, entrepreneurs, and intermediaries.

Individuals who participate in these studies typically are able to obtain copies of the published versions, information not otherwise readily available and costly when it finally is available. Participating in such studies can open the door to proprietary information invaluable to the investor, and ultimately it will get the investor on critical mailing lists for other academic and venture-related events and conferences that can lend immeasurable value to professional development. For these reasons, we urge investors to participate in these studies.

To get on mailing lists for such research studies, contact the authors or researchers of books on our Suggested Reading List (Appendix G) and let them know of your interest in participating in such research on a confidential basis.

Referral-Based Networking

ANOTHER WAY TO GENERATE venture investment possibilities is to make yourself known to key intermediaries and professional service providers who service your targeted market ventures. You can define your target market by geographic region, industry, stage of development, or size of transaction.

As we indicated in the studies mentioned at the beginning of this chapter, most angels already network with friends, family, associates, and colleagues; we encourage developing this first line of referral sources. In addition, alert other angel investors in your coinvestor group that you are, in fact, looking for deals. This networking is particularly useful if you haven't spoken to other investors for a while, because they may have concluded that you are no longer active in this area.

You can learn of key intermediaries and professional service providers through the popular press, academic journals, trade papers, newsletters, and financial tabloids. Also, you can cold-call the professional organizations associated with the group.

Securities attorneys will be aware of companies in their area in need of capital. The business of investment bankers is deal structuring, valuation, and raising capital for emerging and expanding companies. Through their own deal flow and connections with brokerages involved in syndicating offerings, investment bankers will be aware of ventures that may be too small to justify their involvement or fees but that may fit the angel's investment criteria. Focus on investment bankers who specialize in equity financing rather than mergers and acquisitions.

More than 450,000 management consultants operate in the United States. At least 20 percent of these offer business planning services. Through reputable professional associations like the Institute of Management Consultants, you can obtain directories of professional service providers in your region. By introducing yourself to them, you will help them to better market their own services and add value to their consulting.

Certified appraisers are also a resource for deals. While few certified appraisers are expert in "blue-sky" valuation of early-stage companies, a number have developed reputations as resources for companies needing counsel on developing pre-money realistic value prior to embarking on capitalization programs. You can get in early in the process through introductions or referrals from valuation specialists.

Many of the large accounting firms have developed entrepreneurial finance divisions. These groups offer services at a discount for equity or, in some cases, for promising ventures that have good prospects for raising capital pro bono. Listings of the entrepreneurial finance division offices are usually available through any of the large accounting firms, and contact persons are readily accessible. Accountants are sometimes placed in the position of providing some investment banking advice to their clients, and it is natural for them to refer capital sources, especially individual investors. This fertile area is ripe for networking and for nurturing referrals.

Once you have defined your target market, visit the library and examine directories of industrial and trade organizations and associations for a short list of groups to network. Many of these organizations are chartered to help their membership with the major challenges. Raising capital is just such a major challenge for many companies. You will be helping these organizations to better serve their members by speaking to their group, mentoring their members, or writing articles for their newsletters.

Commercial bankers are a major source of referrals. SBA lenders and preferred SBA lenders have local associations that meet to discuss issues and network. These groups will be aware of people involved in ventures, people who may have approached them for loans when, in fact, their ventures were more appropriate for equity investment. Bankers get tired of just saying "no" when a company lacks collateral or would not be able to service debt; it benefits them to have someone to refer a qualified equity deal to when they are unable to service that company's financial needs. If you are interested in turnarounds, a bank workout department is a referral source. Or if you want to buy a business, the trust department might be a resource of businesses for sale. Spend time with commercial bankers in your area to clarify your investment criteria.

Caveats: Deal-Flow Development Approaches to Avoid

LESS THAN 4 PERCENT of the deals that come to you through the active approaches described in this chapter will be worthy of serious concern. That's not bad news; it's just a fact of the early-stage market. Very few of the deals out there justify investment beyond the cradle equity or "gift" loans from founders' families and friends. But that 4 percent justifies the time, money, and energy for mounting active deal-flow development programs. To find a few good deals, we need the opportunity to look at many deals.

Less-experienced angel investors will continue to place classified ads announcing "capital available," or attempt to jump-start their deal-flow development without a strategy by responding to classified ads seeking capital in publications like the *Wall Street Journal* or their local newspapers, or *overrely* on referrals from friends and colleagues. Inevitably, they will find that they have generated hundreds of business plans and ventures to review in this fashion before stumbling upon a single promising venture, a deal that merits the time and expense of closer examination. More experienced and successful investors find the diamonds in their own backyard using the approaches we have described in this chapter. They understand that initiating a deal-flow development strategy takes stamina, perseverance, and persuasive interpersonal skills.

In addition, we offer one last warning. Many individuals operating in the venture market call themselves "finders." These individuals have no qualifications, no financial resource connections, no references, no academic qualifications or professional experience directly related to the money-finding arena. Worst of all, they have no ethics. The finders' arena is an unregulated area filled with rip-off artists, charlatans, and fast-talkers—all of whom ply their trade by preying on both naive entrepreneurs and unwary investors. We urge you to make every effort to thoroughly research any finders or brokers who approach you with deals.

We can't tell you *what* to invest in any more than we can tell you what clothes to wear, but we do plead that you use caution in deciding *how* you go about the investment process. Dress warmly. Investing in this market can bring on a cold chill.

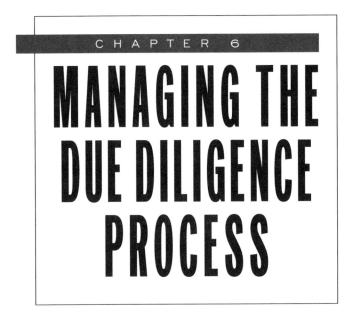

MANAGING THE DUE DILIGENCE PROCESS

Why Due Diligence Is So Important in Today's Angel Market

DUE DILIGENCE IS A VITAL ASPECT of the investment

selection process. From the investor's point of view, one

of the best tests of a deal's practicability and pricing is

whether it attracts and sells to another private investor

at the same price. However, an investor must rely on

solid judgment in evaluating a deal on its own merits. To do so requires comprehensive investigation and analysis. It's important to recognize that angels must rely on their own judgment, especially in such an inefficient market, because much less information is generated by private companies than is produced by public companies, and the quality of information on private companies may not be as high.

Historically, alternative funding resources were made up of informal groups of friends, colleagues, and coinvestors—individuals who invested in a deal in a specific industry at a particular stage of a company's life cycle. Those individuals formed a small circle that pooled its money and shared the mutual responsibility of due diligence. The group also shared the risks inherent in such deals. This informal concept still exists today. It tends to be focused geographically, offering, as always, the benefits of shared responsibilities and shared risk. However, this approach is not enough, because when investors delegate and share responsibility, they may abdicate their due diligence responsibility.

Due diligence is no more than the caution any prudent person would exercise with her own money, or the prudence she would use in managing another person's money. This is the role the lead investors in angel transactions play—that is, the investors on whom coinvestors depend for guidance.

While less sophisticated investors will rely on the technique of asking the entrepreneur "country boy" questions—questions that the investor already knows the answers to and that serve only to test the entrepreneur's knowledge—sophisticated investors recognize that nothing takes the place of a full venture audit, an in-depth assessment of the founder and entrepreneurs, and close scrutiny of the deal elements themselves. To judge the viability of a prospective early-stage direct investment, the veteran investor will require numerous face-to-face meetings with the entrepreneur; thorough reviews of the business plan; interviews with management, customers, suppliers, and competitors; and counsel from relevant industry experts. The sophisticated investor will investigate the principals, including comprehensive background and reference checks, and will conduct interviews with former superiors, peers, subordinates, and business associates.

When financial transactions are involved, a business marriage is taking place, so extensive due diligence is in order. How can we stress strongly enough something that is an absolute necessity? The investor must recognize that 50 percent of businesses discontinue operations. As noted, this doesn't mean they have failed, only that they have not achieved their projections on time. Ninety percent of these companies dissolve voluntarily. Only 10 percent of the dissolutions are involuntary, such as failure by bankruptcy. After all, even marginally profitable businesses will close if they fail to achieve projections on time. Only through due diligence can the investor hope to discover the prospects that can achieve success or have the best chance of doing so.

To be a good investor in other people's businesses, you need first to understand your own strengths and weaknesses; next, you need to avoid investing in people about whom you cannot make a valid judgment. And valid judgment emerges only from research.

Such detailed investigation may seem elaborate, but you should be at least as cautious as a banker or other financial institution. With so much at stake, why do less?

In angel investing, nothing replaces legal and financial audits, a keen assessment of market potential, and vigorous background checks. Investors especially want to know the potential and identifiable risks in the venture and its realistic future profit potential. Clearly, they cannot rely solely on intuition and personal conviction.

Further, we also explain what successful investors do before they invest. They know that what they discover in the aftermath is information that comes too late. Once the sour milk hits the morning coffee, it cannot be strained out. Neither can sour deals. That's why you need to avoid mistakes in the first place.

The basic concepts of the due diligence process apply regardless of a company's stage of development. Due diligence becomes the final exam that the company passes by getting the money; fail that, and you fail. Many of the questions investors raise in the due diligence process are the same ones that should be addressed in creating a business plan. Questions for a start-up or seed company will begin by focusing on the quality of the management team. If the company has an operating history, questions will focus on performance to date and how management has addressed and over-come business hurdles as they have arisen. Next will come questions on the company's effort to identify and quantify the potential market for its product or service, and then will come questions on existing or potential competition, particularly from financially stronger companies.

Our experience demonstrates that entrepreneurs can be, in many cases, overly optimistic about risk factors and weaknesses in the management team, in the technology, and in possible production delays. Entrepreneurs close to their dreams can be blinded by enthusiasm and as a result complicate issues unnecessarily.

By nature, entrepreneurs will minimize the true capital requirements in the deal. Maybe they haven't done the thorough study necessary to recognize all of the possible delays and all of the financial requirements involved. Perhaps they're innately optimistic. Or they may not want to ask for too much for fear of losing the investors and thus their ability to complete their financing round. They may fear a loss of control and the inability to marshal the direction of the company.

Concerning financial projections, the investor must analyze the financial assumptions that drive the projections of the company's growth. The investor also needs to examine the capital required to grow the venture to achieve the projections proposed by the management team. Investors can count on problems with the projections and the time frames within which those projections are realized. Entrepreneurs may be blinded by their ignorance of proper financial analysis or their desperation to achieve capitalization goals. Entrepreneurs can forget that investors have their own fears and concerns and that they are assuming substantial risk in getting involved in the venture to begin with. Regardless, it is the investor who needs to take these possibilities into account. For whatever the reason, the consequences remain, consequences no investor wants to endure.

So throughout the due diligence process, successful investors will exhibit three important qualities: they will be direct, precise, and attentive. Perhaps most important, they will take copious notes to accurately record the statements and promises the entrepreneur makes.

Beware of Dead Ends on the Road to Riches: Case Studies from the Dark Side of Early-Stage Investing

INVESTORS CAN BECOME BLIND to risk when the promise of riches looms large. As we discussed earlier, depending on the investment terms, their investment can tie up their money for a long time. Because it can take that long for companies to get off the ground and become profitable, this type of capital has been called "patient money." Your money becomes locked up, and you might not see a return until you realize equity through the sale of the firm or a public stock offering.

In this market, the investor faces sizable risk. Based on our research, of ten venture capital investments, four will turn out to be partial or complete losers, two will break even or provide nominal returns, and four may bring moderate to potentially phenomenal results. In our own experience, less than 5 percent of the deal flow coming into International Capital Resources merits professional angel investment beyond family, friends, the founders themselves, colleagues, and associates, or through reinvestment of retained earnings. The market for the product may be too small, the management team too inexperienced, or the technology too far-fetched, but the message is clear: Investors should not invest in these nonfamily situations. Besides, because family members are investing in the integrity of and their belief in the entrepreneur, the investment more nearly resembles a loan with no expectation of return.

The promising start-up in which you invest could become a monetary black hole. Besides the amount they initially invest, investors see expenses mount just to get the ball rolling: accountant's fees, attorney's fees, and other costs involved in performing due diligence on the deal. And, inevitably, years after your first outlay, the company may need more capital. You and the other investors may have little choice but to cough up the extra bucks needed to keep the operation afloat or to protect your position from excessive dilution.

But beyond these well-known reasons that justify close examination of potential angel investments, other reasons to be cautious crop up. Too much money is chasing too many deals of questionable potential. Years ago, every entrepreneur you met was toiling away on a résumé. Today, everyone with the entrepreneurial spirit is ready to yank out a business plan from pocket or purse.

The angel is a gatekeeper to making entrepreneurs' dreams a reality by providing capital and adding value through advice and counsel beyond the money he provides. For institutional investors, investment criteria are stricter, with only 5 of 1,000 plans considered fundable—approximately 0.5 percent of their deal flow. Here's the point: These ratios reflect the demand for deals that propel quick judgment—or worse, *bad judgment.* The glamour of a potential new star hides the glare of truth: that investigating potential investments is time-consuming and expensive.

Perhaps a few tales will justify the need to be cautious about due diligence. For nearly a year, *San Francisco Chronicle* reporters Reynolds Holdings and William Carlsen investigated allegations of legal and ethical misconduct in Silicon Valley. They pored over thousands of pages of financial reports, internal company memorandums, government records, and court documents and conducted scores of interviews with corporate executives, government officials, state and federal prosecutors, judges, lawyers, academicians, and entrepreneurs. Only through court orders were the researchers and their organization able to scour previously sealed documents. Their findings were published in the *San Francisco Chronicle* in November 1999.

The thumbnail sketches that follow and that are based on their findings should provide ample incentive to use a studied approach to due diligence, for "Honesty is no longer to be found in the marketplace." This bitter declaration from third-century church father Saint Cyprian has a contemporary ring to it. The number of investor class-action lawsuits attests to accusations against entrepreneurs of lying about revenues and products. Investors have also accused company advisers of playing fast and loose with conflict-of-interest rules and of betraying other investors for their own benefit.

CASE STUDY 1: ASPECT TECHNOLOGY

IN THE RACE TO TAKE a company public, young companies and their boards of directors and advisers may sacrifice laying the foundation for a viable long-term business, according to former SEC Chairman Arthur Levitt. This is what happened in 1998 to Aspect Technology, a maker of sophisticated software for designing silicon chips. Aspect's board and advisers, all shareholders, had been warned by their auditors, a major accounting firm, of accounting problems.

The company's accounting systems were seriously flawed because of unsophisticated financial systems and controls; still, the board ignored the auditors' warnings and filed a registration statement with the SEC for sale of common shares. According to the auditors, Aspect had been booking sales of software that customers never paid for because the company had not met all of its commitments under the contract, and it failed to account for costs to repair faulty software. The result was inflated revenues of more than 21 percent for two-and-a-half years.

CASE STUDY 2: MEDIA VISION, INC.

THE CASE OF MEDIA VISION, INC., is another example. In 1994, six months after raising $246 million from investors, the company filed for bankruptcy, allegedly having faked more than $100 million in revenues by hiding returned inventory, booking sales that never occurred, and not recording millions of dollars in expenses. The attorney and underwriter for the IPO were criticized by investors for not having done a thorough background check on the company's founder, who allegedly had falsified revenues at a prior company.

CASE STUDY 3: VALENCE TECHNOLOGY

VALENCE TECHNOLOGY manufactured laptop and cellular phone lithium polymer batteries that would supposedly last four times as long as standard batteries and cost less to make. The company raised more than $167 million from investors.

Unfortunately, the batteries shorted out, sparked, overheated, and in some cases exploded and burned when pinched by assembly equipment, according to the *San Francisco Chronicle* report. The product was riddled with problems and was dangerous, and the cost to manufacture the batteries was exorbitant—$50 to $60 for a battery the company planned to sell for about $15, the article said.

Information about the batteries' failure and associated costs would not get to investors for years. But news of potential contracts and projected sales would. By then, the founder had sold his stock and moved on. One investor was wiped out after borrowing $320,000 to invest in the company.

CASE STUDY 4: SEAGATE TECHNOLOGY

SEAGATE TECHNOLOGY MANUFACTURED hard disk drives with much more capacity than the standard disk of its time. In 1984 Seagate claimed profits of $42 million. Later that year Seagate executives announced dramatically lower profits and slower growth, a set-aside of millions of dollars to cover obsolete inventory and uncollectible accounts, and the sale of a plant that was built but never used. Later that year, as the company stock dropped further, investors learned that founders and executives had unloaded much of their personal stock for more than $85 million.

By 1987, Seagate had recovered from its financial problems, reaching revenues of $1 billion a year with its new 3.5-inch disk drive. But in 1998, Seagate disclosed that earnings were down 57 percent, and again the founder had unloaded shares when the stock price had been high. Investigators for investors also discovered that Seagate had boosted revenues by claiming to have sold disk drives that were actually stored in rented warehouses. Eventually, the founders paid $5 million to 17,000 shareholders in an out-of-court settlement without admitting wrongdoing.

Greed and the Entrepreneur's Loss of Ethics

WHILE INVESTORS SHOULD invest in what they know—stick to their knitting, as it were—and focus on business they understand from personal experience, angels today simply cannot turn their backs on high technology even after 2000's dot-com shakeout. New technology typically projects extraordinary profits and, thus, extraordinary investor returns. And extraordinary profits also derive because unique technology benefits from "first-in," noncompetitive pricing.

But investors must beware of investing in businesses with which they are unfamiliar. Another potential pitfall is that private companies, particularly privately owned technology companies, don't readily provide information on their business, and their management doesn't viscerally experience the pressure to produce financial profits more quickly than technological development allows.

Although this is not the norm, instead of building sustainable companies—certainly the objective of a true angel investor interested in long-term economic value—some of today's high-tech start-ups and their founders are more interested in playing the capital market for a quick buck. They sell a concept and flip it to an acquirer, thus lining the unethical entrepreneurs' pockets. Only through due diligence can you avoid lining their pockets at your expense.

And for the smart angel investor, IPOs come too late. The reason is that many VCs and investment banks are taking companies public too early, long before any analyst can confidently point to a workable business model. Venture capitalists seem more concerned with building market capitalization than with building companies. Public-market investors are in essence becoming second-tier venture capital investors by paying astronomical valuations for IPO companies with questionable futures. The early liquidity and exit make the money manager look like a genius and make the early investors rich at the expense of pushing the long-term risk onto the public market. The value that must be held by an angel pre-IPO investor is the building of sustainable companies, because that is the only way the angel will get her money out and see a return that justifies the risk taken in the first place. For the true angel, it's the proof of the business model, not another notch in the IPO gun belt of the institutional venture capital money manager.

Following are examples of ethical lapses by some technology

companies in their relationships with investors, as described in a 1999 *Fortune* article:

◆ Large customers exploit their relationship by extorting pre-IPO shares from a software company about to go public.

◆ Companies invest in other companies that turn around and buy services from the investor company to inflate their revenues.

◆ Some Internet firms are grossing up their revenues by reporting the entire sale price a customer pays at their site when, in fact, the company keeps only a small percentage of that amount. Gross bookings do not equal revenues. The motivation for this practice is that e-commerce companies that don't make a profit are valued at multiples on reported revenues.

◆ Companies sometimes recognize revenues prematurely, even before letters of intent are signed.

◆ Companies report barter transactions as revenues. For example, they exchange advertising space on their Web site for ad space on other companies' sites, and they report the value of the trade ads as revenue. When as much as 50 percent of reported revenues are from bartered transactions, this becomes a gray area.

◆ Companies record sales at full value, not the actual price the customer pays when using a company's own coupons or discounts, and record those coupons or discounts as sales expenses. It's not easy to discover the true revenue and marketing costs critical to evaluating the business's potential if this practice is in place and has not been disclosed in advance.

◆ Companies hide fulfillment costs. Those costs include warehousing, packaging, and shipping, and companies record these as marketing expenses rather than cost of sales, which inflates the company's growth profit margin and hides the potential long-term cost structure of the venture.

◆ A customer of a high-tech company announced it would buy $400 million of the company's products. The company went public with a market cap of $15 billion. Six months after deciding to award the company the contract, the customer company gave a half-dozen of its employees options for the tech-company stock—options that after the IPO were worth a lot of money. This friend-and-family stock option was priced at $38 a share and could be sold on the day of the IPO for a profit. The price for most of the first day of IPO trading hovered between $200 and $250 a share.

Angel investors conducting due diligence must be aware as never before of operating in an environment in which the culprits who get caught merely have to plead that they will cease and desist from the borderline unethical behavior and that they weren't aware of doing anything wrong. In an environment where generally accepted accounting principles offer wiggle room for greedy entrepreneurs to exercise financial legerdemain, unsophisticated investors in particular must be very careful.

It's difficult for entrepreneurs trying to make it to remain above the fray, especially when others seem awash in deceitful riches. Indeed, many have lost their ability to say no. Ultimately, that responsibility rests with the investor, and she must have the discipline to say it. Investors are investing in a high-risk situation, but they need to recognize the questionable practices prevalent in today's technology capital market, a market no longer playing by the old rules—if there ever were any.

When customers, suppliers, partners, and advisers are being let in on the action and analysts have become spokesmen for the firms raising capital, how can an investor trust the due diligence process? Conflicts of interest will always be with us, and considering this fact it's best for investors to resign themselves to the worst possible situation.

Government Regulation and Legislation

TRENDS IN GOVERNMENT LEGISLATION enforcement demonstrate clearly that the role of legislation is not to protect investors. In fact, investors are on their own, particularly when investing in the private equity market. The rising tide of alternative mechanisms for bringing investors and entrepreneurs together illustrates the government's role as *reflecting*, instead of driving, change. The government is only beginning to recognize that venture forums, matching services, newsletters, and online introductory services— hosted by nonprofit and for-profit groups alike—facilitate the flow and exchange of capital from respectable institutional investors as well as astute and novice private investors. Further, these venues allow those investors a glimpse of deals they would otherwise be unaware of, and at the same time offer entrepreneurs a precious opportunity to acquire funds they have searched fruitlessly for on their own.

Through grassroots polling and other rising pressures, both the SEC and state Departments of Corporations are beginning to recognize that laws enacted to protect unsophisticated investors from unscrupulous individuals act to inappropriately restrict deals introduced by experienced entrepreneurs, who are often principals in the ventures, to seasoned investors, highly astute financial analysts with industry track records in this type of investing.

Government is also getting the message about the efficiency of going directly to the investor. The California legislature has taken the lead in the United States with its innovative new program, enacting Section 25102 (n) of the California Corporate Code. This section allows entrepreneurs to advertise for angel investors following a simple, inexpensive procedure. It also grants an easing on dollar amounts and number of purchasers, an action that could reverberate nationally. Some believe that regulation is unfair to small companies, that there is no empirical evidence that small offerings are any more fraudulent than large offerings, and that in general compliance is strangling capital formation. However, this new law opens the way for angels to use their own judgment in assessing the risks and rewards of an offering, just as the multimillionaire institutional investor does.

Although regulators and the accounting standards board may try to curb the more aggressive liberties being taken by entrepreneurs seeking investors, most attorneys, accountants, and investment bankers generally agree that they will never be able to keep pace with the financial and accounting creativity of entrepreneurs desperate for capital or wealth. The U.S. Justice Department and the Securities and Exchange Commission have largely failed to enforce laws enacted to protect the market's integrity. During the past decade, for example, the agencies have filed few criminal and civil cases in Silicon Valley, despite warnings that corporate misconduct is thriving.

Screening Opportunities with the Investor-Oriented Executive Summary

THE THRUST OF THIS BOOK has been to focus on angel investing, investing in and building a company to achieve significant capital appreciation on your investment. So the emphasis is not on evaluating entrepreneurs or specific technologies. While these aspects do represent early-stage investing opportunities, conducting due diligence on a business venture requires a broader diagnostic model than looking at a single technology.

The due diligence process needs to be designed so that investors can cut through large deal flows not only to respond properly and courteously to those who submit their ventures for consideration but also to identify select venture opportunities that deserve closer examination as potential investments.

The first step is to ask key questions to determine whether the investment meets your criteria, and whether any "red flags" are present that would preclude spending any further time reading the business plan, only to end up saying "no." In a sense, the pre-screening process is a miniature version of the more detailed pre-IPO audit protocol described in Chapter 7.

The prescreening process is best begun by requiring the entrepreneur to prepare and submit an executive summary to your specifications—a summary that is well organized, concise, clear, and readable, in a format consonant with your expectations. If the entrepreneur doesn't seem to have time to prepare a summary, you should not give time to the entrepreneur's idea. Since entrepreneurs' executive summaries are frequently ill conceived, you should develop your own brief set of instructions for preparing the executive summary that you can easily e-mail, fax, or snail-mail to the entrepreneurs who want you to consider their ventures. This simple step will save hours of handling inappropriate business plans.

You want the executive summary—the introduction to and synopsis of the venture—to explain the company's reason for existence: to entice you to investigate further, to enable you to grasp the viability of the whole notion, to instill confidence that its writer has the will to persevere in bad times, and to motivate you to want to read the entire business plan.

Following is the prescreening executive summary that International Capital Resources has developed and refined over the past eleven years. We use it for preliminary evaluation of a venture before requesting a complete business plan and making a commitment to read it.

- Date
- Name
- Title
- Business Name
- Headquarters Address
- State
- Zip
- Telephone
- Cell Phone
- Pager
- Fax
- E-Mail
- Description of type of business, specifically industry category, stage of development, key goals of management
- Product and/or service: What is the product or service? What is its name or trademark? How does it work, and how is it used? What is its present stage of product development? What problem does the company's product or service solve? What's unique about the business, company, or technology (its competitive advantage)?
- Is the solution proprietary? Is it patented, or is the patent pending? Is it a trade secret?
- Founder/CEO: Is management knowledgeable and experienced in the industry? Is the principal an inventor, entrepreneur, or businessperson with a proven track record? Does she anticipate hiring a new chief executive or chief operating officer in the immediate future? What is the date of the most recent business plan? What is the type and stage of venture documentation (for example, a business plan, a private-placement memorandum)?
- Market: Who or what is/are the prospective customers, current customers, market size, market growth rate, competition, industry

trends? How will the firm compete? Any endorsements? Is missionary selling required to convince the public of the value of the product or service?

◆ Operations: How will the product or service be manufactured or delivered? What is the extent of current facilities and equipment, special processes used, labor skills required? Is a union present?

◆ Channels of distribution: How will the product or service be distributed to customers, and how will it be sold?

◆ Financial results: If it is an operating company, how long has the company been in business? Is the company profitable? If not, why not? Is the cash flow positive? When will breakeven be achieved? If it is a start-up, what are the company's projections for the next three years for sales, profit, and cash flow?

◆ Current financing status: How has the company been funded to date? Indicate how much capital management plans to raise to achieve profitability. How much are they attempting to raise now? Is any additional funding anticipated? Is there a minimum investment the company is accepting from one investor? What are the proposed uses of the funds?

◆ What level of active or passive investment does the company seek? Assuming that an outside investor's training and experience were appropriate, what role or roles could such an investor play in managing the company?

◆ Investor appeal: Are there other investors in the deal? Who are they? Have others expressed interest in the deal? Who are they?

◆ Valuation: What is management's pre-money valuation? Post-money valuation? How does valuation compare with other companies that have completed their transaction? What deal is management offering? For example, what percentage of ownership and equity in the company is currently available for investors?

◆ Exit: How does management foresee returning the investor's capital—for example, by sale, merger or acquisition, maintenance of ownership and buyback, or IPO? Can the company provide an example of another company in the industry that has used this exit mechanism?

◆ Potential return on investment: This is a calculation by management of how much money the company can possibly make and a description of the calculation to achieve it.

After studying the prescreening executive summary, you become informed enough to make a preliminary assessment about the company's and management's strengths and weaknesses to determine what you like and dislike in the situation and so make a decision about whether to request and read the entrepreneur's full business plan and documentation package. Also, if you are not interested, you can provide the deserving entrepreneur with comments or recommendations to assist her in getting on the right track.

Why You Should Require a Business Plan

BUSINESSES THAT FAIL or voluntarily cease operations typically do so because of insufficient planning. This results in inadequate performance, failure to achieve projected levels of results, inadequate capital levels to sustain or grow the business, and general failure to attain the owners', managers', or investors' goals. Failure to plan leads inevitably to a plan to fail. To constantly reassess the original business vision in light of new developments in our fast-moving economy, you need to continually commit to paper the business concept, the business model, and its plan for execution. So avoid unnecessary risk in angel investing: Always require a business plan, a written plan to build, market, and sell at a profit the product or service of a business.

International Capital Resources recently completed a study of 1,200 angel investors. Thirty-five percent stated they would invest in a venture without a business plan. Such risk is unnecessarily dangerous. Where is the line between being bold and being foolhardy? The business plan demonstrates in writing management's hypothesis about its ability to control the business.

The logic, strategy, and support provided in the plan reflect management's assumptions of a cause-and-effect relationship, whereby "If management does X, then Y is likely to occur." Without a business plan, your due diligence analysis of management's hypothesis about its competitive advantage—for example, your assessment of the market potential, which drives all cash flow forecasting—is relegated to subjectivity and speculation. Remember, everything that works is simple, but *achieving* simple is hard. The business plan is your key to opening the door to the company's potential success.

So in due diligence, sophisticated angel investors next assess the business plan. The business plan should contain *at least* the nineteen items listed on the business plan outline below. If the business plan does not contain these elements and you are still interested in looking at the deal more closely, require the entrepreneur to supply the missing information to supplement your decision-making process.

BUSINESS PLAN OUTLINE

1 **Summary of the company's proposed activity, management, and performance**
2 **Present stage of development**
   —Trace the history of formation, product choices, and rules for principals.
   —Describe early problems/setbacks and plans to overcome them.
3 **Product/service description**
   —Distinguishing features
   —Distinctive advantages and disadvantages
   —Targeted customers and cost justification to purchase
4 **Venture objectives**
   —What is to be achieved in the market? Why? What are the sales and profitability goals?
5 **Nature and current condition of target industry and industry trends**
6 **Business strategy (management hypothesis)**
   —Define and explain how the strategy is to be implemented.
   —Explain how it creates a competitive edge.
7 **Competitors**
   —Who are they? What are their strengths and weaknesses and market share? What about probable future competitors?
8 **Existing/potential customers**
   —Who has expressed interest?

—Who has rejected the opportunity?

—How are you in touch with customers?

9 Summary of functional specs of the product

—Attach a photo, drawing, diagram, etc.

10 Key technologies and skills needed to reach development and manufacture

—Is any leading-edge technology involved?

—Do you anticipate problems? How do you plan to overcome these?

—Are there any patents and proprietary rights?

—Are there any built-in barriers to market entry? Are they protectable?

11 What are the sales channels/distribution modes and alternatives?

12 Are there any aftermarket service operations (and any anticipated problems)?

13 What is the cost volume and development cost breakdown: materials, labor, etc.?

14 Manufacturing process

—What facilities are needed?

—What types and quantity of equipment are needed?

—What is the cost to purchase or lease them?

—What are the labor and plant space considerations?

15 Summary of the proposed deal

16 Marketplace

—What is the market attractiveness/driving force?

—Buyers' profile: Who are they? What are their preferences? Does your product solve the customer's problem?

—Positioning (distribution, marketing, servicing)

—Size, growth rate, characteristics of the target market; how will market acceptance be achieved?

—Market analysis (summary) and support

17 Management team

—Do they have experience?

—Do they have any successes?

—Do they have the ability to provide a return?

18 Sources and uses of funds

—What is the financing strategy?

—How much money is needed?

—Will it be equity, debt, or both?

—How will the funds be used?

—Explain how investment relates to achievement of company goals.

19 Financial statements and projections

—A summary of historical financials

—A summary of projections (best case, worst case, most probable). Note key assumptions.

Investigating the Entrepreneur and Management Team

THE PURPOSE OF INVESTIGATING the entrepreneur or founder and management team is to enable you to determine the breadth of the management skills of its members, identify needs for further additions or replacements to the team, and gain insight into the stage at which additional skills will need to be added to the team. This process will also enlighten you about the point at which the coinvestment team may need to become actively involved in the venture to correct problems, provide direction or counsel, consult on a short-term basis, become involved in a board role, or take a more operational-level involvement now or in the future.

Angels accept the truism in angel investing that people get funded, not business plans. The successful angel investor is a master judge of people. She is not investing in an idea, technology, or a plan but in building a sustainable business. More to the point, she is investing in the belief that the people involved can transform the idea, technology, or product into a successful business. Regardless of the validity of an idea, technology, or product/service, we have learned the folly of believing that the world beats a path to the door of a better mousetrap. Most successful angel investors agree that an experienced, successful manager with a "B" product or plan has a better chance of getting returns for the investor than a less-competent manager with an "A" product or plan.

In evaluating the management, consider above all whether the entrepreneur and her team possess direct experience in the industry of the proposed venture. The best criterion is a track record of success in management or having made money for investors. In assessing the management team, remain objective, because evaluating character is very difficult if you become friends with the entrepreneur.

When evaluating a potential investment, you need to determine whether the founder is an inventor or entrepreneur and/or is qualified to be the CEO. Does she have the experience and the temperament? If not, you need to determine early on whether the founder/entrepreneur is open to additions or replacements in the management team. We do not believe that you can rely on founders or entrepreneurs to evaluate their own strengths or weaknesses. Too much is at stake for you to abdicate this assessment responsibility. A harsher truth is that the only insurance against being cheated is to check out the entrepreneurs themselves.

You need to assess each individual in the entrepreneurial team and examine the team itself. From the team perspective, does it have a history of working constructively, or is it a group of "lone rangers"?

We identify below the psychological characteristics that seem to be present in entrepreneurs whom angel investors have funded successfully.

◆ **Vision:** Has the foresight to handle unexpected events and to recognize and take advantage of opportunities.

◆ **Leader:** Has enthusiasm and passion; is charismatic; can communicate the vision and build a team; is able to tell the company story and generate trust, support, and commitment; has the professional competence and technical skills to manage rapid growth in an early-stage company.

◆ **Courage:** Is a risk taker; has placed a portion of her own net worth into making the vision a reality; is open to new technology and new markets, as well as experimenting with new approaches to communicate with customers, suppliers, vendors, and investors; is a pioneer and an innovator, not a follower.

◆ **Optimistic:** Has unbounded belief in the venture and the research and study to back up that belief; has a "no is for now" attitude and does not react defensively to criticism or suggestions. This optimism is manifested as persuasiveness in interactions with others; works constructively with others from a positive position.

◆ **Hard worker:** Is unwaveringly reliable; makes all the sacrifices; is first in, last out of the office; doesn't ask others to do what she hasn't done or isn't willing to roll up her own sleeves to do; lives the dream; has unbounded energy.

◆ **Patient:** Has the long-term view; is in it for the long haul; is interested not in "flipping the company" quickly but in building a venture of substance; listens and considers before acting; relations with others are characterized by consideration.

◆ **Creative:** Is an independent thinker; has developed an original solution to a real problem; has demonstrated productivity in the early-stage environment because she can deal skillfully and quickly with the many new situations that typically arise; is resourceful.

◆ **Integrity:** Is trustworthy and ethical, as demonstrated by a thorough background check.

While many of the examples of psychological characteristics were provided in relation to the work environment, sometimes the best way for the angel investor to get a handle on these attributes or the presence of character flaws is to have at least one meeting at the entrepreneur's home and observe her reputation and conduct in her neighborhood. If this is not possible, then plan to do something together with the entrepreneur. Psychologists believe that you never know a person without some form of shared experience.

Still, the "softer" psychological and characteristic evaluation cannot substitute for a formal background check performed by a professional corporate investigation firm. The formal background check will typically cover the following areas:

◆ Statewide criminal history
◆ County criminal history (including felony and misdemeanor)
◆ Civil court record, including litigations
◆ Federal court record, including criminal, bankruptcy, and civil records
◆ Credit and debt check
◆ Education and credential confirmation
◆ Driving record

◆ Name-link identity check
◆ Reference check, including work and personal references
◆ Compensation history

A release authorization from the entrepreneur will be required to perform a background check of this scope. She will need to sign a form authorizing the background check and provide a name, address, social security number, date of birth, sex, race, and driver's license number. You, in turn, must keep this information in a secure file, separate from any personnel records of the company should you invest in it.

The fees of corporate investigative firms are very reasonable. We urge you to use professional, experienced, independent third parties to carry out all background checks and investigations, particularly the reference check. However, if an investor feels that she must perform the reference check herself, we refer you to the comprehensive protocols for conducting interviews offered by Lipper and Gladstone in our Suggested Reading List (Appendix G). If entrepreneurial background checks do not come out positive, drop the deal, regardless of how good it looks on paper.

Separating Fact from Fiction in Venture Documentation

AFTER A COMPLETE INVESTIGATION of the entrepreneur and management but short of embarking upon the extensive pre-IPO audit (see Chapter 7), you can direct your questions to the business plan and venture documentation—for example, the private-placement memorandum. Why? It's simple. Once the entrepreneur has your money, you can whistle for answers to your questions. The time to ask the tough questions is before you invest. The best way to understand the business proposal is to research the business plan.

Even the best venture offerings are highly risky. So after reviewing the business plan, if you experience a nagging sense of doubt, you probably have good reason for it. Good investments are based on sound business criteria and not emotions. If you are not entirely comfortable, the best approach is usually not to invest. Other opportunities will come along, so do not let an overzealous, highly enthusiastic entrepreneur pressure you into making a premature decision.

As discussed earlier, it is a good idea to size up the management face-to-face. Focus on experience and track record rather than a smooth road-show presentation. If at all possible, take any of your professional advisers or coinvestors with you to help in your analysis. Beware of information that is different in the road show from that presented in the executive summary, business plan, or private-placement memorandum or not contained at all in those documents. If a significant difference cannot be explained, hoist the red flag.

We have already made suggestions about what entrepreneurs should be expected to provide within the context of the business plan, usually a twenty-to-twenty-five-page document with appendices to support assumptions listed within the business plan narrative. In this section, we want to highlight some qualifying criteria successful investors use to guide their reading of business plans, emphasizing what they look for in a venture before embarking on the more complete pre-IPO audit.

As you build up deal flow, be clear about more important criteria in qualifying ventures suitable for more complete due diligence. Remember, it takes only one red flag to justify putting down the plan, suspending further reading, time, and financial expense, and moving on to the next project. And again, the only way to be sure you're investing not just in an idea but in a potentially sustainable business is to read the business plan, including the entrepreneur's explanation of business strategy and the company's competitive edge.

In earlier sections, we have discussed investigating management team skills and background, checking references, and fitting or matching the venture with the investor's personal criteria. The best way to determine whether the venture can provide return *of* investment and return *on* investment, while also meeting other investor objectives—for example, something investors can get involved in, something that excites them, that they can embrace and identify with—is by closely scrutinizing the business plan and investment proposal.

Due diligence is the first stage of preinvestment research to verify the viability of the entrepreneur's proposal. When you analyze the venture documentation, such as the business plan, you will not find a magic formula for making successful investment decisions. But based on our research, successful venture investors consider certain factors to be particularly important. The pre-IPO audit in Chapter 7 will reveal many specific questions to ask; meanwhile, pay attention to the following highlighted elements when you first review business plans submitted for your consideration.

To repeat, there is the review of the management-team section of the plan. This should confirm that the team members possess the requisite skills and experience in the industry, are dream-driven, work well together, generate real chemistry, and demonstrate pride in the enterprise. Most important, remember that the major risks in early-stage investment require management-team members to work together with great acumen, as they face the onslaught of stress and strain during the fast-growth periods and early stages of development.

But although management and technology can be changed, the market remains recalcitrant, difficult to influence. So the market section is one of the first sections we recommend you review when looking at a business plan. Can the market size and growth rate justify the investment in the deal? Is there significant market growth potential? The company's product line or service must exhibit a large enough market potential to support rapid growth. A strong point is a large market, exemplified by qualified buyers and preferably a unique market niche.

Also, is the market ready? Is there a true need for the product? In other words, is the product or service really solving a major problem, or is it going to require missionary selling to get off the ground? What we like to see is proof of market demand, in the form of a survey, purchase orders, or some other verification. The overall consideration is whether the market is receptive at the price on which the projections are based.

In addition, when considering the market, you want to look closely at what we call "channel economics," an analysis investors often skip over in reviewing the business plan. Channel economics assesses whether the management team has demonstrated a detailed understanding of the cost to bring the product or service to market. The question is whether the company has a realistic marketing plan and whether it has planned for the resources to successfully market the product or service.

Another element to consider is whether management has presented a strong case for significant competitive advantage and outlying barriers to competition. We're talking about barriers to competition beyond offering the product or service for free or at a low price. Does the company know the competition? Have customers and suppliers provided interview data, and has the company assessed its competition, particularly large-company competition?

The company also needs a proprietary market position, one that must sustain rapid growth and create the kind of high profit margins necessary to keep it growing. The plan should also capture whether the company's competitive advantage is further supported by patents, trademarks, copyrights, or other exclusive relationships or trade secrets. And although it's more difficult to determine, you need to assess the large risk of whether anything is brewing in the market that could affect the company and its projections. Consider at the business-strategy level whether the market can change and perhaps have an impact on the acceptance or rate of acceptance of the product.

Selecting an industry you are familiar with will help you accelerate your view of this section of the business plan. Is the company in an established or emerging industry? Obviously, if it's not an established industry, the venture represents significantly more risk. Also, it is extremely important for you to understand the industry, or at least the use of the underlying technology. Again, if you don't understand, you should consult with advisers before proceeding. Last, you should request industry-sector research if the company has not supplied it as part of the plan. Many aftermarket industry-sector research reports are readily available, and these can be a valuable yardstick against management's estimates and projections.

To reduce risk, you need to understand that the more tangible the product or technology is, the better it is for you. The first question we ask ourselves about a product, service, or technology is whether it is a real solution to a real problem. To calculate the answer, determine the extent to which the product or the technology has been realized. Obviously, conceptual deals—those only on paper or at the idea stage—represent significantly more risk than ventures already at the alpha, beta, or prototype stage.

Next, ask whether the technology works, whether it accomplishes what the entrepreneurs claim it can. Also, you need to calculate the product's and technology's growth potential. Find out if it is a protected or proprietary technology in the form of a patent, trademark, copyright, trade secret, or private formula.

If the plan is for a manufacturing entity, check whether the technology exists to make the product or whether there is yet another level of risk in manufacturing the devices to create it. Will manufacturing and/or R&D work as planned? These are risk questions, so they are vital. Is the manufacturing capability immediately available to make the product? And how has the research and development proceeded? Has it worked as planned? The most important question is this: Is production currently feasible—and feasible at the rate used to generate the financial projections?

Are you looking at a potentially profitable and sustainable business? Or is the business plan an inventor masquerading as a business in order to sustain a lifestyle? The best way to determine whether a business is profitable and sustainable is to examine the financial statements and the financial pro formas and projections. Are the projections reasonable?

We like to see a minimum of $10 million in sales within five years and a growth of at least 20 percent annually, figures common in the small-business and angel capital market. There must be above-average profit potential, with pretax high-profit margins of at least 15 percent. Profits must be large enough to generate the levels of working capital needed to support rapid growth, and also to create the profits for providing returns to investors on an ongoing basis.

Also, in the case of operating companies, you have to analyze the financial performance of the venture. If no financial history is available, then, as an alternative source of analysis, you can borrow the financial history of companies where the management, entrepreneur, or founders worked before. A red flag we always look for in projections is whether management is dealing unfairly with investors by taking salaries or other benefits that are too large for the company's stage of development or in comparison with their salaries at earlier positions.

Regardless of the diverse motivations that attract angels to early-stage, higher-risk private-equity transactions, investors must see potential for significant investment returns from the proposed deal to justify their loss of access to their capital and the risk they assume. In effect, the economic potential of an angel investment opportunity is equal to not only the amount of money invested but also the additional resources to be invested along with the money, and the risk associated with the investment. The investor must evaluate the circumstances based on the total investment anticipated. That includes the time she will be involved, as well as the money and risk.

Investors often compare expected returns from the less liquid venture with those from another investment of equal risk but with less involvement and more liquidity. Investors we have spoken with aim for a minimum of 25 percent to 50 percent internal rates of return founded on credible projections and supporting assumptions that the entrepreneurs provide, or founded on corresponding financial models that the investors themselves develop when they analyze the venture.

There is also a correlation between the size of the investment and the size of the potential return on the investment. More sophisticated investors are extremely demanding and aim for a tenfold return within a reasonable period of time, from five to ten years. The venture must be solid enough to provide this level of return before they are willing to lose access to their capital and assume the risk.

Another large component of evaluating the potential for return is calculating valuation. Are you being asked to pay more than the shares are worth? We will discuss valuation in much greater detail in Chapter 9. Meanwhile, another aspect that's a more specific example of valuation is to determine from the business plan whether entrepreneurs are retaining an inordinate amount of the company equity compared with the amount investors will receive.

For example, are the angel investors putting up 80 percent of the money but receiving only 10 percent of the company's shares? It is not unfair for investors to analyze the potential need to reinvest further funds in order to minimize dilution of their investment. Obviously, if the venture becomes successful, the investors may want to increase their stake in the company. So when investors consider whether they can afford the investment, they should prudently consider how much additional money might be required in later rounds, in addition to how much will be needed now.

The last critical consideration for the investor is what we call "capital intensity." This is the amount of financial risk or capital that must be put into a company before you see any proof that the company or its technology is workable. One of the reasons that angel investment in biotechnology has fallen off a little is that investors have learned that millions of dollars are required to go through the process of clinical trials and FDA approval, and only then can the company *finally* create a product. Other industry sectors require much less capital intensity.

Less than 1 percent of U.S. businesses are publicly traded. To appreciate the challenge of pre-IPO investing, then, we must understand the requirements of IPO exit and liquidity. One of our requirements when reviewing a business plan is that a believable exit plan must exist. If the company proposes to investors that liquidity will be provided through an IPO, for example, it is incumbent on the investor to ensure that the management's business plan documents the company's growth to the point at which the venture meets original listing requirements for an IPO on a major exchange. No one wants to be listed on the Pink Sheets.

Companies list on major exchanges because they want to secure the best possible market for the trading of their securities. The New York Stock Exchange fills this need by providing today's public companies with an efficient, competitive, and equitable marketplace for their shares. The New York Stock Exchange offers a number of compelling reasons to list with it, such as a broad range of investors, outstanding liquidity and transparency, and the most cost-effective access to the world's largest pool of capital.

Such a listing gives individual and institutional investors confidence that they own shares in quality businesses and that when they buy or sell shares, their orders will be dispatched fairly and efficiently. The original listing requirements that the New York Stock Exchange applies to domestic companies going public are described below. We provide here four different tests for assessing the entrepreneurs' projections and their viability for meeting exchange requirements. Meeting any one of the four domestic financial tests is all that's required:

◆ Most recent fiscal year pretax earnings of $2.5 million, with pretax earnings of $2 million in each of the two preceding fiscal years.

◆ Aggregate for the last three fiscal years pretax earnings of $6.5 million, with minimum pretax earnings of $4.5 million in the most recent fiscal year (all three years must be positive).

◆ For companies with not less than $500 million in market capitalization and $200 million in revenues in the most recent twelve-month period, an aggregate operating cash flow of $25 million for the past three fiscal years (each year must report a positive amount).

◆ Revenues of $250 million in the most recent fiscal year.

In addition to the above requirements, there are also distribution requirements. Underwriters must provide the New York Stock Exchange with a letter stating that the common shares will be sold to ensure that the New York Stock Exchange distribution standards—of 2,000 round lot holders, 1.1 million public shares, and minimum aggregate public market value of $60 million—are met. In addition, if the minimum market capitalization test of $500 million is applied, the New York Stock Exchange will require a letter from the underwriter confirming the value. It's important to note that pretax earnings are adjusted for various items as defined in the New York Stock Exchange listed company manual. Operating cash flow is adjusted to (a) reconcile such amounts to cash provided by operating activities, and (b) exclude changes in operating assets and liabilities, as adjusted for the requirements of the New York Stock Exchange listed company manual.

Knowing When to Say "No"

ON THE SUBJECT of saying no, Arthur Lipper III in *Venture Investing Angels* said it best: "Angels should insist by their bearing and deportment on having authority. Authority in this case [in an angel investment transaction] results from having something, that is, money, that someone wants, whereas respect is earned. This kind of authority is power."

Successful investors know when to say no. If the investor waivers or displays any ambiguity in what he says, be assured an entrepreneur will almost always interpret it in the most positive way, even if this is not the most realistic interpretation. As previously discussed, you can use the prescreening protocol to winnow out deals that are not a fit and that hold no interest. You can use the information gleaned from that preliminary assessment not only to say no but also to provide constructive feedback, gently prodding the entrepreneur to think anew, to put the venture on track or make it more presentable to other investors.

Also the investor can, by saying no, save the entrepreneur from journeying down a path prematurely, one that may in the end be financially destructive for him and his family. We have personally witnessed many entrepreneurs whose vision consumed them and ultimately destroyed them financially, devastating their personal and family lives. Honest feedback early in the capitalization process from an angel whose judgment the entrepreneur respects could get through and change the outcome of a venture.

There are many reasons why investors might think turning down a venture proposal is justified. Below are some quotes from investors we've interviewed:

◆ The potential return for the risk I had to accept was inadequate.
◆ Management did not seem qualified for the task.
◆ I had no interest in the business; it has no social value.
◆ We could not agree on valuation and equity share for my investment.
◆ The venture was a bad idea; it wasn't a plan, it was a wish.
◆ It was a business I am unfamiliar with.
◆ The business was too far away from me geographically.

◆ The market was just too small to be exciting.

We have identified from all of these reasons and others a number of trends for not investing in a deal. The angel who said "no" was clear before investigating the transaction about what he was seeking in a desirable deal. The investor's thinking and his heart were in agreement; that is, when an investor rationally decided he was not interested, he was not emotionally swayed thereafter by the entrepreneur's pitch and appeals. This solidarity with one's own decision is important, because many investors have revealed that "catching the entrepreneur's enthusiasm" is one of the worst things that can happen to an angel.

Again, the enthusiasm of a fanatical dreamer can hypnotize you. You forget the risk, forget that the projections most likely will not be realized, and forgo the more objective and prudent route of performing proper due diligence. This pressure to catch the enthusiasm can be insidious. One can catch the bug not only from the entrepreneur but from other investors as well. For example, a novice investor may feel inferior to a more experienced investor who has already made an investment in the company. By operating in the shadow of the more experienced investor, the novice is vulnerable to sacrificing her own judgment and ignoring the results of her own due diligence. Even coinvestors do not rely on the judgment of lead investors; they still do their own due diligence to supplement the lead investor's evaluation. Whether you use the prescreening questionnaire, the business plan, or the full preinvestment audit as a yardstick, the idea behind venture management is that you must be certain that the market and financial opportunity survive rational assessment.

Saying no is not easy. You should anticipate negative reactions from rejected dreamers passionate to make their vision a reality. Don't assume anything about an entrepreneur's interpretation of "no." For example, don't think that by not returning their call they will "get it" and go away. Entrepreneurs require an authoritative response. If you are sure that there is no fit, get to the point; be direct. Say what you mean: say "no." Failing to do so leaves you open to ongoing contacts from the entrepreneur.

Who Pays Due Diligence Expenses?

AS YOU KNOW, DUE DILIGENCE is time-consuming and exhausting. It is also expensive, depending on how detailed an investigation is required. To no one's surprise, the following activities and professionals cost money: background checks, private investigators, attorneys, accountants, investment bankers, technical advisers, travel, and the incidental duplication, shipping, and telephone expenses associated with preparing and sharing documents. All of this adds up more quickly and higher than the parties usually anticipate. Perhaps no one disputes the presence of a price tag. The question is, who will pay it? Who should be responsible for the investor's expense incurred during the due diligence on a potential investment?

When dealing with seed, R&D, and start-up situations, it is reasonable to expect that the company or the founder is rarely in a financial position to bear the cost associated with investigating the venture for the many investors who will consider investing capital. Angel investors must resign themselves that in early-stage investing, they inevitably will pay.

However, the investor may recover some or all of the expenses incurred during the due diligence process as long as the expenses were properly documented. The most typical situation is one in which the investor decides to invest in the company. During negotiation, the investor can seek an agreement among the parties that upon closing, the investor will be reimbursed for accounting, legal, and other professional fees associated with due diligence on the transaction. Of course, the investor may negotiate for reimbursement in the form of additional equity.

Another occasion when the investor can be reimbursed for documented due diligence expenses is when the investor has offered a deal that has been accepted "in principle" by the entrepreneur. Normally, the parties agree to close the transaction within an agreed-upon time frame. If the entrepreneur should change her mind and decide against entering into the transaction after agreeing to go forward "in principle," then the parties can add a clause to the agreement that requires the investor to be reimbursed.

Finally, a word about confidentiality agreements: During the past eleven years, we have met more paranoid entrepreneurs than we care to recall, individuals overly concerned that someone would steal their idea. While functioning as an intermediary and managing a professional business service, we acquiesced to an entrepreneur's need for a sense of security by signing confidentiality agreements. But it is not in the best interest of angel investors, particularly capital providers embarking upon aggressive deal-flow development strategies like those advocated in this book, to sign such agreements. Nondisclosure and confidentiality agreements, once entered into, can come back to haunt angel investors who invest in deals similar to the confidential ones. Don't do it.

THE PREINVESTMENT AUDIT

The Analytical Research Approach to the Preinvestment Audit

WHEN THEY REVIEW THE FOLLOWING detailed audit guidelines, many investors will at first react by claiming they are overwhelming, unrealistic, or impractical. But what is far more impractical and costly is losing $50,000 to $250,000 in an investment, money that the investor could have invested elsewhere or money with which he could have financed a more deserving, sustainable venture. Angels and their capital are a precious resource, and one way for them to avoid squandering this resource is to consider this alternative: spend a few weeks to complete the painstaking audit to determine the competence and integrity of the management, the feasibility of the business plan and financial projections, and the fairness of the deal.

The preinvestment audit we are about to describe, regardless of how comprehensive it is, does not substitute for the due diligence steps described in the previous chapter—for example, scanning the summary, studying the business plan, and using a professional firm to conduct a background check and character assessment of the CEO and management team. Instead, the audit builds on these earlier assessments in a more organized, detailed fashion. To avoid redundancy, questions posed earlier will not be repeated here.

In this chapter we organize the key queries that need to be investigated and answered. Also included is a comprehensive listing of the miscellaneous documents the investor should request from the company for thorough analysis.

The focus of this questionnaire is to examine the early-stage technology and manufacturing company, that is, companies that have started up and/or are expanding operations. Therefore, the investor will not find the questions and ratio analysis typically posed for more mature operating companies. Clearly, if this audit is used for more established information technology or service companies, the investor will need to improve upon it by adding questions to all of the sections, and by modifying some of the questions listed.

The investor must consider all sections of this diagnostic assessment because failure by the company in any area can increase the risk and create greater potential for failure in meeting projections or investor expectations.

The investor should consider this preinvestment audit within the context of the following six-step analytical research approach:

◆ Collect data directly from the company through documents and interviews with the management. Remember to take notes on what management says in responding to your questions.

◆ Using the comprehensive reference checklist, contact people outside the firm yourself or with the help of a professional corporate investigator to gain another perspective. Supplement this information with secondary documents you obtain from outside the company, using the checklist we have provided.

◆ Compare, contrast, and analyze the information you obtain from inside the company with information from outside resources.

◆ Identify gaps that suggest management incompetence or errors, poor judgment, or lack of integrity; identify strengths and weaknesses in the business plan, the financial data, and the deal. Weigh and compare these different aspects.

◆ Then, compare the results of your analysis with your personal assessment, which is your feelings and intuition about the management, the company, the plan, and the deal. Also, of course, consider the advice of your counselors. Clarify what you like and dislike about the investment.

◆ Last, list all of the gaps you have identified and assess the risk and potential reward the company represents. Compare this gap analysis with your personal risk tolerance to determine how the deal fits with your personal investment strategy.

The following is an organized, analytical research approach to assessing the true feasibility of an early-stage private equity transaction. The categories of data to be collected include management; products and services; industry; market sales distribution; competition; human resources; suppliers; production; research and development; financial analysis of projections, including capital requirements, balance sheet, income statement, cash flow forecast, use of proceeds, list of financial plan assumptions, and risk/return analysis; investors, directors, and advisers to the company; reference checklist; and miscellaneous documents required for analysis.

The Preinvestment Audit Questionnaire

MANAGEMENT

1 Who are the managers of the company? Who holds the major authority? Who is the key decision maker?

2 What are the major achievements of the CEO? How successful were his or her previous ventures?

3 Is the CEO personally familiar with the specifics of the company's operations?

4 How has the CEO dealt with major problems the company has faced before?

5 What are the CEO's financial goals in being involved in the company?

6 What is the management team's background? Do the team members' past industry experiences dovetail with their current job responsibilities? What are the members' reputations in the industry?

7 Have team members been involved in any other start-ups or public companies? Has any member of the management team previously made money for investors?

8 What is the relationship between the management and the board of directors?

9 Who sits on the board of directors? What is their experience and qualifications? Have they managed more developed, successful companies?

10 What is the total compensation of all officers in the company? Their salary, commission, bonuses, loans, expense reimbursements, profit sharing, etc.? What was their compensation in their previous positions?

11 What is each manager's stock ownership, and how much, if any, of his or her own capital has been invested in the company? What is the CEO's ownership following financing? What is the ownership of outside directors?

12 Are there any restrictions on company stock?

13 Is the style of management leadership compatible with the investors' values?

14 Is the company current in all taxes owed?

15 Is the company in compliance with all federal, state, and local laws and relevant agency rules and regulations?

16 Has management made any acquisitions or divestitures?

17 Has a management performance and evaluation system been installed? How is it being implemented?

18 Have members of management worked together before, or are they related? Do they exude a palpable team spirit?

19 Are there any vacancies in the management structure, or is any member of the management temporarily filling a position until a permanent professional is located? What is the plan to recruit and fill positions?

20 If the CEO were not available, is there a suitable replacement on the team?

21 Has any member of the management team sued or been sued within the past five years?

22 Has any member of the management team ever been convicted of a felony?

23 Are there any civil or criminal charges pending against any member of the management team?

24 Has any member of the management team ever been terminated from a management position? Has any member left the company? Why?

25 Has any member of the management team personally filed for bankruptcy or been involved in state receivership within the past five years?

26 Has any member of the management team ever been the officer of a company that has filed for bankruptcy?

27 Has any member of the management team been disciplined by a regulatory agency or professional association within the past five years?

28 Obtain personal and health data on all of the key managers. Are management personnel in good health? Has any member of the management team disclosed any serious difficulties in his or her private life (divorce, psychological breakdowns, alcohol or drug problems)?

29 Is any member of the management team not expendable? If yes, why? What will happen if he or she becomes unavailable?

30 Have there been any SEC problems or violations in the past ten years for any manager, officer, or director? Has the management team signed employment contracts? Do these include non-compete clauses?

31 Have there been any problems within management, and if so, have those problems been resolved? Have there been any changes in the management team within the past two years? How do they communicate now?

32 What reports does management use to run the business? Can you get copies?

33 Will management provide written assurances that the company is in compliance with all federal, state, and local laws and with all rules and regulations by agencies and commissions thereof, including but not limited to safety and health; consumer products safety; and environmental laws relevant to the ownership of its properties, its operation, or its business?

34 What in-house financial systems are automated—for example, inventory, general ledger, etc.? How accurate are these systems? How smoothly do they run? Are they integrated companywide or are there stand-alone systems?

PRODUCTS OR SERVICES

1 What is the current product line? Describe each. How reliable are the products? Are samples available?

2 Which product is the most profitable for the company?

3 How does the product work? What problem does the product solve? Does it solve a "real" problem or fulfill a "real" need?

4 What is proprietary about the product?

5 Has all R&D been completed on the products? What is the timetable for new product introductions?

6 How is the product priced? Who establishes the price and the price structure? What are the past and present price trends in the industry?

7 What is the estimated remaining life span of each of the company's products?

8 If applicable, what is the current status of the patent for the process or product? Is a copy available?

9 When were the products introduced? At what point are they in their lifecycle? Are changes in products planned?

10 Can the product be mass-produced, or does it require customizing?

11 Estimate revenues and the market share for all products over the next twelve months.

12 What are the margins for each product, and how will they change as the market share increases?

13 What are the customer service requirements for each product? Describe any customer service operations. Are any customer services contracted out to third parties?

14 What is the company's warranty policy? What is the current and projected warranty expense?

INDUSTRY

1 What industry (or industries) is the company involved in? How many companies are in the industry? How is the industry structured (product, price, geography)?

2 Are any large players accounting for a significant share of the business in the industry? Describe the market share.

3 How would you define the competitive structure of the industry (fragmented, oligopoly, monopoly, etc.)? Which way are mergers and acquisitions heading (vertical or horizontal)?

4 What is the failure rate of companies in the industry?

5 What has been the annual industrial sales growth rate, and what is it expected to be over the next five years?

6 What has been the annual earnings growth of the industry? What are the projections for the next five years?

7 Is the industry subject to cycles? How volatile are industrial sales and earnings during economic cycles? Indicate the best and the worst possible scenarios.

8 What are the significant barriers to entry into the industry?

9 What is the success rate for new entrants into the industry? Do any company patents suggest the company's industry will succeed?

10 What is the history of the industry? Have any recent events had an impact on it?

11 What government agencies regulate the industry, and does the company expect any future changes in the degree of regulation?

12 To what extent is the industry unionized, and what has been the impact of recent labor contracts in the industry?

13 Identify the key elements influencing future industry growth, for example, market growth changes, economic trends, consolidations and economies of scale, price differences, interest rates, government regulation, environmental issues, technological innovation and product development, foreign competition. How might these factors influence projections for the company?

MARKET, SALES, AND DISTRIBUTION

1 What is the dollar size of the market by product? What is the annual market growth rate by product? What are the projections for three years? What are the data sources?

2 What is the company's marketing strategy? What are the annual advertising expenditures, current and projected? What is the company's selling proposition?

3 What are the central objectives in marketing? How will the strategy be implemented, e.g., is there an array of promotional activities planned?

4 How does the company's marketing strategy compare with the competitor's information (see Competition section of audit)? What market research has the company conducted? Are copies available?

5 How do sales breakdowns/projections by product compare with industry data?

6 Who are the company's customers? What do they buy? How big is the average order? Is there any backlog of orders, purchase orders, or letters of intent? Are customers fiscally sound? To what extent are customers repeat purchasers? How do customers perceive product quality? Is the company dependent on a few key customers?

7 How does the company find customers? What is the time and cost to close sales? Does this fit with projections? Is intensive personal selling required?

8 What are the key variables in the buying decisions? What are the price, quality, terms, etc.? Can customers shift from a competitor to the company, or is it difficult to change?

9 Has the company lost major customers? Who? Why? Have there been or are there now any common complaints?

10 What are the company's credit policies, and how are they administered?

11 Who is responsible for marketing? Is he or she qualified? How is this person compensated through incentives? Who reports to this person? What are their qualifications?

12 What are the sales performances of key salespersons to date? Are their sales currently covering the costs of marketing and sales functions? How are they compensated? How is their performance evaluated?

13 Has their performance been compared with sales projections?

14 Does the company participate at trade shows or conventions?

15 Does the company advertise? What is the average cost? Are there standing orders? What are the advertising expenditures for the past two years, and what are the projections for the next three years?

16 What is the cost of product packaging, and what image does this packaging convey to the customer?

17 Is a sales force currently in place? Is their experience relevant?

18 What types of warranties, guaranties, or service contracts are offered to customers?

19 If there is a customer problem, how is it handled?

20 Has the company established any distribution, joint venture, or technology transfer agreements?

21 How many distributors does the company use? How does the company select them? What is the rate by sales volume? Does any single distributor account for a large amount of the company's sales? What are the remuneration arrangements with distributors? What are the credit terms? Are copies available of distributor marketing agreements?

COMPETITION

1 Ranked by sales, who are the company's largest competitors?

2 Are they fiscally sound, well capitalized, and profitable? What are the present and future respective market shares?

3 What is their focus: Are they expanding niches in the industry? Are they expanding into new markets or diversifying into other industries?

4 How does the company differentiate its product from the competition? What is unique about the product?

5 What are the barriers to entry in the company's industry? Is it easy or difficult to enter this business?

6 How does the company compare to the competitors in terms of product, price, market share, functional expertise, capital resources, and management?

7 Has the number of competitors increased or decreased in the past two years, and do you expect this to change? Are any new entrants expected?

8 How do competitors usually deal with small competitors (push them out of the market, buy them out)? What is their competitive strategy?

9 At what sales level do you believe the company is a competitive threat to other companies, and how much market share does that translate into?

10 How does the company plan to combat the competition, and vice versa? For example, compare product features and price points to those of competitors.

11 Has the company identified any of its competitors in the international marketplace? If so, who are the three largest, and what are their geographic market shares?

12 What research has been conducted on competitive products? Is documentation available on competitors?

13 What competition might the company face from products from other industries that may be substituted for its own?

HUMAN RESOURCES

1 What is the number of nonmanagement employees? Obtain a list of officers, management, and employees.

2 How many employees does the company expect to hire over the next twelve months? Is the supply of skilled labor adequate to meet its hiring goals?

3 Does the company employ any independent contractors? Are such relationships legally structured within federal tax guidelines?

4 How are employees selected (hiring criteria)?

5 Describe all employee benefits, e.g., medical, travel, or any fringe benefit programs.

6 How are salaried or hourly employees compensated (salary, stock, etc.)? Are payroll records maintained and available? Are any salaries or bonuses excessive?

7 How do salaries compare with those of local competitors?

8 How is employee performance evaluated? Are there written policies?

9 Are any employees represented by labor unions? Is unionization pending?

10 How high is employee turnover, and in what areas of the company?

11 Are any employees or former employees involved in litigation with the company?

12 Has management entered into any special contracts with any employees, consultants, or subcontractors?

13 How would you categorize the company's employees?

—Highly skilled labor   _____percent

—Semiskilled labor   _____percent

—Nonskilled labor   _____percent

14 How are employees trained?

15 Are there employee manuals, human resources, policy handbooks, or benefits manuals?

SUPPLIERS

1 Who are the company's major suppliers? Are they fiscally sound? What are the prices paid, total purchases, and terms?

2 What raw materials does the company use? What are the prices?

3 What is the outlook for the suppliers' industries? Are any shortages or delivery problems anticipated?

4 Are they unionized?

5 Are any shortages anticipated in items supplied to the company?

6 Have they caused any problems, such as bottlenecks or shortages?

7 Will they provide credit? Are any special terms arranged or contracts in place?

8 Describe how supplies are received. What receiving systems are in place? Are any quality tests of incoming materials conducted?

9 Who is responsible for purchasing? Are there requisitions and approval procedures?

10 What inventory levels are maintained? How often is inventory taken? Is there a formal procedure?

11 Is inventory theft a possibility or are systems in place to prevent theft?

12 Does any inventory item have only one source of supply?

PRODUCTION

1 Who is responsible for production? Are they qualified? What do they envision as major production challenges?

2 How many production employees are there? Are the needed employees available for hire in areas of operations?

3 Are productivity measures used? Are training, evaluation, and reward systems planned or already in place?

4 Is the company unionized or have there been attempts to unionize? What is the attitude or morale of the production workers?

5 Does the company have a plant? How many? Where? Owned or leased?

6 Has the operation been audited, and what is the age of the plants and equipment? Are plants and equipment appraised? Insured? What is their value? Useful life? Are new capital equipment expenditures needed or anticipated? What are the maintenance costs?

7 What does the company produce? Are there specifications for each product? How is production monitored? Does product design facilitate manufacturing?

8 How long is the production cycle from raw components to shipment to customers? Are there any bottlenecks, such as equipment that could cause production delays?

9 Does the company have the production capacity to meet current and projected demand for the product? How long before capital expenditures will be needed to meet excess demand? Can the production process be changed readily to conform to changes in demand?

10 What are the materials used in production? (See Suppliers section for further questions.)

11 How does management monitor and control, or plan to control, production costs? Are there any historical production cost records? Compile a production cost list.

12 Who is responsible for quality control? Are tests set up to check the quality during the production process? What are the current test results, and what actions are taken when problems are identified? Is there a final quality test before shipment? What is the defect rate?

13 Are there any pending issues related to the Equal Employment Opportunity Commission or Occupational Safety and Health Administration?

14 What type of production process is used, e.g., continuous or batch? What are the major operations? What are the sequence, relative cost, and space requirements for each? What is the extent of automation?

15 What is the length of the production cycle and cost of the setup? Identify the key components in the production process.

16 What is the level of technological complexity of the elements used in the production process? Any downtime problems?

17 Is the process labor-intensive? What could be automated? What would be the cost of automating?

18 What backup systems have been created to deal with possible production problems?

19 Is the company vulnerable in any way to current or projected energy availability from suppliers for its production fuels or for transportation of its product to customers? What means of transportation are used to ship the finished product to market?

20 What kind of scrap or waste is generated by the production process? Are there potential issues with disposal, including environmental pollution? If necessary, check with the appropriate agencies for air, water, waste, and land issues.

21 What production stoppages has management encountered? Are there any alternative sources of production if there is an interruption in the current assembly line?

22 What are the optimum inventory levels for the finished product and for raw materials? Is the current level of inventory at the optimum level?

23 Is any part of the production process subcontracted out? Who are the subcontractors?

24 Compare the data from the above inquiries with available industry data.

RESEARCH AND DEVELOPMENT

1 Who are the key engineers and R&D managers and personnel? What is their technical background?

2 What have been the costs and benefits of the major R&D programs completed during the company's history?

3 What are the current R&D programs and projected costs and time until completion? What are the expected outcomes? How were these programs selected? Why?

4 What new R&D projects are planned following financing? What are the costs and anticipated benefits? How is R&D monitored?

5 How does the company's expenditure (or projections) for R&D compare to industry standards?

6 What is the company's strategy to ensure protection of its proprietary technological developments, etc.? What about its patents, confidentiality agreements, and so on?

7 What is the condition of the R&D facilities and equipment?

8 Has R&D generated reports for management? Are copies available?

Analysis of Financial Projections

FINANCIAL MANAGEMENT CAN BE the determining factor in the survivability and the success of the angel's investment. It is important to carefully analyze financial projections as a way of assessing management's planning for and control of the business. While accounting is essentially a record of historical performance of the business, financial projections or the creation of pro forma financial statements and budgets help the investor think through the financial implications of decisions management made while preparing the business plan.

In this section, the investor will assess in financial terms the strategies delineated by the entrepreneur in the business plan. The past is documented in financial terms (if applicable), and management takes a forward look, forecasting likely conditions to project the allocation of resources that will support future operations.

Can Management Reach the Forecast Objectives?

PROJECTIONS ARE STRUCTURED around the objectives developed by the management team during the planning process. The marketing, sales, and operations strategies and plans indicate the financial requirements. The industry trends analyses imply specific assumptions about likely future conditions.

The key to assessing and evaluating projections is to determine how accurately management has given quantitative expression to the qualitative business proposal outlined in the business plan. You need to critically evaluate the potential for profitability of the venture. Can you believe in the accuracy and attainability of the entrepreneur's projections and, what's equally important, convince other investors and your advisers that the financials are realizable?

If the company has been in business, then you will have past financial data to guide your projections, and baselines to use in comparing data. If this is a start-up, you will need to be creative in seeking out comparative ventures. Be vigilant in analyses of projected cost data, and be realistic in sales projections. If the projections for market share, profit, growth rate, market conditions, sales performance, and/or operating margins significantly deviate from industry standards, you will face an uphill battle in achieving return *of* investment and return *on* investment.

As an investor, you must evaluate the projections using the assumptions behind them. Look for consistency. What are the key assumptions regarding wages, benefits, pricing, production costs, sales, volume, market projections, and inflation? Are they supported as clearly as possible? If assumptions were made in proposed operating budgets, be sure those assumptions or disclosures are honestly reflected in the pro forma statements. Closely study documents and footnotes to assumptions on all of the pro forma statements. This is especially true when entrepreneurs prepare projections using spreadsheet software but without the assistance of a professional accountant or financial adviser. It's important to ask how these projections were calculated and determine how valid the underlying assumptions are.

Interrelationships of Financial Projections

WE RECOMMEND THAT you request pro forma financial statements, cash budgets, and operating budgets. Begin by requesting separate sets of departmental budgets based on current and desired funding. Then management should provide cash flow data, income projections, and last, a pro forma balance sheet and income statements.

Also consider requesting projections on a monthly basis for the first year, quarterly for years two and three, and annually for years four and five. It is critical that management include footnotes describing the significant assumptions they used in preparing any financial statement projection. In addition, request a break-even analysis projecting when the company will begin being profitable, and a cash flow break-even analysis specifying when the company can stop raising equity capital, thus ending dilution for earlier investors. Find out when the company can begin financing itself on retained earnings and through traditional credit financing. Break-even indicates when total revenues equal total costs. For the investor, the break-even point occurs when the amount of money earned equals the sum he has invested.

Begin your analysis of the financial projections with the operating budgets. These projections detail forecasted department revenue and expense patterns. For example, pro forma sales projections and pro forma departmental expense budgets usually are consolidated into a forecasted operating budget for the sales department. The sales forecast projects when sales will occur, the volume of sales, and thus, gross revenue.

Next, request cash budgets or cash flow statements. Cash flow statements (not to be confused with the Statement of Cash Flows) are detailed projections of the cycle of turning sales into cash that, in turn, pay the cost of doing business and, you hope, return a profit. The cash flow statement describes sources of cash and uses of cash. A cash flow analysis and projection will reflect the company's credit and collection policies, trade credit, and other financing activities, as well as the purchase and disposal of fixed assets. This projection informs you when cash will be needed before it becomes a crisis.

Last, require the pro forma financial statements, which include assumptions about future performance and funding requirements—that is, an income or profit-and-loss statement and balance sheet. The pro forma income statement projects the company's revenues, expenses, and earnings over a specific period of time. When you subtract expenses from income, you will have the company's forecasted net profit or loss for that time period. The balance sheet shows the assets and liabilities and equity of the company on a given date. When you subtract liabilities from assets, the difference is the company's equity. Also include in your analysis historical income statements and balance sheets if they are available.

As mentioned above, management should demonstrate understanding of the break-even point, the level of sales that covers the fixed and variable costs of providing the company's product or service. For example, estimate the level of sales needed before the company would break even after implementing management's business plan for new product development and completing the current round of financing. The break-even point in this example can be calculated by dividing fixed costs by the contribution margin (unit sales price – variable cost per unit / unit sales price). To perform this calculation accurately, separate costs into "fixed" (costs that *don't* vary with the sales level) and "variable" (costs that *do* vary with the sales level); group any additional fixed costs with new products planned; forecast a sales price per unit; and calculate variable costs per unit. Forecasts should describe the level of sales volume required to break even and candidly discuss the likelihood of earning at least that much. You will need to know fixed costs (rent, utilities, insurance, etc.), which remain relatively constant regardless of sales. Plus, you will need to know variable costs (cost of goods, sales commissions, etc.), which will generally increase with sales.

The purpose of this chapter is not to offer a textbook on financial analysis. A discussion of the application of ratio analyses, for example, to financial forecasts and pro forma financial statements is beyond the scope of this discussion. We refer the investor who is seeking more detailed guidance to the Glossary (Appendix I) and the Suggested Reading List (Appendix G).

What Are the Company's Expected Financial Needs?

THE PURPOSE OF THESE financial documents is to help you, the investor, assess future performance and funding requirements. After you finish analyzing the projections and statements mentioned above, you will be able to evaluate the amount of funds management is requesting over the time period covered by the business plan; the date when funding will be needed; the information to select the most appropriate types of funding (debt versus equity); and how much the company will have to give up to get the funding. For example, in the case of debt, you will know the loan amount, collateral, interest rate, and repayment schedule; or in the case of equity financing, you will know the percentage of the company to be given up, the proposed return on investment, and the anticipated method for the investor's exit (buyback, public offer, merger, or sale). You will also place yourself on firm ground when you assess how management proposes to use the funding, and you will be able to analyze the use-of-proceeds statement.

How Much Funding Is Sought?

OBTAIN STATEMENTS INDICATING how much money the company is currently seeking, how many investors management is planning for, how it will use the funds it raises, and how investors or lenders will get their money out. It is appropriate at this stage for you to identify potential risks inherent in the enterprise, assess those risks, and consider steps to minimize them.

QUESTIONS ABOUT PROJECTIONS

◆ How did management arrive at its financial projections? Develop a list of key assumptions used by management to prepare the financial projections.

◆ If a company is actually generating revenues, has it met projections to date?

◆ How might ratio analysis be used with the projections?

◆ Should projections be discounted? What impact does such discounting have on the company's valuation and the amount of equity appropriate for the investor?

◆ Are the projected revenues accurate? What are the costs to attain revenues? What are the projected profits?

◆ What is the estimated return based on discounted projections?

◆ What is the past record of actual cost against projected cost?

Evaluating the Company's Stated Capital Needs

ACCURATELY IDENTIFYING the need for capital is central. By logically analyzing these numbers, you will become more confident in projecting the possibility of returns than if you simply accept an entrepreneur's mere estimate of what he needs. In establishing capital need, the company must demonstrate an understanding of the major problems of growth. Rapid growth creates a need to support growth, which means greater capital infusion. Additionally, large volumes usually signal the need for more front-end money.

For you to determine the capital needs of the company, the company must provide data that describe how much money it is currently seeking, the number of funding rounds expected for full financing, and the specific dollar amount being sought in the round at hand. Sources of funds include equity financing, typically in the form of preferred or common stock. Debt financing might include mortgage loans, other long-term loans, short-term loans, or convertible debt. It is also important to determine how much the entrepreneurs themselves are investing.

QUESTIONS ABOUT CAPITAL REQUIREMENTS

◆ What is the company's capitalization strategy? Long term, short term, or both?

◆ How much more capital, based on the company's proposed funding schedule, needs to be raised before the company can finance operations and growth from income and from the use of traditional credit-type financing?

◆ At what point will the company be able to internally finance future growth?

◆ What is the total amount of capital needed for this round?

◆ What will be the total dilution at the end of the funding schedule? Is all equity diluted equally? What securities is the company using or offering?

◆ Is there a timetable for IPO or exit?

◆ Does the company need approval of any entity other than the board of directors for this financing?

Analyzing the Forecast Balance Sheet

THE BALANCE SHEET illustrates the financial condition of the company by showing what it owns and what it owes at the report date. The balance sheet lists the assets required to support the operation of the business. The liability section shows how these assets are to be financed. Every accounting transaction affects the balance sheet. The balance sheet also helps the investor analyze a business. It validates the assets and documents the liabilities, working-capital current ratios, inventory turnover, etc. The validity of the balance sheet is based on information derived from the production schedule, capital expenditures, and occurrence of debt, and from other data outlined in the assumptions.

Description of the Balance Sheet

THE ASSETS SECTION of the balance sheet includes information on current assets, property plant and equipment, other assets, and intangibles. Current assets include all cash of the company. Current assets also include marketable securities at lower cost or market value, accounts receivable less doubtful accounts, notes receivable collectible within one year, inventories, prepaid expenses, and any other current assets. Property, plant, and equipment can provide information on land, buildings, machines, leasehold improvements, furniture, and vehicles, less any accumulated depreciation. Depreciation relates to tangible assets, such as a building, car, and so on. Other assets, such as intangibles, will provide balance sheet information on goodwill, patents, franchises, trademarks, copyrights, and licenses, less any amortization. Amortization is a way of reflecting periodic changes to income to recognize the distribution of the cost of the company's intangible assets over the estimated useful lives of those assets.

QUESTIONS FOR THE BALANCE SHEET

◆ Cash

— How many depository accounts? Identify all cash accounts.
— Average balance per account during the past year?
— Have all bank accounts been reconciled?

◆ Receivables

— What percent of the company's sales are on a credit basis?
— What are the terms?
— What credit checks does management perform before extending credit?
— Are credit reports updated?
— What percent are delinquent? How long before delinquent accounts are collected? Is there an allowance for an account that may be difficult to fully collect?
— Does payee recognize receivables as being due?
— How and when are receivables recognized?
— What percentage of sales are cash versus credit customers?
— What are the credit terms?
— Who makes the decision about extending credit?
— Does the company have any allowance for bad debts?

◆ Inventory

— What inventory valuation method is used (cost or market value)?
— When was the physical inventory last reconciled (present market value)? Was a year-end physical inventory taken?
— What is the turnover rate?
— What condition is the inventory in? Is any of it obsolete?
— Are inventory controls in place? What is the policy or procedure to minimize the amount of money tied up in inventory?

◆ Fixed assets

— Description, cost, and current value of each fixed asset? What is the replacement value for plant and equipment, and how does this compare with the book value or the liquidity value?
— Are depreciation methods used consistently?
— What percent of the company's assets are leased? What are the terms? How does the value of capital leases compare with the fair market value?

— Who approves capital expenditures?

— Are any assets pledged as collateral or subject to liens?

◆ **Other assets**

— Is management expensing R&D, or is it capitalized as an asset and expensed over a defined period?

— Is management invested in marketable securities? Which securities and why?

— Are there any deferred costs or intangible assets? How are these valued?

— Is there a pension plan? Are there any funding requirements?

— Are there any reserve accounts to cover bad receivables or warranty claims?

Liabilities

THE BALANCE SHEET liabilities section covers current liabilities and long-term liabilities. Current liabilities are those that will be due within a year and include accounts payable, notes payable, and accrued expenses; for example, salary, interest, professional fees, insurance expense, warranty and taxes, income taxes payable, and revolving lines of credit. Look at any large accounts payable. Consider taxes in some detail. For example, take the time to understand what the company's applicable federal, state, and local income taxes and excises taxes are and any special industry tax considerations, such as depletion allowances (and write-offs). It's important to understand in reviewing the income tax payable whether the company is current on all of the taxes it owes and whether it has filed all tax returns, whether it has ever been audited, and whether it is in compliance with sales and payroll taxes.

Long-term liabilities—those due beyond a year—include items such as deferred income taxes because of accelerated write-offs, long-term notes, and debentures.

QUESTIONS ABOUT LIABILITIES

◆ How much debt has the company incurred? How many loans does it have outstanding? Request legal loan documents. What is its debt service schedule and payment history?

◆ What collateral has been offered up for loans?

◆ Have there been any personal guarantees or corporate guarantees for loans?

◆ With what companies does the firm have payables due? Is any one company owed more than 10 percent of the payables? How old are outstanding payables?

◆ Obtain a complete list of loans and notes payable and details on each. Gather information on payment histories and any defaults, and on any guarantees for loans.

◆ Are there any off-balance-sheet financings? What are their terms and conditions?

◆ Any unrecorded liabilities or product liability claims?

◆ Are there any accrued liabilities outstanding?

Shareholders' Equity and Net Worth

SHAREHOLDERS EQUITY is the total equity interest all shareholders have in the company. It is the amount shareholders would split up if the company were liquidated at balance sheet value. In the balance sheet, the shareholders' equity section involves a detailed description of all capital stock, whether those stocks are preferred or common, and any additional paid-in capital. Paid-in capital is any amount paid for stock over the stated value or the par value per share of that stock. Also included in the shareholders' equity discussion is information on any retained earnings of the company.

To supplement the shareholders' equity section and provide background on the company's capitalization history, it is important for you to investigate the past financings of the company. Elements that might be included in such an investigation are as follows:

◆ A chronological list of all past financings.

◆ A discussion of why the company raised money and at what valuation.

◆ Evaluation of whether loans are all paid to date.

◆ Evaluation of whether dividends have been provided as promised.

◆ The state of investor relations.

◆ Description of any personal guarantees, assets, or collateral that have been pledged by the company.

◆ Managers trying to pay off company debt or alleviate any personal debt through the financing.

◆ The person (or persons)—if anyone—who will have liquidation preference over the investor's investment.

◆ The company's present capitalization.

◆ Data on all shareholder equity and classes of stock used by the company, including the type of stock, number of shares authorized and outstanding, any voting rights, dividends, warrants and options outstanding, the owners' names, prices offered, and any special terms. Also, determine whether any of the following items are also included: stock option plans, restrictions on stock, preemptive rights, rights of first refusal, convertible instruments, and agreements for further issuance of stock.

The Income Statement
or Statement of Operations

AN INCOME STATEMENT is a record of the revenues and expenses for a given accounting period. An accounting period is usually one year. The forecasted income statement matches amounts the company expects to receive from selling goods and services and other income against cost and outlays incurred to operate the company. The income statement is also called a profit-and-loss statement or—when there is a loss for the period—a statement of operations. The accuracy of a pro forma income statement is directly related to the assumptions used in creating the sales plan.

You can examine the sales forecast, which defines the production schedule and direct costs. Once you know the direct costs and operating level, you can evaluate management's budget for the indirect cost of production and evaluate the general and administrative overhead costs. All of these will be combined to develop the income statement.

The projected income statement can help you analyze operating, sales, and profit information. The operating status of the venture can be determined relative to the objectives established in the plan. You can use this type of analysis to identify critical elements that may need attention, and you can indicate the need for reassessing the underlying assumptions used to develop the projections.

The Income Statement

IN REVIEWING THE INCOME statement, you will see that the primary revenues or gross sales of the company are subject to calculations. These include the deduction of cost of sales (materials, direct labor, and overhead) in order to arrive at the gross margin, or the excess of sales after the cost of sales is deducted. From the gross margin, operating expenses are deducted to calculate operating income. These expenses include depreciation and amortization (the useful value of tangible assets, such as a patent); selling, general, and administrative costs; and development and research costs.

To operating income, other income items such as dividends and interest are added, and from operating income interest expense is deducted to obtain income before taxes. Following the deduction of income taxes, income is calculated, and extraordinary items (if any) that have occurred in the recent fiscal period are applied against income in order to obtain the net income or loss. In operating companies, a further calculation determines the shares outstanding and the equity earnings per share.

QUESTIONS FOR THE INCOME STATEMENT
◆ Sales
— How are sales or revenues or losses recognized?

— Are sales front-loaded—that is, recognized before being collected in full?

— To what extent are future revenues dependent on R&D projects in process?

— At what rate are revenues projected to increase annually for the next three years? How does this compare with industry estimates?

— Are forecasts based on historical results, trends, or any industry analysis?

— How were projections developed? Should they be discounted? Have projections been achieved in the past?

— What method was used to forecast growth: trend projections, market studies, management's best guess?

◆ **Costs**

— How does the company recognize costs of production? Recognize overhead? For example, is it using standard costs that it corrects for rework?

— How are costs budgeted, monitored, and controlled?

— What are the critical costs to keep under control?

◆ **Earnings**

— Is management contemplating any potential future earnings adjustments, such as salary adjustments, different tax provisions, and so on?

— Has management provided realistic best-case and worst-case circumstances for projecting earnings?

— When potential increases in costs are incorporated into the projections, is gross profit percentage maintained in the projections?

Cash Flow Forecast

FOR BOTH NEW AND EXISTING businesses, the cash flow forecast is the most important projection, because it details the amount and timing of expected cash inflow and outflows; that is, it incorporates sources of cash and uses of cash in any given time frame to determine the cash outlay and the net cash available. In effect, the statement of cash flows examines changes in cash resulting from all business activities. Generally, the cash flow in the start-up years of a business will not sufficiently finance the operational needs. Cash inflows often do not match the outflows on a short-term basis. The cash flow forecast will indicate these conditions and enable the investor to evaluate management's plan for cash needs. Also, under accrual accounting, a transaction may be recognized on the income statement when the earnings process is completed, but that does not necessarily mean cash is, in fact, exchanged. Accrual adjustment will not necessarily affect cash flow. The accrual adjustment should be eliminated in any cash flow analysis.

Given a level of projected sales and capital expenditures over a specific period, the cash flow forecast will highlight the need for additional financing and indicate peak requirements for working capital. The investor must assess management's approach to this additional financing and its strategy about how it is to be obtained, on what terms, and how it is to be repaid. This information is all part of the final cash flow forecast.

If the venture is in a seasonal or cyclical industry, or if it is in an industry in which suppliers require a new firm to pay cash, the cash flow forecast becomes crucial to its continuing solvency. A detailed cash flow forecast that you understand and use during due diligence enables you to direct your attention to potential or impending operating problems. Cash flow forecasts should be made for each month of the fiscal year of operation during the first three years or until breakeven is forecast.

The Forecasted Cash Flow Statement

CASH FLOWS ARE CLASSIFIED in the pro forma statement by business activity, that is, investing, financing, and operating activities. The cash flow statement starts with net income, adjusted to reconcile net income to net cash. Adjustments from operating activities are made to reflect the effect on cash availability as a result of transactions, such as cash collected from customers, interest paid and received, salary and insurance paid, depreciation, amortization, accounts receivable, inventory, prepaid expenses, accounts payable, income taxes payable, dividends payable, and accrued expenses and compensation, as well as deferred taxes.

Net cash from operating activity after the above adjustments is then further adjusted for financing and investment activities. These adjustments would include changes in net income related to the receipt and payment of funds provided by creditors and investors, for example, issuance of debt or equity securities, repayment of debt, or distribution of dividends. Also, adjustments would be made to net income for such investment transactions as asset acquisitions or building, land, or equipment purchases. Net cash for operations, investing, and financing transactions is used to adjust cash and determine net increase or decrease in cash, and to help the investor compare cash available at the beginning and end of each period under consideration in the projections, for example, by month, quarter, or year.

QUESTIONS FOR THE CASH FLOW STATEMENT

◆ How many depository accounts are there? What are the balances in those accounts? How much cash does the company have?

◆ How much cash flow does the company handle monthly?

◆ Does the company have multiple collection points?

◆ How many disbursement accounts does the company have? Who authorizes payments? Who is in control of disbursements?

◆ At what point in time will cash flows become positive?

◆ What is the monthly cash burn rate, and how will this forecast fluctuate pre- and postfinancing?

◆ At what rate are earnings projected to increase over the next three to five years?

◆ Is the company taking advantage of discounts for early payment when available?

◆ Is the company maintaining the minimum cash balance required in its operating accounts?

Use of Proceeds

WHY DOES THE COMPANY need capital now? How will the company use the funds currently being raised? These questions are answered in the use-of-proceeds statement. Normally, the uses of proceeds cover such capital expenditures as purchase of property, leasehold improvements, purchase of equipment and furniture, and other types of capital expenditures. In addition, in a use-of-proceeds listing, working capital commonly will be required for such activities as purchase of inventory, staff expansion, new product line introduction, additional marketing activities, and other business expansion activities. In some instances, debt retirement or establishment of cash reserves will be the focus of the use-of-proceeds section.

QUESTIONS FOR USE OF PROCEEDS

◆ If the company has raised money in the past, how did it use past funds?

◆ Why does the company need money now? Specifically, how will it use the money? Spell out each item that the company plans to spend money on.

◆ Are there any broker fees that portions of the proceeds will go to pay?

Financial Assumptions

THE FINANCIAL PLAN must be accompanied by a written list of the assumptions used by management in the preparation of the financial forecasts. The foundation of any financial plan is to identify the relevant assumptions used in formulating the financial projections. How were these assumptions developed? Are the details believable? Proper assumptions are based on realistic estimates of future operating outcome, so they should be neither overly optimistic nor overly conservative. They may not only adequately assist policy formation and decision making but also indicate financial feasibility to the investors. Additionally, you can identify potential major problems by studying them.

The primary reason you should focus on assumptions is to help you compare potential risk with potential return. Based on your consideration of the assumptions, you should ask the following questions:

◆ What are the chances of the company's achieving projections?

◆ What major problems did you identify in the projections, and what are management's plans to overcome them?

◆ Can the problems be realistically solved within your time frame to achieve returns?

◆ If the company fails to achieve financial objectives and must be liquidated, what is your downside recoverability?

◆ Based on further financial requirements for the company that have been identified, are you prepared to reinvest in the future?

Also, based on financial analysis of the company's pro forma financial statements, more general questions might include:

◆ Is the company's valuation justified?

◆ Under the worst circumstances, what would be your return (loss)? Can you sustain such a loss?

◆ Calculate the internal rate of return, cash on cash. Is the return possible, as well as acceptable, for the risk exposure per the financial analysis?

Company Investors, Directors, Advisers, and Resources: Lists for Reference Checks

HAVE THE COMPANY supply names and contact information for the following:

◆ Institutional investors and lenders

◆ Any investment banking firm involved in the transaction

◆ Law firm and corporate legal counsel

◆ Names of the accounting firm(s) for the past three years

◆ Bank(s), banker, and any private credit source

◆ Board of directors, officers, and advisory board

◆ Broker dealers or underwriters involved in the transaction

◆ Private and corporate investors and any other stockholders in the company

◆ Finders or financial intermediaries assisting the company

◆ Consultants, past and present, who advised or analyzed the company

◆ Appraisers involved in valuation of the company

◆ Key customers

◆ Landlord

◆ Public relations, marketing, promotion, or advertising firm retained by the company

◆ Institutional industry analyst following the industry and venture capital firms investing in this industry

◆ Key competitors

◆ Top three publicly traded companies in the industry

Miscellaneous Documents Required for Analysis

ALONG WITH THE BUSINESS PLAN, financial plan highlighting best- and worst-case situations on three years' worth of pro forma projections, balance sheet, income statement, cash flow statement, and use-of-funds statement, you will want to obtain copies of the following documents when available:

◆ a capitalization table disclosing pre- and postfinancing ownership

◆ an organization chart describing corporate structure

◆ a marketing plan with product samples
◆ résumés of key management personnel (with at least five business and personal references)
◆ purchase orders, contracts, or letters of intent from current customers
◆ certificate of incorporation
◆ minutes books, bylaws
◆ business licenses
◆ comprehensive organization chart with names, job titles, and salary data
◆ job descriptions for each person in the organization
◆ list of officers, directors, and advisory board members
◆ any special employment contracts
◆ list of employees
◆ all noncompete agreements
◆ list of all stockholders in the company, the number of shares owned, and the price paid
◆ sales and technological literature
◆ any joint venture or essential business contracts
◆ union contracts
◆ diagrams of production
◆ list of suppliers
◆ any leases or property or capital equipment appraisals
◆ insurance policies
◆ all business licenses and permits
◆ fee agreements with director or officers
◆ fee agreements with brokers or finders
◆ all tax returns for up to three years, including
  — federal taxes
  — state taxes
  — local franchise and income taxes
  — payroll taxes
  — real estate taxes
  — personal and business property taxes
  — sales taxes
  — results of any tax audits by federal or state agencies
  — analysis of the tax basis of any assets being acquired

◆ Materials on any past, threatened, or outstanding lawsuits, proceedings, or litigation to which the company, its management, officers, or directors were or are party to

◆ List of all company insurance policies; e.g., property, key officer, etc.

◆ Patents, trademarks, and copyrights

◆ Details on all authorized and outstanding stock and management stock ownership

◆ All loan documents where the company is borrower or guarantor, especially loans to or from management

◆ List of the primary trade associations and periodicals in the company's industry

◆ Marketing reports, list of sales, price list, promotional literature, and representative agreements, list of distributors, marketing and advertising budget

◆ All reports by R&D on engineering progress/problems

◆ List of R&D projects underway

◆ Copies of management incentive compensation plans

◆ Prospectuses of publicly traded companies in the venture's industry

◆ Any past SEC registration filings

◆ Any management letters from auditors or corporate attorneys

◆ List of all depository accounts

◆ Credit report

With all that goes into the preinvestment audit, little doubt remains about its importance, making every minute you spend on it well worth your effort.

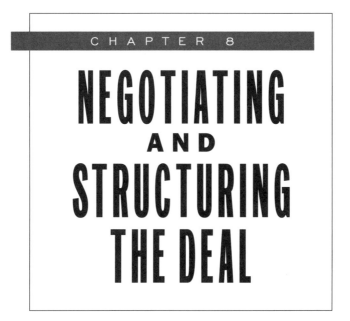

CHAPTER 8

NEGOTIATING AND STRUCTURING THE DEAL

Definition of Negotiation

NEGOTIATION IS SIMPLY THE PROCESS by which the investor, entrepreneur, and their advisers reach an interdependent mutual decision that the transaction is a good deal. This involves clarifying and agreeing on what the investor and entrepreneur will give to and receive from each other in completing the transaction. What is the bottom line? Each wants to get a good deal! All of the parties must appreciate their interdependence; thus, negotiation is not a win-lose relationship. Each person must understand and consider the other person's concerns.

Angel transactions are not routine, and if investors have followed our lead, they will be rich with due diligence information. This makes these transactions special situations. Arthur Lipper III says, "Those with the gold, rule," but those with the power of the investor in negotiations must beware of their own haughtiness, because this power might make entrepreneurs concede more. This is behavior the investor may pay for later in entrepreneurial anger or resentment about the terms of the valuation or deal structure. In his *Notebooks,* the nineteenth-century English writer Samuel Butler put it this way: "It is not he who gains the exact point in dispute who scores most in controversy, but he who has shown the most forbearance and better temper."

Central objectives of the negotiators are to achieve a fair deal and give the investor some protection if management fails to meet its stated projections. Given the length of time the investor and entrepreneur will be working together, neither wants to discover later that she has been taken advantage of.

Market Inefficiencies Make Negotiation a Must

THE NEGOTIATION PROCESS is time-consuming, can involve legal and financial advisory costs, and is far from easy and conflict-free, yet it is still mandatory. In *Finding Your Wings* (1996), we stated that in an efficient market, a willing buyer and a willing seller negotiate a fair price and deal structure by arriving at a price at which assets should be exchanged between them when neither is acting under compulsion and both have equal access to all relevant information. The inefficiencies that pervade this market influence the private equity transaction. The inefficient marketplace for early-stage company stock is characterized by an absence of analysts, severely limited market information on companies, inconvenience for buyers and sellers alike, expensive fees for advisory counsel, no real-time liquidity, no clearly defined exchange method nor company history available for due diligence since financials are all blue sky. So the search for and the evaluation and completion of transactions require time and money. Because of these factors, the inefficient market for early-stage company stock mandates that angel investors give high priority to negotiations.

Negotiating the Transaction

WHEN DUE DILIGENCE IS completed, and if the investor has decided to go forward with the transaction, the next stage in the investment process is for the parties to negotiate the structure of the transaction, establish a preliminary understanding, and then specify the terms of the investment into legal documents. The parties involved must decide on key issues like control and incentives, the value of the company, and the equity share of the company the investors receive for their capital. Typically, the transaction terms are negotiated between the entrepreneur and the lead investor, who will also be responsible for drumming up interest among other coinvestors in her circle of contacts. We discuss the process of determining valuation in detail in the following chapter.

One way angel investors protect their financial downside when associated with early-stage investments is by negotiating terms and conditions of an investment agreement or simple investment contract that allows the investors some degree of influence and control in decision making. Investors can achieve this objective by managing the negotiation process, matching the investors' and entrepreneurs' conditions, and accurately transferring the verbal agreements between the parties to formal venture investment documents.

Negotiation Mistakes Made by Angel Investors

DR. MARGARET NEALE, professor of organizational behavior at Stanford Graduate School of Business, has created a model of negotiation as decision making. From this model, we have identified a number of elements that have blocked angel investors from getting the best deal possible.

1 The investor gets caught up in winning the negotiation. He may develop an offer that he focuses on too much, pressuring the entrepreneur to accept it over any other.

2 The investor has spent time and money in finding and evaluating the investment and is now determined to recoup the spent resources, so he has locked recovery of these costs into the negotiation.

3 For some reason, the investor and entrepreneur have entered into a battle of egos, and as a result winning has become more important than arriving at a mutually beneficial deal for all the parties involved. This dead end occurs when one party seems preoccupied with coercing the other with contract terms.

4 The investor overemphasizes risk, unconstructive aspects of the deal, and possible losses that have an undesirable impact on negotiations. It is best to focus on "minimizing losses." That means framing negotiating terms so they propose to reduce risk of loss and reduce loss of time in a nonprofitable investment.

5 The investor poses an unrealistic first offer, assuming that such an offer will result in a better deal at the end of the negotiation process. But the offer insults and alienates the entrepreneur. If, however, the entrepreneur immediately accepts the investor's first offer, the investor can be confident he has valued the company too highly and has not allowed himself room to adjust to the entrepreneur's reaction to his offer during the negotiation process. The best approach is to start with a reasonably lower price and adjust upward during negotiation.

6 The investor focuses on the deal and forgets to be attentive to the entrepreneur's behavior and reactions to the various offers and terms. Not being careful and attentive to entrepreneurial behavior during the negotiations, and focusing on incorrect factors in the transaction, the investor blocks a beneficial negotiation process and outcome.

7 The investor sets an unreasonable time frame to reach an interdependent decision with the entrepreneur. Artificial or unrealistically short deadlines to reach a deal can contribute to the perception that the best deal was not negotiated. It is in the investor's interest to not rush negotiations.

8 Misinterpreting the posture the entrepreneur struts during the negotiations, that is, a "poker face," as hostility or apathy.

To reiterate, the negotiation process is not adversarial. Rather, it is interdependent and has more of the essence of consensus building than of win-lose.

Simple Guidelines for Professional Angel Investment Negotiations

NEGOTIATION IS A PROCESS that investors should emphasize as much as do entrepreneurs. One study by Mason, Harrison, and Allen in 1995 found that while 78 percent of entrepreneurs seek professional advice from lawyers and accountants in drawing up investment documents, only 38 percent of angel investors use such assistance. Negotiation involves such factors as being aware of the needs and concerns of all parties with a stake in the outcome, an objective and respectful evaluation of all the alternatives and options available, and a consensus on choosing the most mutually beneficial priorities from among these options. For example, when the final structure of the deal is determined, it must reflect the company's need for capital and cash flow, provide for capital return and liquidity for the angel investor, and establish monitoring procedures and control mechanisms should management fail to meet objectives.

Some sample guidelines for angel investors to make the negotiation process more professional are listed below:

1 Be clear and accurate in expressing your terms. What are you looking for in the deal? Obviously, it would be helpful to clarify this before the negotiation meetings.

2 Take your time; since risk begins after the investment, don't rush negotiations. This is especially true in angel investing, since it is much easier to invest in a transaction than to exit a private company. Allow yourself one to four weeks to negotiate deal structure and price, depending on the size of the investment, the total portfolio of the investor, and the number of coinvestors involved in the deal.

3 Bring attorneys in after you have reached verbal agreement with the entrepreneur. The attorney's role is to create accurate investment documents that reflect the verbal agreements the parties have reached. The attorney can also counsel the investor on the risk and tax consequences of the agreement before he makes a commitment. Of course, angels should use attorneys for advice and counsel before meetings to better prepare for negotiation, much like entrepreneurs are doing.

4 Always negotiate the transaction, particularly valuation. Never accept and always walk away from a fully structured deal offered by the entrepreneur or a broker, because such a situation precludes the negotiation process. Negotiation is critical in establishing the relationship that will exist after the entrepreneur has obtained the investor's capital.

5 Always negotiate for yourself. Do not let a third party negotiate in your place. The successful angel must learn the art of negotiation and the evaluation of investment contract terms and conditions. The investor can always use legal and financial counsel to discuss the investor's thoughts about deal structure and valuation before negotiating with the entrepreneur.

6 The angel investor doesn't have to invest! It is this circumstance that makes the angel different from a banker or venture capitalist, those who must invest their money under management. Before an angel says "no," if she is interested in the deal, she should attempt to renegotiate by specifying the terms and conditions under which she would accept the deal.

7 During negotiation, refrain from rejecting the entrepreneur personally; instead, decline specifics of the valuation or specific terms or conditions of the deal itself, or of the contract agreement. If you must reject something, specify the object you are rejecting so that it is clear you are not rejecting the person.

8 Always attempt to find out the terms negotiated by entrepreneurs with other investors in the company before investing yourself.

9 Wait as long as possible during the transaction before disclosing (a) how much you are able or willing to invest, (b) what equity stake you seek for your capital, and (c) how long you will allow the offer to stand before the entrepreneur must accept it; that is, the date after which you will withdraw it.

The Private Placement

BASED ON RESEARCH by International Capital Resources of more than 480 completed deals, 65 percent of transactions concluded at the seed, R&D, and start-up stages used the private placement with informal venture investors. It is no accident that the transaction structure most commonly used by angels is the private placement. The private placement investment typically involves cash for equity and includes all types of offerings not publicly sold. The private placement is the issuance of Treasury securities to a small number of sophisticated private or institutional investors. The common exempt offering involves either equity and/or debt investing by private investors.

These direct participatory investments accommodate transactions for a smaller amount and are generally more quickly arranged than public offerings. Besides, because of the lack of Securities and Exchange Commission requirements, these more flexible structures let the company circumvent onerous public offering requirements while accessing the nonaffiliated market without full regulatory compliance. So these investments prove much less expensive.

Private placement investments consist of anything that is not a public offering. Such leeway allows investors to test the limits of their creativity and negotiating skills. Herein lies the strength of the private placement and the main difference between an institutional private placement investment and an angel's direct, participatory investment. The former is primarily debt; the latter is not. Private placement investment usually means a subordinated debt transaction in the institutional market, but for angels it most often means an equity transaction between an individual and the company, a transaction that brings with it several advantages and responsibilities.

Private placement investment has the advantages of confidentiality and lower costs. First, with their less stringent disclosure requirements, direct investments enable private investors, who keenly prize their privacy, to maintain confidentiality in their financial transactions. Second, reduced cost causes a glint in the investor's eyes when choosing direct investment, especially compared with public offerings.

Also, with most early-stage investing, private placement investment deal structures tend to be equity or equity-related, including the ability to accommodate subordinated debt. Even when subordinated debt or convertible debt is involved, these structures offer convertibility into equity, so that the investor can share in the upside possibilities should the venture become successful.

Finally, private placement investment offers flexibility during negotiations between the private investor and the entrepreneur, flexibility unavailable when purchasing stocks of public companies. There are chiefly three practicable structures, with equity fundamental to each. First is preferred or common stock. The second is convertible debt, a structure much more common to the institutional transaction, typically involving some type of interest payment arrangement. And third is some form of long-term debt with warrants, a debt situation applicable only to later-stage ventures.

In almost all cases, the only way investors in these types of transactions can benefit from the risk they have assumed is to share in the upside potential if the venture proves successful. And the only way they can do that is through equity. So, at bottom, all structures relate to equity. We see investors relying on preferred stock for several reasons. It is senior to common stock; therefore, it provides leverage to influence management when things go askew. Also, preferred stock requires the entrepreneur to remain in contact with the investor. This provision creates warning mechanisms that permit the investor to change management or set time frames and conditions for making changes when they become necessary. Preferred stock can also provide some income through dividends, although this is not a circumstance that usually arises in early-stage ventures. However, preferred stock is redeemable by the corporation, which may set up a sinking fund and establish compulsory payment. The preferred stock is convertible to common stock, so if the company is purchased or does go public or experiences some other liquidation event, the holder shares in the success.

Choice of Securities for Angel Investors

ANGEL INVESTORS USE four categories of securities: common stock; preferred stock; convertible preferred stock; and, of course, convertible notes. The most common security used both to take advantage of upside capital appreciation and to provide downside protection is the convertible preferred. Investors universally use this security. Though not as common, some investors will also use convertible notes. Investors don't view convertible notes as optimal because they carry a negative impact on the balance sheet. Preferred stock is equity and makes the balance sheet stronger. Also, many investors believe that start-up companies should not be paying interest if they possibly can avoid it. In their transactions, angels most often use a convertible preferred security.

Preferred stock usually carries a number of preferences, which include dividends, liquidation preference, voting rights, convertibility elements, and redemption. Generally, preferred stock does not carry mandatory dividend rights. Preferred shareholders will usually participate with common shareholders when the company declares dividends. If the angel's investment objective is a dividend preference, then the company may pay returns on a cumulative or noncumulative basis. Obviously if a start-up lacks cash flow, the investor needs to consider the likely effect on the company's ability to pay dividends.

Preferred shareholders will have a priority claim over common shareholders to the assets of the business if the company suffers difficulties or liquidates. This liquidation preference will typically equal the investor's original purchase price of the security, plus any accrued dividends that the agreement arranged for. When the company liquidates, preferred shareholders may also be in a position to obtain additional distributions by sharing the remaining funds with common shareholders after it satisfies the liquidation preference. This liquidation preference normally will not change over time, except as dividends accrue. Also, preferred shareholders are often permitted to elect liquidation treatment in the event of a merger or acquisition in which the company is not the surviving entity.

Preferred shareholders often vote with the common shareholders in all major matters and are entitled typically to one vote for each common share, into which the preferred shares may be converted. Also, preferred shareholders voting separately as a class may have the right to veto certain corporate transactions affecting preferred stock—for example, the issuance of senior securities, merger, or acquisition. Preferred shareholders may also have special voting rights, such as the ability to elect the majority of the board of directors upon any breach of the terms in the preferred stock purchase agreements, such as the failure to make mandatory redemptions or some default in performance of financial milestones.

Preferred stock is normally convertible into common stock at the discretion of the holder except where automatic conversion obligations have been agreed to. Automatic conversions usually are tied to certain events, such as the completion of a public offering. This convertibility will also occur at a specific price per share or at the attainment of some prespecified financial goal. The ratio is usually expressed by a formula based upon the original purchase price. The ratio is typically adjusted to take into account any stock splits, dividends, and consolidations and sales of common stock at prices lower than those paid by the preferred shareholders.

Redemption features offer the investor a way of recovering the investment. It also allows the company the opportunity to eliminate preferential rights that some shareholders might hold. Redemption can be optional or mandatory after a number of years. In some cases, a stepped-up redemption price or redemption premium is built into the investment agreement to provide investors with a certain return on the investment. One implication of mandatory redemption or redemption called by the company is that such a clause may force the preferred shareholder to exercise conversion or lose the upside potential of his investment. So investors need to be very careful with such clauses.

The Role of Legal Documentation in Private Equity Transactions

VERY SIMPLY, LEGAL DOCUMENTATION delineates the deal. The legal documentation could be the private placement memorandum and subscription agreement, term sheet, stock purchase agreement, shareholder's agreement, and ancillary agreements, for example, employee confidentiality agreements. (The business plan is not considered one of the legal investment documents.)

It is important to place the legal documentation within the context of entrepreneurial capitalism, that is, high risk/high trust. The best legal documentation will not salvage a poorly investigated investment into a nonviable, nonsustainable company. All the clauses, covenants, representations, warranties, and legal agreements mean nothing if the venture falls to creditors. Second, following due diligence on the management team and its plan, the investor who decides to go forward must take the full risk, and that means trusting the entrepreneurs to do the best they can and encouraging them to "go for it."

Saturating the relationship with a multitude of legal agreements is no substitute for good judgment in people, business plans, and investment deals. The successful angel investor looks into the character of management, makes a decision to trust it, and sets up board-based monitoring mechanisms to help ensure success. It is perhaps better to emphasize board representation—if the investor is willing to serve and will accept the liability exposure of directors and officers—or advisory board representation and reduce emphasis on the more onerous legal documentation. As you will see, we view angel investing as team investing, and the legal documentation and negotiation of it should be an extension of the team-building atmosphere. Operationally, this means meeting, talking, and working things out before and after the deal is done. These activities lead to a successful investment.

Misuse of Business Plans as Investment Documentation

IT IS WORTH NOTING that some entrepreneurs are using business plans as their deal documentation. Unfortunately, while some entrepreneurs strapped for cash are using business plans as substitutes for private placement memoranda, they are not written for that purpose, so investors must beware.

Typically at pre-seed and seed stages, an entrepreneur along with a group will invest $25,000 to $100,000 themselves, as well as a lot of "sweat equity," which they will ignore, because if they take stock for it, it becomes taxable as ordinary income. Next, using just a business plan, they will embark on a direct offering. In other words, the corporation will act as the issuer and raises the money without using an intermediary. A business plan is not a private placement memorandum. Business plans are oriented in favor of the company and management. The plan reflects no empathy for the minority-shareholding angel investor. Angels, who usually will not have the benefit of a stock purchase agreement to protect themselves, become vulnerable. The business plan is really not investor-friendly, yet many entrepreneurs use it as the primary money-raising tool.

Overview of Legal Documents Used in Venture Investment Transactions

SOME LEGAL AGREEMENTS are more suitable to the realities of angel transactions than others. While the private placement memorandum does spell out the particulars of the deal and is commonly used along with an investor's subscription agreement, its primary function is to prevent a charge of fraud and misrepresentation, protecting the entrepreneur, management, and company by specifying primarily the risks and, secondarily, other aspects of the deal. A well-written private placement memorandum can be useful to the angel investor. To qualify, it must specify up front the investment concept. Namely, the private placement memorandum must clearly state why the investor should invest, not just provide a laundry list of boilerplate clauses defining the risks of investing. It should also answer four basic questions:

1 How much money is the company trying to raise?
2 What is the company offering to investors for their capital?
3 How will the investment money be used?
4 How will the investor get her investment back, and what is the exit to provide the investor liquidity and return on investment?

Also, in certain instances, there is a compliance requirement. For example, if a company has even one nonaccredited investor when using Rule 506, the company must use a Reg. A offering document and audited financials. So not all angel investments require or need a private placement memorandum.

The primary objective of a stock purchase agreement is to set out the terms of the deal, such as issuance of stock in situations in which the investor will dominate management—whether an institutional venture capital firm or a small group of angels is investing a large amount of money. This is not the overriding characteristic of most angel investments, in which investment amounts by each investor are smaller and the quality of the relationship is more egalitarian. So stock purchase agreements are highly unusual in transactions below $5 million.

The stock purchase agreement—heavy with representations and warranties, as well as with various positive and negative covenants—is used when the investor is the boss. Many entrepreneurs and their advisers view such agreements as onerous. Although venture capitalists who use stock purchase agreements are also building a team, they are building a very different type of team, what we term an "arm's-length" team. The angel investor, on the other hand, is building an "arm-around-the-shoulder" team, usually because, except for the lead investor, no individual in angel investing is a dominant investor.

When fifteen to twenty investors are involved in a deal, no one has the whip hand. In most cases, the entrepreneur who believes she has a good deal and has decided on the angel market as the primary source of capital will not tolerate the onerous legal provisions of a stock purchase agreement. William Evers, a highly respected securities attorney in San Francisco, sees a stock purchase agreement barely once in thirty angel deals. Stock purchase agreements are not to be confused with employee stock purchase agreements, which provide for the sale of common stock to key employees under standard vesting terms.

A shareholder agreement is a contract between different shareholders and the entrepreneur or management. This agreement specifies details related to the company's ongoing responsibilities and to managing control of the company—for example, how stock might be voted to appoint an individual to the board of directors. It is not solely focused on the terms of the deal but covers instead registration rights and other covenants of the transaction.

The shareholder's agreement is designed to control the transfer and voting of the common stocks of the company by key shareholders so that stable ownership and management of the enterprise may be maintained for the term of the investment. This type of control may be accomplished through restrictions on the sale of the stock by insiders, restrictions that have the effect of limiting the shareholder group to persons who are known to the investors, and through voting agreements, which assure that the composition of the board of directors will be perpetuated.

Employee confidentiality agreements or proprietary information and inventions agreements are important to have so that employees are aware they have a duty to not use the company's trade secrets. These agreements can provide the company with various rights concerning employee-developed inventions and can offer certain protection in connection with the company's inventions and trade secrets. Especially in a high-technology deal, confidentiality agreements are prevalent. After all, intellectual property is the cornerstone supporting the viability of a technical investment. Blocking the employee from using trade secrets serves the same purpose as anticompetition agreements, since you can stop competition during employment. However, after employment the only enforceable anticompetition agreement occurs if the investor buys the business and pays for goodwill.

Aside from theoretical discourse on what should be used or academic analysis of documents used in traditional institutional venture capital deals, angel investors use particular documents. When dealing with transactions of less than $5 million, the investor is almost always concerned with developing a positive longer-term relationship with the entrepreneur. In our experience, the danger here is that entrepreneurs often look at the investor as a necessary evil, and they fail to keep the investor informed, not realizing that angel investors are, in the long run, their best friends. As we previously discussed, the negotiation process should encourage a team feeling among investors and entrepreneurs. But the investor cannot forget that she is vulnerable as a minority shareholder. Neither is she the boss, as defined by typical legal agreements used in the institutional venture capital arena. For example, in a stock purchase agreement, institutional venture capitalists, even as minority shareholders, will negotiate the right to throw management out if they don't think it is hitting projected goals.

For angel investors the term sheet is the principal legal document used for structuring the transaction. While term sheets need to fit the situation and to be precise, our experience suggests they are not so much contracts as working documents. The purpose of the term sheet is to effect a meeting of the minds about the specifics of the deal to which the investor and entrepreneur are willing to commit. The term sheet helps the negotiations proceed more efficiently and, therefore, becomes a most useful tool. If the investor fails to use a term sheet, inevitably he or she ends up tip-toeing, then waltzing, around conflicting issues. This tuneless dance continues around the unresolved issues, until after wasted weeks of negotiations, the parties realize that the deal is going nowhere, an insight they could have used early in their discussions. It is fair to say that without a term sheet, a deal favorable to the investor becomes negligible. The parties never reach a meeting of the minds. The deal dies.

Using a Term Sheet to Structure the Angel Investment

INTRODUCTION

THE TERM SHEET, usually in an outline form, defines the key business elements of the transaction and sets forth the understanding the parties have reached. A term sheet contains the following general aspects of the deal:

◆ Valuation of the company and percentage of the company that the investor will receive

◆ Type of security, price, and amount of investment

◆ Vesting

◆ Dilution

◆ Representation on and composition of the board of directors

◆ Employee stock purchases

◆ Other clauses used less often in angel investment term sheets

The investor, not the entrepreneur, prepares the term sheet. Perhaps the best advice to guide the investor in structuring a deal is to isolate the biggest risk in the deal and to structure the initial investment terms so that capital is used to eliminate or minimize that identified risk. Practically speaking, it's much better to set up remedies in advance rather than later—in court, or after the business has failed and the investment or any part of it becomes non-recoverable.

VALUATION OF THE COMPANY

THE VALUATION OF the company is one of the major issues in an angel investment transaction. We will discuss what determines valuation in detail in the following chapter. For now, suffice it to say that the range of valuations depends on a number of elements. Such elements and their accompanying risks are all taken into account by the angel investor in determining valuation. Angel investors are intimately familiar with the values that certain types of companies in certain industries with certain management teams receive.

The process by which investors value a company is complex, as the reader will learn. The investor must require that any entrepreneurial group seeking the angel's investment assess the value of the enterprise from the perspective of the investor, so that the entrepreneurs will appreciate the dynamics of the investor/company relationship. Of course, entrepreneurs want to raise as much money as they can while relinquishing as little ownership as possible. The angel investor, on the other hand, seeks to maximize the return on investment by investing as little capital as possible and obtaining the greater share of ownership. Through the negotiating process, the investor and entrepreneur resolve these opposing perspectives.

TYPE OF SECURITY

THE MORE SECURITY in a transaction, the less need for equity instruments. The riskier the deal, the more appropriate equity becomes. Most angel investment transactions result in the issuance of common stock to the founders and management team and preferred stock to the angel investors. Angels typically prefer to invest in a senior security, security that is convertible into or carries rights to purchase common stock. A convertible senior security affords the angel investor downside protection—the opportunity to recover the investment on a priority basis through redemption, repayment, or liquidation preference. It also has the upside potential of common stock, which may appreciate in value. However, common stock carries the most risk. With common stock, there is no protection. This security is less flexible and offers the investor no return until the stock is sold.

Preferred stock is the investment security most frequently involved in angel financings because of the flexibility it offers a company in tailoring the critical issues of the investment, namely, management control and investment return. The preferred stock investment vehicle is a compromise between common stock and debt structures. Preferred stock has more protection than common stock but less than debt financing. It also allows a pricing differential with the common stock in order to provide cheap stock to the company's employees. It is in the interest of the founders and management for investors to buy senior securities that can be valued at a higher price than the company's common stock to avoid negative tax consequences of investors paying significantly more for a common stock, thereby creating a "bargain" for tax purposes for founders and management (Section 83[b] of the Internal Revenue Code).

Selection of the appropriate investment security for a specific transaction will depend upon the comparative importance to the investor and the company issuing the securities of a number of different elements, including risk associated with the venture, the investor's investment objective and strategy, any and all capital requirements of the company now and in the future, the relative interest and contributions of other investors previously involved and currently considering getting involved in the deal, the liquidity of the securities, and the degree to which investor control of management is desirable.

Practically speaking, preferred stock is used in early-stage transactions specifically because the equity base beneath any existing company debt improves the balance sheet for potential creditors. Also, angel investors are rarely concerned about current return— for example, dividends—since their objective is capital appreciation. So dividends or cumulative dividends rarely burden the preferred stock, allowing the company to plow back any profits to achieve faster growth. Finally, the preferred stock security offers the investor a senior position in liquidation.

VESTING

SINCE AN INVESTOR'S decision to invest in a company is influenced by the competence of the management team and its ability to work and continue to work together, the angel investor will take steps to ensure that the management team members will remain with the company for a certain period of time after the investor's infusion of capital. Commonly, angel investors assume that the founder or principal entrepreneur will be the company's CEO. Consequently, the investor frequently demands either that shares be issued to the management team members over time or, if the founders' shares have already been issued, that the company have the right to repurchase them if the executive leaves the company. Obviously, entrepreneurs prefer to purchase the shares up front and be 100 percent vested without the company having any repurchase rights. Therefore, it is extremely important to negotiate a compromise between the investor and the entrepreneurial team, a compromise by which the founder and management will be partially vested at the time of investment and then receive the remainder of the shares vested over time. In addition to the negotiated clause, the parties should hammer out an arrangement whereby the unvested portion of shares would be subject to repurchase by the company if any member of the management team terminates employment.

DILUTION

IN THE INVESTOR'S never-ending quest to match the possible reward to the risk, he or she will also negotiate dilution terms. Based on our research, it's not uncommon for entrepreneurial ventures to seek as many as five rounds of financing beyond the capital provided by family and friends. As a result, many companies require multiple rounds of financing. Angel investors are reasonably concerned about having their equity position diluted relative to the entrepreneur's share. Investors will typically address this issue by requiring certain protections to prevent such dilution. Adjustment of the conversion ratio is one mechanism for achieving this protection. The nature of the antidilution adjustment can have a significant effect on the number of common shares issued when the angel investor's preferred stock is converted.

Two major price-adjustment alternative formulas are used to prevent dilution issuances at prices below those paid by the first-round investor. The "rachet-down" antidilution provisions reduce the conversion price to the price per share of the lowest sale price for any shares of common stock or other securities. Because this formula obviously favors the investor, the company views it suspiciously. The "weighted-average" antidilution provision adjusts the conversion value by applying a weighted average of the purchase price of outstanding stock and newly issued stock. Any antidilution provisions will also arrange for a predetermined pool of shares, which may be issued to employees without triggering an adjustment of the conversion ratio.

The longer the earn-back period—or period of time to earn back the investment and returns—the greater the pressure to negotiate antidilution terms. This increases the impact of proximity of earnings. For example, in the case of a start-up company, earnings are in the future, and so the chance for things to go wrong before the investors recover their investment increases, while the potential need for further rounds of capital can also grow. These conditions bring greater importance to the antidilution protection rights that have been negotiated.

REPRESENTATION ON THE BOARD OF DIRECTORS

TO MONITOR MANAGEMENT and influence critical decisions that affect financial viability of the venture and ultimate liquidity— reflecting the investors' penchant for protecting their downside— angel investors will seek terms regarding representation on the board of directors. The board of directors' role is to offer caution to management and to constructively assess its work, taking corrective action if it becomes necessary. Unfortunately, many times boards, overcome by their own greed, will exercise their vested interest and focus on growth on earnings at the expense of prudence. It has been said many times that growth is the job of management, while reining in management is the job of the board. To attract top board members, the company may have to offer directors and officers liability insurance because of their fiduciary responsibilities to creditors and shareholders. Such liability coverage, hard to get and expensive besides, explains the increasing popularity of advisory boards.

The representation of the investor on the board of directors is handled in a number of different ways. Angels rarely view themselves as mere shareholders—nothing akin to their public-equity counterparts. They perceive themselves as owners, not just shareholders, a view that explains their concern with board representation. Some investors are satisfied with the representation obtained through voting their preferred stock on major matters. Other investors may be satisfied with the contractual undertaking by the issuer to nominate a certain number of investors or their representatives to the board.

Another alternative is the provision in the articles of incorporation specifying the number or percentage of directors to be elected by each class or series of stock. This provision can address some investors' fears about the dilution of representation rights that subsequent stock offerings might cause. Until certain objectives are met, more aggressive angel investors may seek to obtain proxies from entrepreneurs on entrepreneurial stock.

Angels may also seek to negotiate the right to appoint corporate counsel and a corporate secretary, and may also require "key-man" insurance on the founder. The insurance will buy time and help cover costs to replace the founder if she dies or becomes disabled. Some angel investors have negotiated terms that provide investors' rights to appoint more voting directors if the company's management fails to meet financial projections and milestone objectives.

EMPLOYEE STOCK PURCHASES

IN PLACES LIKE SILICON VALLEY, a major incentive for a founder, management, and quality employees is the opportunity for equity participation in the venture, not just a large salary. So conditions under which founders and important employees acquire stock should be covered in the term sheet—including the number of shares to be made available, price, consideration to be paid, allocation of shares to employees or employee stock purchase plans, vesting terms, and any repurchase options and restrictions upon transfer.

Model Term Sheet Checklist

IN THIS SECTION, we list the principal features of an angel term sheet and the categories of information it typically includes, and we clarify various preferred stock provisions.

◆ Type of stock identified at the head of the term sheet

◆ Amount of the financing round

◆ Number of shares

◆ Price per share

◆ Valuation

◆ Dividends (if appropriate)

◆ Liquidation preference

◆ Redemption: price per share, date proposed for redemption, and percent of shares to be redeemed

◆ Conversion features: price conversion ratio/formula to be used, voluntary options, automatic conversion events (for example, IPO), antidilution protection (including any exceptions), price, and so on

◆ Voting rights: number of votes equal to number of shares, terms for election of directors

◆ Protective provisions, restrictions, and limitations: repurchase of stock, issuance of securities, asset transfers, and so on

◆ Employee stock purchases: allocation of shares available for employee incentives, price, for what consideration or what period of time (vesting), restrictions upon transfer

◆ Other terms and conditions:

— Information rights for periodic financial reports

— Registration rights (for example, demands rights, piggyback registration, termination of registration rights)

— Board of directors composition, selection, expense reimbursement

— Right of first refusal, co-sale (take me along)

— Key man insurance
— Patents and noncompetition agreements
— Vesting
— Other conditions to closing
For a model term sheet, see Appendix C.

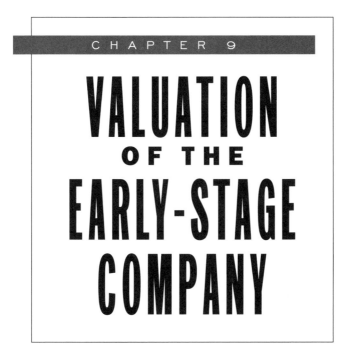

CHAPTER 9

VALUATION
OF THE
EARLY-STAGE
COMPANY

Pricing as Good Judgment, Not Formulae

ONE ELEMENT THAT characterizes all early-stage ventures

is their illiquidity. In our previous book *Angel Financing,*

we suggest that the best test of a deal's practicality and

pricing is whether it can attract and be sold to another

private investor at the same price, although not necessarily the highest price—in other words, sold at the same valuation to another investor. In addition, investors could do worse than to seek opinions from their network of coinvestors to obtain the bids of other respected, experienced investors. Estimates from others that reasonably approximate an investor's own appraisal can increase confidence in valuation assessment. Ironically, the value of an illiquid company may be more a function of finding an investor than of financial formulae and calculations.

Regardless, investors must rely on their own judgment in valuing a deal, a judgment mandating considerable investigation and analysis. Some factors have an obvious effect on value (i.e., low risk means higher value); computing value is a complex affair fraught with problems. Valuation is not a precise form of financial analysis; it is more akin to an art form or, at times, even horse-trading. In valuation, subjective factors simply eclipse objective factors. The mass of intangibles is often overwhelming and weighs heavily on investors, causing two sophisticated investors to reach two different estimates of value. For example, to the extent that investors are familiar with the business, they might give the entrepreneur a higher valuation because they perceive their risk as being lower, whereas the investor who is investing in a business about which he or she knows nothing will not. Since value is in the future, definitions are limited. Limited too are calculations influenced by incomplete information, rapidly changing environmental factors, unproven management, untested technology, and undeveloped markets. Determining value in early-stage investing is highly subjective because so much depends on something that has not yet happened. In addition, the negotiation skills of the investors and entrepreneurs themselves can become a factor in the valuation outcome.

Thus, no unchanging Euclidian formula guides valuation. The best that valuation can offer are rules of thumb. And again, all investors may view such rules differently. How investors perceive risk, or stage of the venture, relates to value. In other words, the higher the risk investors perceive, the higher the return they will require; and the higher the return they require, the lower the valuation is likely to be. The farther along you are, the less risk investors perceive. Put another way, investors are willing to pay more for what an entrepreneur already has.

In the wake of market fluctuations, the spotlight now falls more than ever on the vagaries of valuation. Public-market companies with little-established earnings had been trading at 1,200 times earnings, and 5 percent of the entire stock market contributed 70 percent of the wealth by the end of 2000. It seemed that even public equity players threw caution to the wind. Public enthusiasm pushed valuations very high by historic standards, especially since a number of start-ups had been more successful than anticipated.

Warren Packard, a director of the Draper Fisher Jurvetson venture capital firm in Redwood City, California, laments that "[d]uring the past few years investors have lost sight of fundamentals and have come up with newfangled ratios, like twenty times forward-loaded revenues, to justify market valuations."

The astounding multiples at which many Internet start-ups with no earnings or immediate potential for earnings had been valued has only served traditional valuation models used to reemphasize early-stage technology company value. Investors are relying on common sense for guidance, using comparative analysis of similar firms to ascertain proper funding levels, valuation, and equity share. If the venture fails, any valuation is irrelevant. In private investing, survival is everything. As we have reiterated, smart investors are risk averse, regardless of what entrepreneurs believe! The foremost thing they want to know is not what their return on investment will be in five years but whether the company will survive at all. Entrepreneurs can talk glory, but if the company cannot survive the first eighteen months, negotiations about value become immaterial. So first the entrepreneur has to convince an investor that the company will survive.

Finally, we want to reiterate a point we made in the negotiation chapter, one that is especially important when the investor invests a larger percentage of the total financing round and plans to be more active in the company after investment. The investor can choose to be an aggressive negotiator, that is, don the guise of the stereotypical Wall Street investment negotiator and beat the entrepreneur down to get the best possible deal, squeezing everything possible out of him. But this strategy is myopic. The chemistry between the entrepreneur and investor must be there in order to make the early-stage investment work.

An investment relationship suffers from inherent fragility because it's so risky. It's folly then for an investor to try to squeeze every last dime out of the entrepreneur, first because valuation is so subjective, and second because such behavior destroys the chemistry essential to a healthy working relationship. Be assured that the entrepreneur will remember bad treatment. These partnerships require the investor and entrepreneur to work together for a long, long time. And no investment transaction can long endure a backlog of resentment by either party.

Factors in Valuing Potential Investments

IF YOU WERE TO VALUE a publicly held company, you would conduct the valuation based on statistics and calculations. In the case of the early-stage company, the situation, as we have said, is subjective. Rather than attempting to divine a specific value, perhaps it is more realistic for you to compile *probable* values. In our experience, entrepreneur forecasts often prove faulty. Their elaborate, high-math calculations can engender a false sense of precision, because their forecasts are sometimes based on questionable assumptions. Such values would depend on the investor's targeted rate of return or expected earnings. They would determine targeted rate of return or expected earnings based on macroeconomic factors and subjective criteria.

Valuations in the public stock market, supply of capital and level of capital demand, current and projected interest rates set by the Federal Reserve—all are examples of macroeconomic factors that might determine an investor's valuation. Meanwhile, more subjective determinants, that is, individual investor requirements, can significantly influence the valuation calculation, a calculation that might include the risk profile of the investor, the risk associated with various company characteristics (for example, stage of development, management experience, and time to liquidity), the deal structure, the level of investor involvement, and the dilution.

Valuation is part of negotiation. As we have said, in the valuation negotiations, the parties are trying to come up with percentage ownership between the investor and entrepreneur. The objective of the negotiation is to bridge the gap between an entrepreneur's high expectations and an investor's valuation model. It is in the interest of both parties to use multiple valuation methods in trying to arrive at a mutual value. Since early-stage investors are risk averse, they appreciate the risks involved in early-stage investing and intend to manage those risks through due diligence, valuation, negotiation, and close monitoring of the venture after they invest. Additional valuation tools successful investors use include correlating desired return with time to liquidity, discounting projections, establishing realistic desired multiples for cash-out in advance, and correcting equity share with dilution factors.

Macroeconomic Forces in Valuation

FOR CURRENT OR POTENTIAL angel investors, a number of macroeconomic determinants can influence their valuation of a company. The following checklist may help in weighing those factors:

◆ **The stock market.** While the stock market obviously determines the value of a publicly held company, it also affects privately held companies. The higher and more buoyant the stock market, especially IPOs, the greater the impact on early-stage company valuations. Internet companies serve as prime examples. The problem in the late '90s was the absolute explosion in IPOs, primarily Internet companies. That explosion was compounded by the compression of time. In the late '80s and early '90s, the standard waiting period from seed stage to either an acquisition or an IPO was three to five years, usually closer to five than to three. In the case of Internet companies, market watchers in the late '90s viewed one or two years as a long time.

◆ **Money supply and capital demand.** Right now a huge supply of money, including institutional and private funds, is available for increasing numbers of start-up companies. Venture capital funds are being formed weekly, and newspapers report major angel investments on a daily basis. When we began writing our first book, *Finding Your Wings,* in 1992, $50 million was a huge institutional venture fund; today $500 million is average. In 1992, studies by International Capital Resources showed that average angel investments were less than $50,000; today they average approximately $100,000 per investment.

◆ **Interest rates.** By mid-May 2000, the Federal Reserve had raised interest rates six times in less than a year. For the previous several years, interest rates had been historically low and relatively stable. A lower interest rate theoretically will lower the "hurdle" rate for equity returns in general, and the returns for venture capitalists and angel investors in particular. When interest rates rise—that is, when the risk-free rate increases—investors expect and demand higher rates of return for use of their capital; the result is that valuations on early-stage deals will be brought down to ensure better rates of return. In effect, valuations of private companies are inversely correlated to interest rate trends on investment instruments such as Treasury bonds. While we do believe there will be a lag in the impact of interest rate increases on private company valuations, when an investor can earn 8 percent in a five- or ten-year lower-risk or risk-free investment, that investment's availability will remove some of the discretionary capital from the early-stage investment market, with a corresponding reduction in valuations when investors do decide to take the risk.

Subjective Determinants of Valuation

EVERY DEAL HAS THAT soft underbelly mentioned earlier, its weak areas; otherwise the high returns venture investments offer would not be possible. But many entrepreneurs do not want to confess those weaknesses. They will claim that everything is great; they have been known to play games with financials to inflate valuation. For example, if a company by dint of its retail sales has an extensive e-mail address list, that asset is evaluated against future sales, even if the company has a negative balance sheet. In other words, a company in debt may have its market cap increased. But the sophisticated angel investor knows that holes exist in every deal, because unknowns lurk everywhere. To spot the weaknesses, the investor must avoid getting swept away in the entrepreneur's enthusiasm and fantasy. He must not lose his objectivity. Entrepreneurs can be persuasive—and well they should be if they believe in their venture.

As we have indicated, subjective factors do figure prominently in the valuation mix. But other items can swing the pendulum toward objectivity. For example, a term sheet would delineate other issues as the entrepreneur attempts to gain financing for a venture. In addition, detailed issues for further consideration would include the risk profile of the investor, company-specific risk, deal structure, investor involvement, and dilution.

RISK PROFILE OF THE INVESTOR

DIFFERENT TYPES OF INVESTORS have different risk profiles. Things will be different among private investors, amateur investors, and professional investors. And things will also be different within each group. Moreover, these risk profiles are often hardwired, or tough to readjust.

Angel investors' orientation to risk is not monolithic. So valuation of the same venture can vary significantly depending on which individual investor is making the deal. If he is an institutional venture capital investor with a billion-dollar portfolio and he is investing $1 million in a company, he is probably willing to take more of a valuation risk. If he is an angel investor, and this investment is one of only three, and he is investing 50 percent of his available capital in the deal, this calculation will affect the investor's risk profile—and thus the valuation.

COMPANY-SPECIFIC RISK

STAGE OF DEVELOPMENT, experience of management, time to liquidity, and projected return multiples are just a few of the elements at the company level that can have an impact on valuation. For example, early-stage companies, unproven management, longer time to liquidity, and returns not significantly above those available in the public market will all serve to reduce an investor's valuation of a venture.

The stage of a company's development is a measure of investment risk and is an important aspect in valuing a company. In fact, the stage of development may be more important in describing the risk than the current round of the investment. The success of investments in start-up companies is subject to the whims of the capital markets, because these companies have to raise money frequently, and if market conditions are unfavorable, severe dilution can result. On the other hand, later-stage companies are subject to the whims of the new issue window.

Potential risks and rewards vary substantially during the different stages of development in a new venture. Despite every entrepreneur's confidence in this "sure thing," more new ventures fail than succeed. However, investors need only a few big winners to offset the losers. Depending on the risks involved, compound rates of return from 25 percent to 50 percent per year or more constitute targeted expectations. There is a direct relationship between stage of development, as defined earlier, and market value, as calculated by the angel investor. This gets translated into variation in expected rates of return—for example, 60 to 100 percent rates of return for seed or start-up companies, and 20 percent rates of return for bridge or mezzanine financings.

The pricing curve shown in "Venture Price Curve," below, captures this relationship and to some extent explains the angel's penchant for earlier-stage deals. If the angel investor gets into the deal on a start-up basis, he will pay a lower price (lower valuation) and correspondingly take on a lot of risk, but with the potential for higher returns to compensate that risk. Development- and rev-

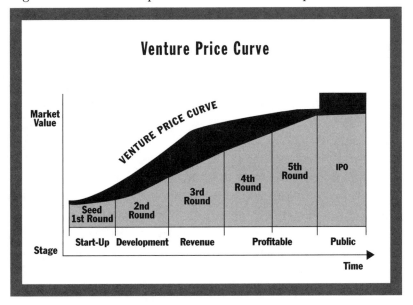

enue-stage companies have many of the same risks as a start-up; that is, the investor does not know if the companies possess all of the ingredients necessary for success. Yet, as the chart illustrates, the valuations are significantly higher than the start-up, with less potential for high returns because of higher valuation.

DEAL STRUCTURE

TWO IMPORTANT INFLUENCES on valuation are timing and duration until payback. If the company can afford to pay a current interest rate, and the investment is structured as a 10 percent convertible debenture that pays current interest to the investor, the investor will probably put a higher valuation on that company. This higher valuation would translate as a lower percentage equity share than if it were a preferred stock at 7 percent paying no current dividend, and all of the investor's return was going to be at the back end, based on some future event that may never happen. And speaking of future events that may not occur, acquisition or buyout is the predominant method for achieving liquidity for small-company shareholders. Mergers and acquisitions remain a feasible alternative to an IPO. VentureOne reports that 276 venture-backed companies were paid more than $40.9 billion for completed M&A deals in 1999. We have already pointed out that the primary method of achieving liquidity is not the IPO—far from it. But that misconception remains. Too often, entrepreneurs and their business plans project a public company in five years. Odds are that such an event will not occur. So investors need to consider how they are realistically going to achieve liquidity.

INVESTOR INVOLVEMENT

ESPECIALLY RELEVANT TO the angel investor is the degree of involvement in the company that the investor will take after he invests. It's natural for former entrepreneurs, now angels, to become active in a company in which they invest; for example, as director or consultant, or even in an operational management role. If the investor can have some degree of influence or control ("control" being the operable word here) over the direction of the company, most would be inclined to give that company a higher valuation, because they are involved. Conversely, if the investor is a minority shareholder, that is, a passive investor vulnerable to the whims of the entrepreneur and especially other investors (who may come aboard in future financings and gain control of the deal), he will most likely place a lower value on the company.

When the investor takes this tack, he needs to also determine whether the private investor's added value lessens the risk. Investors involved in negotiation will tell you the answer to this question: NO. Investors will not trade money to the company for their expertise because their added value, they feel, is their contribution to the process, and they want to be compensated for that contribution. Moreover, the extent to which they are familiar with the business will lower their perceived risk. If the venture is in the software business, for example, and the investor used to work for Microsoft, his familiarity will work to the entrepreneur's favor, because the investor knows the risks and the people.

DILUTION

WHILE DILUTION MAY NOT be at the forefront of every valuation calculation, many angel investors have learned from painful experience that entrepreneurs rarely, if ever, perceive that the company will need a lot more capital than anyone had estimated. Just a little calculation will help investors understand that for their investment to obtain their targeted and justified rate of return, they need X percent of the company. If the entrepreneur has miscalculated, and significantly more money is needed than has been projected, investors will suffer significant dilution and fail to make their targeted rate of return. That is why any discussion of dilution cannot be separated from negotiation of deal structure to protect the individual investor's share, should more money be needed later.

Less-experienced angel investors commit a relatively common oversight in their failure to recognize the difference between pre-money and post-money valuations. According to Perry Pappas, a partner in Buchanan Ingersoll, P.C., valuation of the company is called "pre-money" because the value was established before taking into account new investment, for example. In other words, the value is based on a view of the current climate for the company in a specific industry or based on current revenue and some multiple of projected revenue for the year. For instance, if a company has a pre-money valuation of $10 million, the angel investing $1 million would purchase 10 percent of the shares of the company outstanding before it issues shares to the investor. When the $1 million investment is added to the $10 million pre-money valuation, on a post-money basis, the investor will hold approximately 9 percent of the outstanding shares of the company, with a post-money valuation of $11 million.

Though we have no hard figures, our experience suggests that 90 percent of the deals worked out will need more money than originally projected. The result is dilution, best explained this way: If a deal calls for $1 million, twelve months later it will need more money. An investor with a 40 percent ownership for the first million dollars is faced with three options, if, say, another $500,000 is necessary. The investor can put in $500,000, or he can put in a portion of it, or he can choose not to put in any more money in at all, in which case, to survive, the company has to raise the $500,000 from somewhere else.

With all three options, the investor suffers dilution. He has to put more money in to maintain his 40 percent ownership, or his stake will shrink. Come liquidity, how much of the company will the investor own? The answer is that the investor will own less than when he started out. This illustrates the dilemma a company creates when it needs additional money. This scenario dramatizes dilution—something else for the investor to seriously consider in the valuation process.

Fundamentals of Valuing Start-Up Ventures

IN EARLY-STAGE COMPANIES, as we have said, value lies in the future. Such subjectivity renders less useful the established valuation formulae, which depend on more precise data and calculations. ICR's resident valuation expert John Cadle offers instead an expanded real-world definition of value for the small early-stage business: "That point at which an investor's fear (risk profile) is in equilibrium with his greed (return requirements)." Ultimately this is accomplished by coming up with the percentage ownership between the investor and the entrepreneur.

In the real world, then, an equity ownership position should produce an expected annualized rate of return over a reasonable time proportional to the investor's tolerance for risk. Valuation in this context does not depend on hard assets, prior "sweat equity," intellectual property, book value, or similar items. These considerations enter into the equation only to the extent that they can generate future value. Valuation depends on the creation or expansion of a going concern into a marketable commodity through an event that provides liquidity for the investor, such as by acquisition or IPO. Valuation also depends on the amount of risk that has already been mitigated by the company in product development, marketing, customer franchise, and cohesion of the management team.

CORRELATING RATE OF RETURN WITH TIME TO LIQUIDITY

ONCE THE INVESTOR has looked over the deal and feels comfortable with the risk, he is in position to develop an expected or desired range of returns. Next, based on due diligence and deal structure negotiations, he can estimate the amount of time to liquidity. In the case of the early-stage company without cash flow, earnings will likely come at some future date.

Investors correlate time to liquidity and expected rate of return, so that the longer the period of time until liquidity, the more the investor expects as a return. The higher expectation helps justify to the investor his increased investment risk and the loss of access to his capital. But seed, R&D, and start-up companies rarely, if ever, have cash flow or earnings, so calculations normally used to deduce valuation, like net asset approaches, don't apply.

Also, technology companies derive their voracious appetite for capital from the same growth rate that lets them offer high potential investment returns. So early-stage technology companies are loath to pay dividends or interest during the term of the investor's hold. Instead, these companies will reinvest any cash surplus into their own high growth. Again, liquidity, return on capital, or investor profit is dependent on the future. This suggests that attempting to calculate a specific value is difficult at best.

DISCOUNTING PROJECTIONS

AS A GROUP, ENTREPRENEURS rarely achieve projected sales as soon as expected, and they incur more costs than anticipated. Therefore, they usually need more capital sooner than they anticipated. This entrepreneurial planning failure boils down to dilution for the angel and a negative impact on returns. One technique the investor uses to ensure his percentage ownership when he analyzes projections for valuation is to give them a "haircut."

In other words, successful angel investors are skeptical and always discount projections and develop their own cash-flow models when they consider an investment proposal, paying particular attention to the possibility of unforeseen additional financing needs. The principals of early-stage enterprises rarely forecast cash requirements accurately, not because they are bad managers but because the situation is fraught with circumstances beyond their control. When entrepreneurs say $1 million absolutely will do the job, sophisticated investors are thinking otherwise—and with good reason. The sophisticated investor's mental cash register is clicking away as it adds numbers to the entrepreneur's modest valuation appraisal.

Angels discount the optimistic entrepreneur's projections by 25 to 33 percent or more when they calculate venture valuation, and the entrepreneurs have been willing to give away more equity to get the investor's capital. Even present-value formulae for calculating value incorporate a "discount rate," using interest rates combined with a risk allowance to discount cash flows. Regardless of the fact that both institutional and angel money supplies have increased in recent years, investors cannot forget that they have substantial leverage in valuation negotiations, especially for smaller deals that do not meet the criteria of institutional venture capitalists. Whereas a venture capitalist or angel might use a risk premium of 39 percent for an early-stage equity deal, an institutional investor scheming a traditional debt private placement might limit the discount to 18 percent.

Start-up companies normally require several rounds of funding before they are financially mature enough to qualify for sale, merger, acquisition, or IPO. Common sense dictates that as a company survives and grows, the risk premium will drop. Based on historical statistics presented in May 2000 by Professor Robert Keely of the University of Colorado, a seed-stage company with six years to IPO can have a 21 multiple and a discount rate of 66 percent. A start-up with five years to IPO could have a multiple of 10.5 and a discount rate of 60 percent. He considers these reasonable values, based on historical analyses. Into the analyses, he has incorporated the fact that immature companies are conducting IPOs.

MULTIPLES

ANOTHER CONSIDERATION that enters into the investors' valuation calculation is the multiple that future buyers will be willing to pay. We can no longer rely solely on earnings or cash flow multiples in all valuations. Internet companies with no earnings have valuations based on multiples of sales or revenues. The investor must develop some sense of how realistic his targeted returns are, especially when the time comes to cash out, whether by sale of the company, buyout by company management, or IPO.

The investor needs to get a feel for what the market will bear, regardless of the liquidity mechanism. For example, the investor might say, "If I invest for X years, I'll need to make Y times my investment." What all markets pay can be measured as a multiple of the original investment. Of course, we are talking about the *probable* price here, not the highest price. Identifying other companies in the same industry with comparable market value is not an exact science.

To begin this comparative analysis, the investor must use the reports that explain valuations in completed mergers and acquisitions. IPO data are readily available in the public domain to help calibrate market value conditions. These reports indicate what multiple of earnings, cash flow, or sales is typical in valuations of other private and comparable firms in the industry. While this approach may seem to be based more on intuition than on objectivity, it can provide the investor with benchmarks and guidelines on current market value. The key is using comparable companies!

In ICR's own research, we see investors targeting multiples of five to ten in seed-stage, three to six in start-up, and two to four in development-stage companies. In contrast, institutional investors are targeting multiples of ten for start-ups, four to eight in the development-stage, and three to five in profitable-company investments. It is important to note here that the angel and institutional investors are not evaluating the projected performance of an investment using ROI. Instead, they measure how many multiples they can make on their money over what period of time.

Rates of return on early-stage venture investments are time sensitive. Sophisticated investors spend time and energy considering liquidity—that is, how they are going to get out—before they invest. The graph below, "Correlating Rate of Return with Time to Liquidity," shows what happens to ROI over different time periods for a given multiple on an investment.

You can see from the table on the following page how important it is to the early-stage investor to turn over the money as soon as possible and realize the gains. ROI for higher multiples for longer hold times do not justify the risk exposure of longer-term investments.

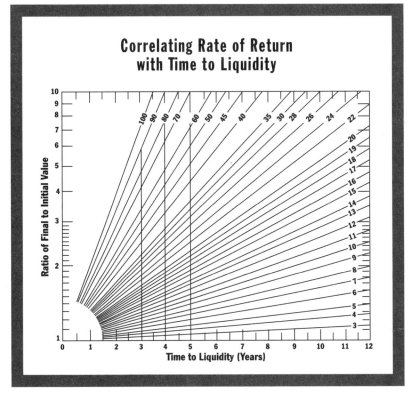

Internal Rate of Return on a Multiple of Original Investment Realized Over an Assumed Time Period

Years	2	3	Multiple 4	5	6
2	41	73	100	124	145
3	26	44	59	71	82
4	19	32	41	50	57
5	15	25	32	38	43
6	12	20	26	31	35

SOURCE: TA ASSOCIATES

DILUTION FACTOR

THE NEXT ELEMENT THAT THE sophisticated angel investor will consider during valuation—in addition to desired returns and time to liquidity, discounting of projections, and clarifying multiples— is an assessment of how much additional capital a company will need to get to the point that the envisioned liquidity event can or will occur. More often than not, the investor is best served by being skeptical about an entrepreneur's claims of what it will take to get to breakeven and to the point that operations and growth can be funded from internal cash flows and traditional credit lines. So it is prudent for the investor to create a dilution factor in the valuation process.

Wouldn't it be wonderful if investments unfolded in a straight line, and all projections were attained on schedule? Of course it would, but that rarely happens. It would be a useful exercise for the investor to prepare a matrix that correlates time to liquidity with desired return, that is, in either ROI or multiples, to help demonstrate the equity share of the company required by the investor. This would be most useful if it was completed before negotiations. This would prove to be a handy little tool for explaining to the entrepreneur the elements that have a negative impact on your valuation calculation and for demonstrating how your discomfort with certain projections and valuation elements translates into your expectations for an ownership percentage.

How can the investor arrive at a dilution factor? As an example, let's say that the investor and entrepreneur agree that the company can achieve $2 million in earnings in three years. They also agree that in three years buyers can be found who will pay twenty times earnings for the company. Therefore, based on these assumptions, in three years the company would be worth $40 million (that is, 20 x $2 million = $40 million). Let's also assume that the investor has offered to invest $1 million, and he has decided to seek a 30 percent return compounded annually over the time period. What percentage of equity in the company does the investor require in order to obtain the targeted ROI? Using his handy calculator, he determines that at 30 percent compounded annually for three years, the $1 million should be worth $2,197,000. Therefore, based on the above calculations, the investor will require a 5.5 percent equity stake in the company ($2,197,000 ÷ $40 million).

However, the investor not only needs 5.5 percent equity in the company today, he needs 5.5 percent in equity three years from now as well to ensure the return. Here the dilution factor comes into play. If the investor is uncomfortable with management's forecasts and determines that more capital may be needed than is projected, he can incorporate a dilution factor into the equity share calculation.

Let's assume that the investor estimates 20 percent more capital will be required than management projects. To protect himself, the investor must increase his equity ownership percentage to ensure that in three years he will attain the targeted return. The investor must therefore correct the 5.5 percent equity percentage figure to account for the increased capital that will be required. This is accomplished as follows: 5.5 percent = 80 percent x (where x = equity share, corrected for dilution). The 80 percent figure is derived by subtracting the 20 percent additional capital required from the original 100 percent of value. Therefore, the investor will seek a 6.9 percent equity share (5.5 percent ÷ 0.8 = 6.875) to ensure his 30 percent return in three years. The dilution factor accounts for unanticipated needed capital.

TRACKING FOLLOW-ON ROUNDS OF FINANCING

MOST ANGEL INVESTORS invest less than $250,000. In ICR's most recent study, only 15 percent of 9,850 investors in its proprietary database of angel investors have invested $250,000 or more in a single deal. Most angels are relatively small investors in terms of their percentage ownership of the enterprise. Since the ultimate capital needs of the company can be significantly greater than even a substantial angel investment of $250,000, it becomes incumbent on the angel to seriously consider the company's track record for raising the future rounds of capital necessary to get the company where management and investors want it to be. This task eclipses in importance premature attention to exiting the investment.

The question poses itself: Who will those other investors be? This is especially pertinent for the earliest investors after the entrepreneur has exhausted his resources of family and friends. At this early stage, the company is not ready for institutional capital, whose average investment is much higher; therefore, it is reasonable to require some discussion with the entrepreneur about where the future capital will come from. Who will my ultimate coinvestors be? Imagine the frustration and disappointment of discovering after investing and helping to build the company for years that the sources for large future capital infusions you counted on to coinvest are not interested. Instead of daydreaming about an unrealistic or premature IPO strategy, perhaps the venture's management and the investor group would be best served by recognizing that before exit, a successful company will likely need an institutional venture stage of financing.

Sweat Equity: The Investor's Perspective

VALUATION IS AN EMOTIONAL issue with entrepreneurs because their egos are involved. They want value for their "sweat equity," the time and effort they have previously invested in the venture. Understandably, the entrepreneur wants the highest value for the hard work he has already invested. Most angel investors appreciate that sweat equity enters into the negotiation, because it is a way the entrepreneur shows investors how dedicated he has been. Investors, of course, want somebody who is willing to do anything to achieve a projection. *Perceived* sweat equity is important in the investor's evaluation of the entrepreneur.

But attributing monetary value to that sweat equity in a valuation calculation is difficult, if not impossible. Sweat equity gets translated into specific value in this way: If the investor is comfortable with the management, the investor will decrease the estimated risk of this deal, resulting in a higher valuation. This move by the investor results, in turn, in more equity for the entrepreneur. For example, the entrepreneur might want to be back-paid, saying, "I could have gone to company X and earned half a million dollars a year. I've been doing this for five years now, and I've only been paying myself $50,000 a year, so I want to be back-paid for the $450,000 per year I gave up. In other words, I want $2 million." This proposal is ludicrous. Successful investors are more sophisticated than that. They simply don't play that game anymore.

The investor appreciates that entrepreneurs have chosen years of sweat equity instead of a salary, that they may have mortgaged their home, and so forth. But the smart angel investor judges that sweat equity only on what he will realize *from this point on*. The arrow points to the right, not backward to the left. What is on the investor's mind is how far along the entrepreneur is in the process and what the investor can get in the future for his investment.

The early-stage private-equity investment culture has changed over the past ten years from sweat equity, whereby entrepreneurs will work in their garages and take salary cuts in exchange for equity, to entrepreneurs working in palatial buildings and taking handsome salaries as the angel investors continue to pump in money. If improved rates of return are to be achieved by investors, the equation will have to change. The fact is an entrepreneur may be able to find some investors who are unsophisticated or who just do not care about their money and thereby gain an unrealistically high valuation. But an initial ego gratification of a $5 million valuation on sweat equity belies the essentials of a long-term partnership, a partnership built with investors who understand the business and the process, partners who will be there to smooth the bumps in the road.

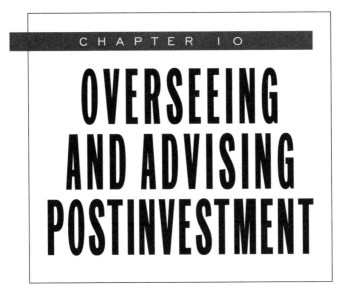

OVERSEEING AND ADVISING POSTINVESTMENT

Definition of Monitoring the Investment

INVESTORS MONITOR AND EVALUATE their investments for simple reasons. First, failing to do so can spell financial disaster. Angels experience a total loss of their investment 11 percent of the time; 24 percent of the time they experience a partial loss. In other words, more than one-third of the time, investors lose investment capital, and the early-stage company experiences perhaps twice as many failures as developed or revenue-generating companies. Second, in addition to trying to ensure their financial returns, angel investors also wish to add value and be part of the company's growth and, they hope, its success. For most angels, it does feel good to be part of growing a company.

To manage risk after making the investment, investors implement monitoring and evaluation techniques to track the performance of the venture. Monitoring techniques are designed to identify potential problems before they require drastic action to rectify them.

Think of the instrument panel a pilot uses to monitor a flight. Like pilots in a fog, investors can find themselves flying in bad weather because projections fuel most of what has lifted their investments off the ground. Little is based on historical financial fact or current reality. Fueling an investment are conjectures based on assumptions. Given the circumstances, investors need to create their own instrument panel. By doing so they put in place an early-warning system capable of alerting them to dangers so they can take corrective action. Investors have to know how to set up an instrument panel whose dials they can read. This ability to read the panel means that investors establish their own instruments—instruments appropriate to the venture and with which they are familiar.

WHY MONITORING IS REQUIRED IN ANGEL INVESTMENTS

ACCORDING TO PROFESSOR William A. Sahlman of the Harvard Business School, the monitoring oversight and advice that investors provide to their investee companies is an important element of financing start-up companies. It's important for us to understand that investors provide more than money to new firms, and this added value is central to appreciating the importance of the private equity investor to our current economic development.

Monitoring angel investments is a form of control mechanism. Why are control mechanisms necessary in angel investments? Investors have shared with us the major reasons that motivate their need for controls on the entrepreneur and management: reservations about the entrepreneur; lack of faith in projections; insufficient time; an incomplete management team; the investor's skill set; and the investor's needs for affiliation, proximity to the venture, and legal structures used in private equity transactions.

Instead of focusing on onerous covenants in the investment agreement in order to strap management down, most angel investors choose to trust management. They recognize that they have to do so to make the proper judgments, perhaps in association with a board of directors. They believe that there is something inherently wrong with trying to do this in writing, and that such action might compromise the relationship with the entrepreneur. The absence of legal constraints and contractual clauses leaves the investor with only monitoring mechanisms to fill the void created by the absence of such agreements.

Since most entrepreneurs are impassioned by the task of raising capital, they are not likely to make conservative projections, which creates unreasonable expectations on the investor's part. How accurately projections and assumptions were developed and presented will affect the investor's need for controls.

If an investor has time on his hands, he will want to be involved in the venture. If he still works in another career, or if he has other investments or familial or social obligations, he will be less likely to be involved.

Early-stage technology ventures rarely have assembled complete management teams. Investors commonly find that critical functional skills are wholly absent. If holes in the management team do appear, angel investors will feel the need to step in and fill the gap until the company is far enough along in development, capital raising, or cash flow generation to attract and compensate top talent.

Closely related to the level of executive involvement is the skill set of the investor. While we can advise the entrepreneur to ferret out investors who can add the value necessary to round out the management team, such a match is not always possible. The closer the fit between the investor's skills and the need for certain management skills at the venture-specific stage of development, the greater the temptation for the investor to get involved in the operation.

Another element that motivates investor involvement is the need for affiliation. Some angels have been called "nurture capitalists."

This term reflects the need to affiliate with entrepreneurs with whom the investor shares certain values. As we have discussed, investors have multiple motivations for investing in high-risk, early-stage deals. Meeting their needs to belong and to help grow a venture spices their desire to be more involved.

Many angel investors want to be physically close to the venture. Whether this is within a few hours' drive or flight depends on the individual's health and attitude towards travel. But the investor hedges risk by keeping his thumb on the pulse of the company he has invested in. So the closer the investor is to the company, the more likely he is to seek direct, regular contact with the entrepreneurial and management team.

Last, some investors become more involved in their investee companies because of the deal structures they have negotiated. Early-stage technology companies receive multiple infusions of capital—usually smaller, more frequent rounds instead of fewer large rounds. The reason is to better manage risk; investors are negotiating the staging of their investments into the company. Staging the investment accomplishes control, in effect saying to the entrepreneur, "The next chunk of financing is not forthcoming unless you meet your goals or make certain changes." Staging the investment gives the investor the opportunity to influence management decisions. Many times at the end of the day the only control an investor has left is to say, "Yes, I will put more money in, but for me to do so I will require certain changes!"

That said, investors can use a hedge to acquire a greater percentage of the investee company based on its results. Basically, the investor receives a warrant to purchase additional shares of the company that becomes exercisable if the company fails to perform according to plan or does not meet its milestones. But staged closings that provide for multiple closings of the investment reduce the risk to the investor up front, when he is unwilling, for whatever reasons, to put up the whole investment. Investors can implement this safety mechanism by agreeing to an initial investment amount, to be followed by specific dates for additional infusions of the investor's capital based, for example, on achieving revenue or income levels.

As one investor said to us, "What also gets my attention is an action plan from someone who demonstrates that once the company receives the money, he or she can enumerate over the next 90 to 180 days what exactly he needs to do to make this business go. The more specific those kinds of milestones are, the more comfortable I am in knowing that I can measure progress after I have made the investment and calibrate how I should react—that is, whether I have made a mistake or whether I should put money in if I'm asked. This is a very good way to monitor the investment and to assess how management is doing and what I can do to help them."

Passive Monitoring and Evaluation Techniques

INSTRUMENTS FAMILIAR TO angel investors fall into two categories: "passive" and "active" monitoring and evaluation techniques. Passive monitoring and evaluation techniques individually and collectively constitute instrument-panel components that supply information so investors can provide help when help is needed instead of waiting until serious problems crop up.

Hands-off monitoring and evaluation takes time and discipline and includes periodic review of financial performance information and participation by the board of directors. Never give in to the impulse to let advisers monitor the investment for you. Keep tabs on every deal in which you have an investment.

PERIODIC REVIEW OF FINANCIAL PERFORMANCE INFORMATION

TIMELY COMMUNICATION OF financial information precludes wishful thinking. Tracking financial performance against forecasts and milestones, knowing how management is using the funds invested, and comparing the performance of the company against business plan goals and objectives—all will go a long way toward helping the investor maintain vigilance. The investor can require the company to create monthly reports and chats to identify negative trends, positioning the investor to take necessary corrective action.

The data to track might include sales, costs, earnings, profit margins, new contracts sold or order backlogs, timeliness of new product introductions, number of employees hired, expenses as a percent of revenues, and conformance to budget and borrowing schedules. This last point is very important. Just as disease occurs in the human body most often where tissues come together, it's most often at the juncture of investor-entrepreneur refinancing that relations break down.

The investor can use this information to determine whether there are problems, such as failure to meet projections or the need to revise the business plan. He can assess whether the company needs some help or whether more drastic actions, such as replacing management, are necessary.

The investor should be organized and keep good records of all meetings with the entrepreneurial and management team. Take notes on conversations, assemble them in a notebook, and discuss your findings with your advisers and coinvestors.

The investor should listen to entrepreneur presentations but must read every financial statement and chart for herself. It's a good habit to develop rather than delegating the task to an accountant, adviser, or another investor. If something is not clear, note your concerns and ask questions of management. It is the entrepreneur's responsibility to answer every question put forth by the angel investor. At the end of this analysis, the investor must constantly reassess any revised estimate of performance in this investment vis-à-vis what other angel investors are getting as a return in similar investments. This is especially true before deciding to put additional funds into the venture. But remember to give the entrepreneur a chance to respond to questions or concerns before taking any corrective action.

BOARD OF DIRECTORS' PARTICIPATION

THE SECOND PASSIVE monitoring and evaluation technique involves the board of directors. Directors from venture-backed companies make up most start-up technology-company boards. These individuals provide capital, contacts, and product development support. On the other hand, large public companies recruit directors from the outside, individuals who bring industry-related expertise. The primary function of the board of directors is to monitor and evaluate the performance of management and take the actions necessary to correct any situation for the good of the company and the benefit of the owners. Private companies often demand a great deal more of their board members than do public companies. Board members of private companies, especially earlier-stage start-up ventures, may be expected to roll up their sleeves and get intimately involved in company operations. This could include providing access to prospective customers, locating creditors or bankers, identifying new investors, and helping recruit managerial talent and other individuals or institutions that the company might need.

Obviously industry experience is critical, as the board may be involved in decisions about initiating new projects, seeking further financing, determining whether and when to sell the company, removing or replacing management, recruiting management talent, stopping a product line, or closing the company altogether.

The board is especially important in early-stage companies that lack a complete or industry-experienced management team. Whether the team is incomplete or the first CEO lacks critical skills, these weaknesses can force more intensive mentoring by the investor, and the board strategy does offer a mechanism by which the investors can exercise some degree of influence on decisions and pass along successful managerial and executive processes and techniques. In addition, the board permits the investors a nonexecutive role to function as a sounding board and to provide advice.

How to distribute voting equity within the board of directors is a central issue. If a small group of angel investors is investing the majority of the capital of a round of financing, it may be able to significantly influence the constitution of the board. For example, in high-risk situations the investors might seek to appoint three of the five directors, and management would appoint two, stipulating that this allocation remain until the company achieves breakeven or positive cash flow. More aggressive angel investors might seek a legal agreement before investing to assure the right to vote shares of the entrepreneur or any third parties under certain negative conditions, for example, loss of sales, denial of patent, or unauthorized borrowing.

Most angel investors agree that effective audit committees play a critical role in the financial reporting system by overseeing and monitoring management and auditors. Angel investors often add additional skilled board members at critical junctures in the firm's development. These board members contribute important advice and credibility to the company in the marketplace.

Active Monitoring and Evaluation Techniques

ACTIVE MONITORING AND evaluation techniques allow investors to add value and protect their investment by offering assistance and providing follow-on support to perhaps influence management decision making through such means as their network of contacts, management recruiting, consulting work, and expanded access to coinvestors. The "hands-on" approach usually involves the investor working at some level in the company.

DIRECT INVOLVEMENT IN THE VENTURE

IT IS RARE TO FIND early-stage company management teams fully staffed with all of the necessary functional skills required to grow the company. Approximately 25 percent of the time, angel investors will step in to fill these gaps in the management team in the companies in which they have invested until the company has sufficiently developed. The investor may take a temporary position, or work part-time or full-time in an executive role.

Active involvement or intervention is common when things go seriously wrong. As projections slip or management fails to realize projected milestones, the successful investor will use contingency plans to deal with potential problems. Investors often become angry that entrepreneurs have failed to make their touted forecasts. While such slippage is to be expected, the failure isn't any more palatable. No investor enjoys the affirmation of bad judgment.

Regular meetings between investors, entrepreneurs, and their advisers demonstrate active involvement. "Regular" can be defined as daily contact during times of severe problems that require intense coordinated response. These meetings present investors with the opportunity to ask questions and express their concerns. Investors can complain as long as their complaints are grounded in specific details and not personal attacks. It is also a time to reassure the entrepreneur of your support and applaud any positive performance. In the event of a short-term problem, the investor may function as a consultant by providing informal counseling.

Obviously the degree of investor involvement will increase as the investor becomes aware of the possible loss of his investment. Normally, investors are part of a team including the entrepreneur and his advisers, such as his attorney, accountant, and investment banker, among others. The investor will want to facilitate communication among the members of the team whenever they face changes or problems. And all of the investors need to make sure that they are checking with each other periodically to ensure that everyone is well informed and can make contributions and suggestions based on the same data.

HARVESTING RETURNS: EXIT ROUTES TO LIQUIDITY

Planning for the Angel Investor's Financial Reward

ALTHOUGH ANGEL CAPITAL is frequently referred to as "patient money," the opposite is the norm. We have never heard an angel investor who was unable to cash out of a deal say, "Gee, I wish I had spent less time thinking about exit and liquidity before I invested." An exit route is the means by which an investor leaves an investment and through which he is able to realize returns. Investor returns are long-term capital gains, so an investment provides little or no liquidity for a long time. The method and timing of liquidation expectations are important variables in a venture capital investment decision.

Investors should quickly voice their interest in liquidity at the highest price achievable within a specified time frame, usually five to eight years. This interest needs to be more than a verbal agreement; terms should be clearly specified in writing as part of the investment's legal documentation. In developing a strong set of terms and conditions during negotiations, do not underestimate the importance of auditing, monitoring, and engaging good legal counsel.

Certainly, the investor can help the privately held company achieve certain goals, especially in developing an appropriate exit strategy. The investor should consider any number of factors in developing an eventual exit plan. The exit is the only means by which the investor can capitalize on the years he has lost access to his capital and justify the risks to which he has subjected himself.

Some investors choose family-owned companies or closely held private corporations that clearly are not likely to go public or be sold out within a reasonable amount of time. They may believe alternative exit routes exist through which to achieve their targeted returns. If it lacks multiple routes to cash-out, the venture is probably not a good investment, even if it has good prospects otherwise. Remember, the entrepreneur may find such a situation acceptable, since management of an even marginally successful private company may receive a good return indefinitely through salaries and bonuses. However, unless the angel sees a clear exit, sufficient profits to pay dividends in line with the long-term investment are unlikely.

A Contrarian Perspective on Liquidity in Public versus Private Markets

SOMETHING VERY INTERESTING occurred on Friday, April 14, 2000. The Dow Jones Industrial Average and Nasdaq Composite Index experienced the biggest one-day point loss ever. The Dow plunged 617 points (5 percent), Nasdaq dropped 355 points (10 percent), and the Standard and Poor's 500 Index fell 84 points (6 percent).

While media analysts attributed this meltdown to increased interest rates, rising consumer prices, inflation fears, and increases in margin calls by securities houses, the reasons go much deeper and are more insidious. We can find the answer to understanding the public market by understanding the dynamics of liquidity in both private and public markets. Liquidity, liquidity, liquidity—it is the mantra of stockbrokers, the reason the public market is touted as a better place than the private equity market for investors to place their capital. Many brokers believe that the private market's greatest risk is its "lack of liquidity." Liquidity is the "sword in the stone," but few private companies can boast of a young King Arthur. In fact, fewer than 1 percent of all U.S. companies will ever get close enough to see Excalibur, much less near enough to clutch its hilt.

However, does public market liquidity truly overshadow the risk of liquidity loss inherent in the private equity market? The value of public market liquidity becomes questionable when an investor must stay in a stock for fifteen to twenty years to justify and eventually realize reasonable appreciation and returns. The liquidity seems illusory if you really can't liquidate the stock to take profits for such a long time; liquidity means little in a market where companies have achieved valuations of 1,200 times earnings or more. For example, before market corrections, the Nasdaq Composite was selling at 400 times earnings; not long ago, multiples of 40 times earnings were viewed with extreme skepticism. Hoping to cash in on the then frenzied IPO market, nouveau entrants to the market bought into the media hype that touted "no end in sight" and were blind to the reality that venture capital firms, investment banks, and brokerage firms prematurely brought to market companies of questionable value. In effect, the actions of the institutional players served only to pass on the risks of these dubious ventures to the Johnny-come-latelies.

Take a moment and consider the circumstances of the so-called liquid public stockholders staring at their computer screens trying to make an online trade that most likely will never be completed at the price they see quoted. Contrast this situation with that of another investor. This investor pinpoints the companies that interest him and actively seeks those that meet his criteria. After reviewing many ventures, he selects a few in industries with which he is intimately familiar. Then he analyzes the management, the business, the business plan, the financial model, and the valuation. He identifies a company whose risk level matches his own risk tolerance. Then, with the help of astute legal counsel, he structures a transaction with a return that matches the risk and negotiates the right to take control of the venture if it goes south before he receives that return. In addition, he negotiates a number of terms and conditions that will help ensure liquidity should the company falter.

Last, like a pilot responsible for the safety of crew and passengers, the angel investor is responsible for his coinvestors and, to some extent, the welfare of the entrepreneur. Therefore, he monitors closely the company's progress toward his goal of returns, taking action during this flight as needed. He may need to make three to seven investments, because some will fail due to unanticipated circumstances, but through diversification and hedging strategies he will eventually prevail on some of the investments, reaping handsome returns and covering the losses.

A fairy tale?

Not quite.

It's happening every day as angels close the capital gap between the growing number of start-ups and the increasing personal wealth in the United States. Angel investing is not about IPOs but about creating sustainable companies of enduring value to shareholders, the economy, and society. And that is the problem in planning liquidity, because many angels, unlike institutional venture capitalists, are more concerned with creating sustainable companies than planning exits.

It is true that the angel may be locked into the investment for an average of eight years in order to realize the level of multiples that constitutes his investment objectives and to justify the risks he has taken with capital. But as you contrast the "liquid" public shareholder in front of the computer screen and the angel investor actively involved in monitoring and guiding the performance of his chosen company, you see the important differences in liquidity and control between these investors and the impact that they can have over their respective investments' fates.

We are not suggesting that investors avoid investing in public securities or become full-time angels. However, for an astute investor with 60 to 85 percent of his investable net worth in stocks and bonds, his allocation decision to diversify 5 to 15 percent of his portfolio into private equity investments—depending on time and money—may be the only sane strategy in a characteristically irrational investment market.

The Importance of Identifying Exit Strategy before Investing

THAT 30 PERCENT OF ALL IPOs in the United States are completed by professional-venture-capital-backed firms is no accident. This statistic reflects the institutional venture capitalist's policy to emphasize and clarify potential exit routes before investing. In contrast, many angels focus on making the business succeed, because they believe that building a sustainable company ultimately will help them achieve their return. Perhaps angels can learn something from institutional investors—that is, spell out in advance the mechanism of getting your return, even though such returns are calculated on speculative projections. Projecting realistic exits with some degree of certainty is difficult. Regardless, we must attempt to define the exit. This permits flexibility so we can modify the exit plan as the company develops and its possible exit becomes clearer.

Start early in the negotiations to specify steps that will ensure future value when the day comes to cash out. Waiting until the last minute will be costly. Before you put your money into any venture, determine how and when you will get it out. Identify alternative exit strategies early, including IPO, acquisition, buyback, and so on. Do not skip this important part of the negotiations. Getting your money out in the future is one of the key goals of angel investing. Discuss with entrepreneurs realistic and worthy exit routes to guide your venture planning.

Reasonable Expectations for Investment Return and Hold Time

IN OUR 1999–2000 STUDY of 1,200 angel investors queried on internal rates of return from their last liquidated investments, we found that over the term of the hold—a mean of eight years—39 percent reported total loss or partial loss of investment, 19 percent reported break-even or nominal returns, 30 percent reported cumulative returns of 50 percent or more per year, and 12 percent reported returns greater than 100 percent. The returns were all cash on cash, plus capital gains.

Before the recent market corrections, angels and potential angels were bombarded with information about the then hot IPO market and about the rises in stock market prices. Huge IPOs were flaunted in the press, such as those in the first half of 1999 by Healtheon Corporation and Priceline.com. Capturing the public imaginations were reports of increases of 862 percent and 622 percent, respectively, above the IPO offering price. Typical of press reports was the rise in stock prices, as was the 77,000 percent return on Benchmark.com's investment of $6.5 million into eBay following its 1998 IPO. Such news served only to create unrealistically high bars for return on investment expectations.

So private investment returns must surpass those available based on historical analyses in the public market, such as Nasdaq-level returns. Private investments must compete with public investment returns. Private technology companies usually are the only kinds of firms that can hurdle those rates. This is true because new technology can command a premium price in the market over outdated competition, greatly enhancing revenues. They have also become the only type of business venture that can reliably offer investors a profitable exit strategy.

These statistics help angel investors establish reasonable expectations for rates of return on investments. Angels do so well partly because they diversify their technology portfolios; they don't specialize in one industry. In addition, we believe that the more successful angel investors are making multiple investments as well.

Most investors we have interviewed over the years indicated they aimed for a minimum 30 percent internal rate of return for investments in start-up ventures. If they make only one or two investments, they are less able to absorb losses. So making multiple investments, establishing reasonable return-on-investment expectations, and defining strategies to avoid making bad investments seem to be prevalent concerns among angels.

It is also important to have realistic expectations about timing the exit. We have seen a wide range in the acceptable time frame for exit. The hold times for angels through the 1980s and 1990s ran from five to ten years. Although for institutional investors the goal is always to liquidate within three to five years, reality sets in for angels, making the wait much longer before creating a substantial liquidation event. The mean holding time to liquidation for successful direct private placements in our study was eight years. The feasible time horizon of the holding period can vary significantly, a function mainly of the industry. For example, the time frame is longer for biotech and shorter for e-commerce and business-to-business ventures.

The angel should also be aware of entrepreneurs' tendency to underestimate time to liquidity and the implications of that tendency. Much as CEOs in public companies are perhaps pressured to provide short-term gains to influence public stock prices, entrepreneurs are sometimes tempted to sacrifice strategic growth for the overall benefit of the venture in order to provide more palatable exit time frames for angels. Both these strategies can reduce the long-term growth potential of firms, whether public or private.

Evaluating Your Returns

ONE WAY FOR ANGELS to measure the success of their investment is to compare their returns with those of other investors. Angels can use qualitative elements in assessing how fulfilling an investment has been, but quantitative measures of performance are much more useful in determining whether the angel can, on another day, return to the private market as a player.

You can assess the value of the exit strategy by studying liquidity events in the investee company's industry. Select companies in the same geographic region of the country. Also try to identify liquidity transactions similar in structure to your own exit, such as IPO, merger and acquisition, buyback, sale to third party, and so on. How have these other private-equity-backed companies achieved liquidity for their investors, and at what multiples? You can provide a baseline for comparison against your own exit strategy and results through an informal comparative analysis, using public domain information. Focus on detecting profitable opportunities in investments that have already occurred. And you can investigate other transactions through comparable postmortems.

Realistic Exit Routes

GRASPING THE EXIT OPPORTUNITY

TO THE OLD SAYING that "the best time to sell is when you're doing well," we would like to add, "*and* when you can persuasively predict doing even better." While greed can conquer, making it difficult for investors and entrepreneurs alike to let go, there will come a time when it is best to exit the deal: when a company is profitable and able to pay its obligations and offer dividends. Or, from a negative standpoint, it may be time to get out when the company is failing.

When this time comes, good or bad, investors must remember that not all private companies are IPO candidates, and not all owners should go public or sell out through merger or acquisition. It is at this moment in the enterprise's life cycle that the investor finally sees possible returns in the form of liquidity. At this time, all concerned parties should consider the benefits and costs of the options available for providing an exit and liquidity for the investor and ensuring ongoing financial viability for the company after the angel's exit. In essence, the end of the angel's involvement signals the beginning of involvement for the next provider of financing, the late-stage investor. Or it may mean the company's management is assuming financial responsibility.

Exiting options run a gamut, depending on such factors as the nature of the business, the need for the owners to receive as much cash as possible from the sale, the founders' interest in carrying on the business, and the owners' continued involvement after the sale.

Ideally, before contemplating exit, a business owner will have built a strong asset base and a reliable cash flow to strengthen the value of the business. Usually this can be done through the years by acquiring real estate (associated with the business) and other assets, creating intellectual property (technology), gaining significant market share, and so on.

Patience and exit expectations shared among the investors and the entrepreneurs are critical for ventures with limited prospects for a public offering or acquisition by a larger firm within the typical exit horizons of venture capital investments. The primary exit routes used by private companies to provide investors liquidity are initial public offering; merger, acquisition, or corporate buyout; later-stage private equity financing; company buyback; and secondary sale.

INITIAL PUBLIC OFFERINGS

THERE ARE 22 MILLION private companies and only 30,000 public companies in the United States. Approximately one-tenth of 1 percent of U.S. companies are traded on major stock exchanges. The initial public offering (IPO) is simply the resale and distribution of the company's stock in the public securities market for the first time. From 1996 to 1998 the number of IPOs declined, according to VentureOne Corporation and PricewaterhouseCoopers. In 1996, venture-backed IPOs reached a ten-year high, with 260 deals that raised $11.8 billion. In 1998, liquidity via IPO for venture-backed companies dried up to a total of 77 deals that raised $4.2 billion. But then the number and value of initial public offerings skyrocketed in 1999, fed by a rush of Internet deals and the myth propagated by the media that all IPOs provide investors with instant wealth.

According to Thomson Financial Securities Data, there were 546 IPOs in 1999 for a total value of $69 billion, compared with 380 IPOs in 1991 with a value of $15 billion. To date, according to Thomson, the group demonstrates an average 74 percent gain from the offering price.

When a company is fabulously successful, the IPO is a possibility. However, a number of circumstances that create variability in the IPO market and that are beyond the company's control can make the IPO route not only unattractive but also unattainable. Furthermore, vesting requirements can block investors from selling all of their shares. Listing the company's shares on a publicly traded financial exchange can allow investors who funded the firm in early stages to realize returns from their long-term investment. Those returns can be diluted by certain conditions: the rigorous listing requirements of the exchange, the high fixed costs associated with an IPO, the complex regulatory requirements to do an IPO offering, the requirement that the company has been successful and grown large enough to float its stock on a major exchange, and the requirement that the IPO offering itself be large enough to create a market of $20 million to $50 million.

The IPOs of Internet companies do not diminish the daunting nature of these requirements for most companies, as we can see by the recent cooling of the IPO market. This was because too many nonsustainable firms rushed to the public markets in 1998 and 1999. These are some of the reasons that fewer than 1 in 1,000 start-up companies will ever reach IPO status. Despite naive business-plan claims that the IPO is the primary exit vehicle, it would be risky, even foolish, for angel investors to assume the IPO is the most probable exit five to ten years beforehand.

MERGER/ACQUISITION/CORPORATE BUYOUT

AS THE IPO FRENZY COOLS, interest in alternative liquidity routes has reemerged. In 2000, thousands of companies merged and acquired their way through $1.4 trillion in closed deals.

Merging the investee company with a large corporation or being acquired by the same and receiving cash and marketable securities for the sale are time-tested exit routes for angel investors. Trade sales, or the sale of one firm to another, are rare unless there are strong strategic reasons for the transaction. Also, the joining companies need to be complementary and synergistic in terms of product or technology. This is why it is so important for investors to focus on technology companies with niche strategies to increase the possibility for such an exit. Also, since angels typically aim for less of a return than institutional venture capital firms, the merger, acquisition, or corporate buyout strategies are also more likely.

Merger and acquisition of venture-backed companies has consistently kept pace as a liquidity route. In 1996, 227 mergers and acquisitions generated $44.1 billion in liquidity for institutional investors. In 1997, 198 deals yielded $12.8 billion, and in 1998, 190 deals generated $12.6 billion for investors in venture-capital-backed firms.

Corporate venturing is fueling the M&A exit route. Twenty percent of *Fortune* 1000 companies have established their own venture firms. For example, in 2000 Cisco Systems announced plans for twenty-five acquisitions a year, doubling what it did in 1999.

For companies left standing at the IPO altar, merger and acquisition and later-stage corporate investors continue to be a prominent source of capital and liquidity. Former candidates for public stock offerings can be very attractive to price-sensitive private funds and merger and acquisition groups. Many entrepreneurs and investors who previously contemplated IPOs are turning to corporate buyout funds and merger and acquisition specialists. For example, Advanced Telcom Group is a Santa Rosa, California, company that received a large capital infusion from an institutional venture capital firm early in its development. It raised $175 million, including a major investment from Texas Pacific Group, a merger and acquisition specialist. Venture capital firms in the fourth quarter of 1999 invested $40 million to $175 million each into twenty-five different companies, jumping into the later-stage financing opportunities presented by firms no longer seeking an IPO.

LATER-STAGE PRIVATE EQUITY FINANCING

LATE PRIVATE FINANCING ROUNDS are helping fallen IPO hopefuls to raise as much money as they can by selling shares to the public. For example, One Coast Network, an Atlanta wholesaler of gift items and home furnishings, raised $39.5 million in financing from private investors, and Trintech, an Internet commerce and credit card software firm, secured $20 million in private capital. For investors and companies that don't want to be held hostage to the fortunes of the IPO and stock market, later-stage private equity placements can be an important source of liquidity.

In May 2000, *Wall Street Journal* reporter Suzanne McGee wrote, "With IPO theaters shuttered, dot-coms act out cash pleas for private patrons. Amid the rubble in dot-com stocks, hundreds of upstart companies are being forced to find different ways other than IPOs to get financing. Many are doing the equivalent of launching an off-Broadway show, for a limited audience, when Broadway itself turns up its nose. Instead of struggling to pull in large crowds for their initial public offerings or follow-on stock sales, these companies are raising money from private investors."

The recent market conditions that caused IPOs to be postponed created many opportunities to invest in companies looking for financing through private offerings. Since these offerings are available only to qualified institutional buyers, the transactions are subject to Rule 144A of the Securities Act of 1933, which specifically covers the resale of restricted securities of an issuer and securities held by affiliates of the issuer.

Turning to wealthy individuals for angel capital not only for seed financing but also for later rounds is now increasing. As their cash requirements balloon, fast-track companies frequently link with corporate investors for financial as well as strategic support. For example, in its last private financing round, Telocity got $57 million from such institutional venture capital firms as Bessemer Holdings and Soros Private Equity Partners. However, it raised even more—a $70.5 million package of cash and production services—from private investors that included General Electric, NBC, NBC Internet, and Valuevision International.

According to the *Asset Alternative Corporate Venturing Report,* corporate venturing mushroomed in 1999. Driven by the need to ensure long-term competitiveness, corporations in 1999 announced the formation of capital programs totaling $6.3 billion, up from $1.7 billion in 1998. Of twenty-eight corporations surveyed, nineteen had committed at least $100 million to their business development venturing programs. Corporations are motivated to do this type of investing to gain access to technology or other strategic benefits, promote their own services or products, and act like a lead investor in order to leverage their expertise and raise additional capital from outside sources.

COMPANY BUYBACK

THE LONG-TERM OR SHORT-TERM buyback is the exit route whereby the investor expects to cash out by selling securities back to the founders. If he plans to use this route, he should be sure that the terms and conditions of the sale are tied to the operating performance and cash flow of the venture.

The company buyback occurs when the founder, entrepreneur, or management purchases shares back from the investors. The leveraged buyout (LBO) is the company buyback using a high level of debt. The LBO is used frequently when the company is marginally successful. The company buyback can be a long-term arrangement in which the owner/founder may or may not remain involved. One way to exercise the company buyback exit is through the prearranged takeout.

Although viewed by some as overly legal and contractual, the prearranged takeout provides angels with a fighting chance to recover their investment in a marginally performing business. The method involves the angel setting aside by preinvestment agreement or tendering to the company a percentage of the company shares. These are held at a price that relates to a predetermined multiple of earnings or cash flow. In the case of Internet companies, revenue levels could also be used as the factor for determining the value of shares to be repurchased. The entrepreneurs can have a call that could be exercised at some multiple value after they have successfully achieved agreed-on levels of earnings or cash flow. It is the angel's responsibility to negotiate this option. To make a prearranged takeout work, an agreed-on percentage of company earnings can be dedicated to purchase the specific segment of securities issued by the company, or to redeem preferred shares.

SECONDARY SALES TO THIRD PARTIES

SOME RESEARCHERS AND ANALYSTS claim that secondary sales of private company stock, or the sale by the investor of all or some shares to a third party, provides an often-used liquidity route for angel investors. Our research findings do not support this contention. In our experience, if the investor no longer wishes to remain involved in a deal and sees no hope of generating return or enough return to stay the course, he will be hard-pressed to find a savvy investor of value to the company and acceptable to his co-investors who will willingly take such a loser off his hands.

The Living Dead: Coping with the Marginally Performing Investment

WHEN WE FIRST STARTED our research on private equity investing in 1989, we came across something called the "two-six-two" rule. This generalization about results from venture capital investments suggests that two times out of ten, investors lose their investment; six times out of ten, the investee companies fail, or if they survive, they provide break-even or nominal returns; and two times out of ten, investors realize high returns on the investment. Of course, as we have already shown, investment returns to angels are much more complex than "two-six-two" would suggest, and survival rates and return rates for angels have improved dramatically. But marginal returns continue to be the outcome of a significant number of investments.

If the company has not positioned itself to provide outstanding returns within five to seven years, the chances of stellar returns decrease the longer the investor holds the investment. If an investor invests in a company, he becomes a partner. And if the investor can never obtain liquidity from the investment, a problem emerges for that partner. The business may be doing well enough for the entrepreneurs to make a living. But the investor views the investment as a failure because he cannot get his money out at an appropriate multiple of the original investment.

The investor needs and wants a liquidity event. If an investor is evaluating a deal and thinks he can get liquid in two years, he will probably accept a lower rate of return rather than accept a long-range development project that may not be liquid for eight years. He can achieve liquidity through a number of different mechanisms, as we have discussed in the previous section. But if none of these alternatives works, the investment becomes categorized as a member of "the living dead." No investor wants to suffer in financial purgatory by being left in a venture without liquidity. For many investors, being part of a "living dead" deal has been a dreadful financial experience—hanging in limbo, not wanting to slip backward but unable to move forward. The money is in, but the investor has no way to get it out.

When an investor has lost faith in management, sometimes salvaging part of his investment is the only alternative left. A number of structures, if negotiated prior to investment, can help the investors manage exit risk, should they ultimately find themselves invested among the living dead. As we discussed, even in the marginal situation, entrepreneurs will be receiving a salary and other benefits as well. So the investors should first negotiate the means of getting their investment back. Next, they should negotiate arrangements to split any additional monies made by the company. This can be done through arrangements that will force the entrepreneur to take money out of the firm after a certain time or after the entrepreneur has achieved certain financial milestones. Other investors will opt to search for more equity during negotiation and hold it until the investor is paid back, after which the equity could be made to revert to the entrepreneur.

But more aggressive investors may negotiate the right to force sale of the company or its assets and require identification in advance of possible buyers of the company. Management and the board of directors determine when a company should be sold, to whom, and on what terms. Even if an investor owns 51 percent of a company, a two-thirds to three-quarters vote of shareholders will be required to sell. Under certain conditions—for example, failure to achieve projections—angels can negotiate the right to sell the company or to sell shares back to the company at a predetermined price.

Restricted versus Free-Trading Stock

SOPHISTICATED INVESTORS want liquidity. They want to have free-trading stock. Contrary to popular misconception, IPOs are not nirvana, especially for insiders, because in many cases officers and major shareholders are not legally free to immediately sell all of their shares. Free-trading stock is grossly overrated, because you can own free-trading stock but not be able to trade it. There must be a market maker.

Following an IPO, a 180-day restriction normally is placed on the sale of stock. Such a restriction, called a "lockup," is initiated by the market makers to prevent stock prices from being pushed downward at issue by a float of a larger number of shares in the rush to cash out.

Let's discuss this type of restriction. When a company is planning to go public, the underwriter will normally insist on a lockup for six months. This is not an SEC regulation; it's an agreement between the underwriter and the insider investors with more substantial holdings of shares. The underwriter will most likely be the market maker, who will look to avert at all costs any dumping of stock as insiders sell and take profits.

The reason investors and entrepreneurs acquiesce to the underwriter's requirement for a lockup is that the importance of a committed market maker to achieving liquidity through the IPO cannot be underestimated. In fact, in our experience, one market maker may not be enough, and in order to have a truly successful IPO, two or three may be required. The reason is this: if you have an unrestricted, free-trading stock without a market maker, it doesn't do the owner of the stock much good. Sure, restricted stock can ultimately be sold if the owner himself finds a buyer, but free-trading stock will sell only if there's a market maker. If no broker is there to make the market, liquidity becomes an illusion.

Large blocks of stock can be floated on the market after such lockup agreements expire, and this may explain why IPOs are not doing as well a year after the highs they experienced at the time of their offering. Especially in today's highly volatile technology stock market, the stock prices can significantly decline below offering price, reflecting additional risk to insiders who were forced to hold the stock during the lockup. Furthermore, in a company going public, the Securities and Exchange Commission may restrict the stock up to a year—six months longer than the lockup agreement. This prevent insiders—that is, officers and controlling shareholders—from manipulating the stock and dumping it right away on an unsuspecting public. So while the underwriter may have let the insider off the hook, insiders—even those holding small blocks of shares—could be restricted from trading for an additional six months by the SEC. The SEC's and underwriter's restrictions are not connected; they are separate.

Transforming Investment Losses into Tax Gains

WHAT SEPARATES ANGELS from the institutional venture capital money managers and lenders is that they don't *have* to invest. This difference provides another benefit for angels: They also don't have to apologize to anyone for an investment mistake. When an investment decision turns into disappointment, sometimes the only remaining exit route with dignity is liquidation or the search for tax benefits from the negative return or loss.

In a positive situation, investors may want to discuss with their tax advisers the potential benefits from rolling over any capital gains to another investment, in order to avoid having to pay capital gains taxes after the exit. Also, as we have written, the government has created attractive incentives for private investors under very specific circumstances to reduce their capital gains taxes, the impetus being to stimulate investment in early-stage companies. The Omnibus Reconciliation Act of 1993 allows investors who hold "qualified" small-business stock for at least five years to exclude 50 percent of the capital gains realized on disposition of the stock—essentially reducing the tax burden on many investment dollars to about 14 percent.

But when outcomes are not favorable, different strategies become necessary. When a company fails or is closed, about 5 percent of the time liquidation or the sale of the firm's assets will occur, a condition that entails a distribution of the sale proceeds to creditors and preferred shareholders. The investors in this situation may seek trade interest through liquidation of the patents or assets such as real estate, buildings, or equipment, if they are present.

When no assets can be liquidated and a negative gain or loss occurs because of the failure of the investment and/or the closing of the company, the investor can gain some advantage in unsuccessful private equity transactions through active accounting and tax approaches to structuring the deal. This procedure will help him in realizing the benefits of write-offs. This process begins with how the corporate entity is structured before the investors invest their capital.

Two types of corporate structures dominate angel investments: C corporations and S corporations. The critical difference is that a C corporation is responsible for paying its own taxes, while an S corporation passes the tax liability through to the individual shareholders. It resembles a partnership in that respect. The S structure offers an advantage to the investor; if the nascent corporation incurs losses, the shareholders gain a tax benefit, because such losses are passed on to individual shareholders, who then can deduct those losses on their individual tax returns. So, generally, a startup company incorporating in anticipation of issuing stock and raising capital would probably elect to form as an S corporation in the early stages when it forecasts losses. After having gone through the loss period and showing profits, management and the investors may find it better to switch the company to a C corporation and have the corporation start paying taxes at its own corporate rates, which are higher than individual rates.

Corporate structure has important implications for exit strategy. A C corporation has a problem when liquidating because it is subject to double taxation. So if a corporation holds assets that are appreciating, it must recognize a gain above its costs on those assets when liquidating. That is, the corporation will have to pay taxes on those gains. This is true even if management doesn't sell but plans to distribute those gains without going through the liquidation process. Individual shareholders will recognize an additional gain on the sale of those assets. That is one of the reasons some companies do not put appreciating assets in a corporate structure; they leave them outside. Real estate is an example of an appreciating asset and is usually owned by the shareholder, not the corporation. The shareholder leases the asset or the building, for example, to the company. In this way, he avoids the problem of double taxation upon liquidation. This strategy is common.

Another method used by angel investors to minimize tax exposure is to realize that companies can always incur losses they can pass through; for example, management could accelerate those losses by taking write-offs instead of capitalizing things and by being aggressive with write-offs for their expenses, whichever are feasible and legal.

Ventures don't necessarily have to structure as S or C corporations; they can be set up as a limited liability company. The investors would be more like partners instead of shareholders in such a situation. This structure is similar to an S corporation in that regard. The limited liability entity has been in existence for only a few years. We see it in use more often in service companies, such as law, accounting, or consulting firms, rather than in high-technology and manufacturing companies. Such a structure provides more benefits in insulating the principals from various liabilities, instead of offering more tax benefits if the company should fail.

CONCLUSION

THE ANGEL INVESTOR'S HANDBOOK

MANY PEOPLE KNOW THAT the term "angel" as we use it today harkens back to the wealthy individuals who graciously backed Broadway shows during the golden age of the "Great White Way," eighty years ago. Those individuals were dubbed "Broadway Angels" by the grateful performers. Far fewer, however, know that the tradition—if not the term itself—dates back quite a bit further. After all, putting on plays has always been an expensive proposition—no less so in our time than during another era, the one known as the Golden Age of Greece.

Then as more recently, the financial burden of putting on plays fell on the wealthiest citizens of the polis. And one of the most costly trappings of every production was outfitting, training, and maintaining the Greek chorus, an essential voice in the great dramas of Aeschylus, Sophocles, and Euripides.

For coming to the rescue of a production, a generous citizen was granted the honor of leading the chorus onstage. He was known as the choragus, literally "leader of the chorus." Angels today still show the way, leading a different type of chorus, to be sure—but one no less important to our times than the choragus was to his.

And knowing the many angels we do—and the critical part they play in the country's and the world's economic survival—we're not at all surprised that they carry on a long, honorable, generous history.

INTERNET DIRECTORY

◆ **Angel Capital Group** (www.acg.com.hk). Begun in 1993, ACG coordinates the venture capital interests of its founders and now is dedicated to sourcing high-quality investment opportunities for a selection of international investors. It bridges the relationship between investors and investees. ACG works with companies unable or unwilling to access funds through conventional venture capital markets.

◆ **The Angel Network** (www.angelnetwork.com/index.html). The Angel Network appeals to investors interested in getting in on the ground floor of high-risk/high-return private and public offerings. Its goal is to develop the largest database of sophisticated, accredited investors; its mission is to seek strategic, entrepreneurial companies willing to sell an initial stake in their ventures for the capital they need.

◆ **Angelstreet** (www.angelstreet.com). Angelstreet.com is a full-service investment bank and Internet address for obtaining private capital, connecting high-net-worth investors with private capital. It creates and organizes a private-capital marketplace for accredited investors to access screened companies looking for capital. It also offers its members a diversified portfolio as well as the potential to invest with venture capital professionals.

◆ **Business Partners** (www.businesspartners.net). Business Partners is a nationwide Internet-based service connecting potential partners, angel investors, investment bankers, and venture capital firms with start-ups, businesses, and entrepreneurs. Its services to its members include, among other things, a full listing search, private and federal grant searches, business incubator searches, business partnering, business buyers and sellers, and business consultants.

◆ **Capital Solutions Network** (www.capitalsearch.net). Capital Solutions Network was formed in 1998 to create a network for entrepreneurs and accredited investors to do joint ventures on projects of mutual interest. It serves start-up or existing businesses seeking capital from the private equity market. It gives investors access to emerging companies that seek financing and offers information to entrepreneurs on business-related topics.

◆ **Capital Southwest Corporation (CSWC)** (www.capitalsouth west.com). Capital Southwest, formed in 1961, with its wholly owned small-business investment-company subsidiary, has provided capital to support the development and growth of small and medium-sized businesses with exceptional growth potential in many industries. Capital Southwest focuses on capital appreciation from early-stage and expansion financing, management buyouts, recapitalization, and industry consolidation.

◆ **The Entree Network** (www.entreeltd.com). Entree is a virtual network of retired and active *Fortune* 500 executives who provide professional incubator services to client companies, including assistance in acquiring funding, term-sheet offers, partnering arrangements, competitive analysis, acquisition suitors, management, board members, new clients, and modeling services. All of their deal flow comes from associates, the Internet, or by word of mouth.

◆ **The Illinois Coalition** (www.ilcoalition.org). The Illinois Technology Resource Center, maintained by the Illinois Coalition (concentrating, obviously, on Illinois), is a center for information, resources, and services to help start and grow technology companies. It is a nonprofit, nonpartisan organization of people from business, government, labor, and higher education formed to strengthen the state's economy by encouraging technology-based economic development. It provides private financial resources for technology-based start-ups, including venture capital, investment networks, and angel investors.

◆ **Information Technology Innovation Center** (www.iticweb.org). ITIC provides a collaborative environment among the U.S. Army Communication Electronics Command (CECOM), New Jersey Commission on Science and Technology (NJCST) universities, small and new businesses, and large companies, enabling them to develop dual-use information technology products and services. ITIC converts innovative ideas and technologies in research, business, and military products.

◆ **International Capital Resources (ICR)** (www.icrnet.com). ICR is a for-profit business introduction service with an extensive, prequalified proprietary database of accredited business angel investors in North America. ICR was founded to help entrepreneurs reach sophisticated, qualified, accredited, and experienced business angels and informal venture capitalists. ICR also assists angel investors in expanding their deal flow and coinvestor contacts.

◆ **Investor Angels** (www.investorangels.com). An "Internet community" for creating Internet companies, boasting a shareholder community made up of programmers, database administrators, graphic artists, mass marketers, day traders, professional venture capitalists, stockbrokers, engineers, translators, doctors, and scientists.

◆ **On-Line Ventures** (www.on-lineventures.com). A member of the Band of Angels, On-Line Ventures is a group of individual investors formed to invest in closely held, early-stage high-technology businesses. On-Line Ventures helps develop business models, identify success formulae, and foster in-depth market positioning, sales, partners, channels, corporate governance (board of directors, etc.), pricing, and alternative exits, among other considerations.

◆ **Point North Angel Investing** (www.denver-mall.com/angelinvesting.htm). Point North funds small to medium-sized Internet businesses. It is involved in private placements, shell corporations, bridge financing, IPOs, second public offerings, mergers and acquisitions, and business consulting.

◆ **Private Equity Links (Envista's Web site)** (www.privateequity. com). Envista's Private Equity Links Web site is a sponsor-supported clearinghouse of online information serving venture capitalists, buy-out specialists, lawyers, accountants, consultants, investment bankers, and others involved in the private equity market. Its site contains a resource list for entrepreneurs. Also, individuals can nominate their Web sites for inclusion in the Private Equity Links database and their events for inclusion in its calendar.

◆ **VCIndustry** (www.vcindustry.com). VCIndustry offers free information on venture capital consulting companies, VC organizations, angel investors, financing sources, going public, VC consultants, and VC publications.

◆ **Ventureline** (www.ventureline.com). Assists in providing financial analysis, locating angel investors, and preanalyzing investment opportunities. Ventureline's "MBA" ("My Business Analyst") analyzes financial statements, with comparisons to other companies in the industry, and analyzes and offers business opportunities. In addition, Venturline writes business plans and conducts professional business valuations.

◆ **Venture-preneurs Network** (www.venturepreneurs.com). A network of business professionals opening doors for each other, linking opportunities and resources. Its central focus is to assist emerging growth companies in fulfilling their needs for funding by connecting entrepreneurs, investors, opportunities, and resources through a syndicate of private investors, management consulting, workshops on guerrilla financing and guerrilla entrepreneurship, and Internet contacts.

◆ **vFinance** (www.vfinance.com). vFinance describes itself as a financial opportunity exchange. For those seeking funds, vFinance boasts VCs, angels, lenders, and investment banks. To investors it offers prequalified business plans and private placement opportunities, as well as the Financial Opportunity Exchange.

◆ **Virginia Business** (www.virginiabusiness.com). As the name indicates, Virginia is the focus of this site, which provides online resources for business-to-business information. It offers the latest in mergers, promotions, and deals made by Virginia businesses. Its "Golden Egg" is a directory of the state's technology business community, and its new "Virginia Now!" offers to expatriate graduates insight on what's happening with the state's new "Knowledge Economy." The site also offers its "List of Leaders," which ranks the state's best companies. Virginia Business Online delivers market research; education and training resources; and lobbying, legislation, and public policy information.

ANGEL INVESTING CONFERENCE/FORUM DIRECTORY

Alley to the Valley Conference. New York City's young high-tech companies present their business plans and network with West Coast investors and industry members in San Francisco. Sponsored by the New York City Economic Development Corporation.

AlleyCat News   Fax: 212-966-3558
580 Broadway, Suite 1011
New York, NY 10012
www.events@alleycatnews.com

Annual Conference for Private and Institutional Investors. A gathering for investors interested in mission-based investing, including private investors, pension managers, foundation treasurers, religious treasurers, family-office heads, and investment managers. Sponsored by Calvert Group, Capital Missions Company, and others.

333 7th Avenue, 9th Floor   212-967-0095
New York, NY 10001-5004   800-599-4950
info@srinstitute.com   Fax: 212-967-8021
www.CapitalMissions.com

Arizona Venture Capital Conference (AVCC). A forum for the exchange of information between venture capitalists and investors from across North America and developing businesses. Sponsored in Arizona by the Greater Phoenix Chamber of Commerce.

201 North Central Avenue, 27th Floor   Fax: 602-495-8913
Phoenix, AZ 85073
www.phoenixchamber.com/avcc

A.S.A.P. E-Business Alliance Summit. Features new models and practices for the formation and management of e-business alliances. Sponsored by the Association of Strategic Alliance Professionals.

P.O. Box 812-027   781-263-0066
Wellesley, MA 02482   Fax: 781-263-0027
reg@strategic-alliances.org
www.strategic-alliances.org

Barbarians on the Net Conference, presented by Strategic Research Institute's Private Equity Group. Conference on valuations, trends, pricing, exit strategies, deal sourcing, emerging sectors, and investors. Sponsored by Alston & Bird.

Strategic Research Institute   212-967-0095
333 7th Avenue, 9th Floor   800-599-4950
New York, NY 10001-5004   Fax: 212-967-8021
info@srinstitute.com
www.srinstitute.com

Business Incubator & Technology Showcase. Features New Jersey incubator start-up companies that are developing unique high-tech products and services and are interested in developing partnering relationships. Sponsored by Venture Association New Jersey (VANJ).

177 Madison Avenue   973-631-5680
Morristown, NJ 07962-1982   Fax: 973-984-9634
clara@vanj.com

California Venture Forum. Showcases start-up and early-stage companies to an audience of potential investors. The forum is sponsored by Southern California Edison.

> 20505 Yorba Linda Boulevard   714-235-8655
> Yorba Linda, CA 92886-7109
> www.calventureforum.org

Central Coast Venture Forum. An all-day conference for venture investors and growth companies in Santa Barbara, Ventura, San Luis Obispo, and Northern Los Angeles counties. Sponsored by Central Coast Venture Forum.

> 800 Anacapa Street   805-966-6644
> Santa Barbara, CA 93101   Fax: 805-568-1955
> forumnidamaloney.com
> www.ccvf.org

CEO Global Breakfast Series. Has assumed management of the Defense Space Consortium (DSC). Sponsored by Santa Clara University Center for Innovation and Entrepreneurship.

> Santa Clara University   408-551-7071
> alcarr@scu.edu

Corporate Investment & Strategic Alliance Conference. A gathering of business development officers of companies open to emerging, growing, and middle-market companies seeking equity funding and strategic alliances.

> c/o OCBC, 2 Park Plaza, Suite 100   800-628-8033, ext. 220
> Irvine, CA 92614   949-476-9240
> www.cisaconference.org

Corporate Venturing and Strategic Investing. Features corporate strategic investors who tell how they set up their venture capital arm. Sponsored by International Business Forum.

> 100 Merrick Road, Suite 500   516-594-3000, ext. 25
> West Building   Fax: 516-594-5979
> Rockville Centre, NY 11570
> stephanies@ibforum.com
> www.ibforum.com

DealQuest Private Equity Markets Summit. Links CFOs, industry players, administrators, fund managers, advisers, equity sponsors, institutional investors, buyout specialists, and venture capitalists. Sponsored by O'Sullivan Graev & Karabell, LLP.

IIR, P.O. Box 102914
Atlanta, GA 30368-2914
register@iir-ny.com
www.iir-ny.com

888-670-8200
941-951-7885
Fax: 941-365-2507

Diamond Venture Forum. Designed to successfully match investors with companies and to help entrepreneurs polish their business plans and work on presentation skills. Sponsored by Southern California Edison and others.

www.diamondventure.com

909-781-2345, ext. 14

Emerging Technology Business Showcase. Showcases technology-based Florida businesses, attracting growing and mature technology businesses seeking strategic alliances or capital funding. Sponsored by Enterprise Development Corporation of South Florida.

3320 NW 53rd Street, Suite 202
Ft. Lauderdale, FL 33309
sdemarco@edc-tech.org
www.edc-tech.org

561-627-2555
Fax: 954-486-2809

Entrepreneurship Capital Conference. Seasoned entrepreneurs share their experiences with novices, who also meet venture capitalists and angel investors.

10995 Le Conte Avenue, Suite 517
Los Angeles, CA 90024
www.uclaextension.org

310-206-1409
Fax: 310-825-9242

Family Office Forum. Presents interactive discussions on investment opportunities, hedge fund investing, real estate returns, and the like, between professionals and those with family portfolios. Sponsored by Banc of America Securities.

IIR NY, P.O. Box 3685
Boston, MA 022241-3685
register@iimy.com
www.iir-ny.com

888-670-8200
Fax: 941-365-2507

Global Alternative Investment Management Forum (GAIM). Offers information on hedge funds, market-neutral strategies, event-driven investments, fund-of-fund alternatives, private equity, venture capital, real estate, managed futures, technology funds, healthcare funds, emerging Asian markets, Latin American private equity, Japanese real estate, and timber. Sponsored by Citibank and Banc of America Securities.

1549 Ringling Boulevard, Suite 500
Sarasota, FL 34236
www.iir-ny.com

888-670-8200

Global Alternative Investment Management Forum (GAIM). Conference on alternative investments for asset allocators and their advisers; speakers include economists and academics; traditional asset managers in alternatives; hedge funds, CTAs, and private equity managers; and advisers.

ICBI, 8th Floor, 29 Bressenden Place
London SW1E 5DR, UK
icbi-registration@icbi.co.uk
www.icbi-uk.com/gaim/

44-20-7915-5103
Fax: 44-20-7915-5101

Greater Long Beach Venture Forum. Assists entrepreneurs and promising high-growth companies in successfully reaching the financial resources they need to build their businesses; features pre-screened companies to potential investors and resource providers. Sponsored by the City of Long Beach, Southern California Edison, Ernst & Young LLP, Don Knabe, and the *Press-Telegram.*

c/o Long Beach SBDC
200 Pine Avenue, #400
Long Beach, CA 90802

562-570-3863

Illinois Venture Capital Conference. A not-for-profit corporation dedicated to promoting capital information in its region by introducing interested persons to presenting companies.

180 North LaSalle Street, Suite 2001   312-855-0699
Chicago, IL 60601   Fax: 312-855-9356
ilvcconf@aol.com
www.ventureconference.com

International Energy Project Financing Conference. Brings together financing firms, power/energy developers, and government financial institutions to share information on energy projects in international markets. Sponsored by the California Energy Commission.

www.energy.ca.gov/export   916-654-4719
916-654-4708

Israeli Venture Capital Breakfast. Several of Israel's venture capital firms present the latest venture capital developments and opportunities in the country's high-technology industry. Sponsored by the Israel Economic Consulate, U.S. Northwest Region.

S400 Hamilton Avenue   650-833-2267
Palo Alto, CA 94301   Fax: 650-327-3699
cnicholson@gcwf.com

Marin Technology Venture Forum. Introduces technology companies to the Northern San Francisco Bay Area investment community. Sponsored by the Sausalito Chamber of Commerce.

29 Caledonia Street   415-331-7262
Sausalito, CA 94965
www.marinventure.com

Massachusetts Software Council Investment Conference. Attended by angels, private investors, venture capitalists, investment bankers, and nontraditional financiers looking for information on technology businesses.

info@swcouncil.org
www.swcouncil.org

Mergers, Acquisitions, and Business Valuation Seminar. Two-day seminar for understanding the drivers behind M&A activities. Sponsored by the National Center for Continuing Education (NCCE).

967 Briarcliff Drive	800-635-9615
Tallahasee, FL 32308	Fax: 850-222-4862
www.nccetraining.com	

The Natural Business Financial, Investment, and Market Trends Conference for Natural, Organic, and Nutritional Products. A gathering of CEOs, marketers, analysts, investors, and decision makers for natural, organic, and nutritional products. Sponsored by Natural Business.

P.O. Box 7370	303-442-8983
Boulder, CO 80306	Fax: 303-440-7741
info@NaturalBusiness.com	
www.NaturalBusiness.com	

New Jersey Venture Fair. Brings together emerging businesses to meet investors and entrepreneurial supporters. Sponsored by the New Jersey Technology Council.

500 College Road East, Suite 200	609-452-1010
Princeton, NJ 08540	Fax: 609-452-1007
hlevy@njtc.org	
www.njventurefair.njtc.org	

New York City Venture Capital Conference and Exposition. Enables New York City's entrepreneurs to showcase their companies to venture capitalists and investors from around the country. Sponsored by Strategic Research Institute.

333 7th Avenue, 9th Floor	212-967-0095
New York, NY 10001	800-599-4950
slitzow@srinstitute.com	Fax: 212-967-8021
www.nycvc.com	

Northeast Venture Conference. Matches early-stage regional technology companies from the Boston area, New York City and State, the metro area of Washington, D.C., and Philadelphia with venture capitalists. Sponsored by AlleyCat News.

580 Broadway, Suite 1011   212-966-4242
New York, NY 10012   Fax: 212-966-9371
www.northeastvc.com
www.alleycatnews.com

The Private Equity Analyst Conference. Networking with 1,000 senior-level institutional investors, venture capitalists, buyout specialists, deal originators, senior and mezzanine lenders, and other industry professionals. Sponsored by Asset Alternatives Inc. Conference.

170 Linden Street, 2nd Floor   781-304-1500
Wellesley, MA 02482   Fax: 781-304-1540
www.assetnews.com

Private Equity in Transition Conference. Features presentations from VCs, buyout specialists, institutions, angels, incubators, and other private equity professionals. Sponsored by Strategic Resource Institute.

333 7th Avenue, 9th Floor   800-599-4950
New York, NY 10001   212-967-0095
info@srinstitute.com   Fax: 212-967-8021
www.srinstitute.com

Private Investment Strategies Summit. Brings together individuals from the investor, investment, consulting, and financial communities, including accountants, attorneys, tax advisers, and investment directors. Sponsored by Institute for International Research (708 Third Ave., 4th Floor, New York, NY 10017-4103).

P.O. Box 102914   888-670-8200
Atlanta, GA 30368-2914   Fax: 941-365-2507
register@iir-ny.com
www.iir-ny.com

Private Placement Industry Conference. Investors, issuers, and intermediaries explore timely issues affecting private markets today. Sponsored by Institute for International Research, New York.

P.O. Box 102914   888-670-8200
Atlanta, GA 30368-2914   Fax: 941-365-2507

Southern California Technology Venture Forum. Offers premier companies an unparalleled opportunity to position themselves competitively in the search for private investment. Sponsored by Ernst & Young LLP; Southern California Edison Investor Forums; Troop, Stuber, Pasich, Reddick & Tobey; Jones Day; and Wedbush Morgan Securities.

515 South Flower Street, 32nd Floor   213-236-4845
Los Angeles, CA 90071   Fax: 213-622-7100
shouston@laedc.org
www.laedc.org/sctvfmain/html

Springboard Women's Venture Forum Series. Brings together angels, venture capitalists, corporate investors, and representatives from service firms with people from private technology and life sciences companies. Sponsored by Springboard Enterprises.

2020 K Street, NW, Suite 375   202-887-1967
Washington, DC 20006   Fax: 202-887-1987
www.springboard2000.org

Tax, Accounting, and Documentation Requirements for Private Investment Ownership Seminar. Two-day seminar on mastering effective tax, accounting, and documentation requirements for private investment partnerships. Sponsored by Institute for International Research.

P.O. Box 102914   888-670-8200
Atlanta, GA 30368   Fax: 941-365-2507
register@iir-ny.com
www.iir-ny.com

Tax-Advantaged Investment and Planning Strategies to Optimize Wealth Forum. Forum for wealthy families and their advisers on tax-advantaged investment and planning strategies. Sponsored by Institute for International Research.

708 3rd Avenue, 4th Floor
New York, NY 10017
www.irr-ny.com

888-670-8200
Fax: 941-365-2507

Venture Capital Financing Conference. A conference for attorneys and legal staff, investors, entrepreneurs, intermediaries, business owners and executives, technology and intellectual property managers, and software developers and publishers. Sponsored by CLE International.

CLE International
1541 Race Street
Denver, CO 80206
registrar@cle.com
www.cle.com

303-377-6600
800-873-7130
Fax: 303-321-6320

Venture Forum, publishers of *Venture Capital Journal*. Presents sessions on the most critical aspects of the venture capital industry, as well as numerous networking opportunities. Sponsored by Testa, Hurwitz & Thibeault, LLP, and Bank of America.

Securities Data Publishing
40 West 57th Street, 11th Floor
New York, NY 10019
colleen.a.gallacher@tfn.com

212-333-9281

VentureVest Capital Corporation Venture Forum. Brings together angel investors from Arizona with emerging companies seeking additional capital to achieve their corporate goals.

2929 N. Central Avenue, Suite 1500
Phoenix, AZ 85012
ventvest@aol.com
www.venturevest.com

602-263-4778
Fax: 602-263-4779

Women of Silicon Alley Summit. Features representatives from venture funds that focus on financing women-owned businesses and leading women entrepreneurs. Sponsored by Harvest Consulting Group, AlleyCat News.

580 Broadway, Suite 1011   212-966-4242
New York, NY 10012
www.events@alleycatnews.com

A MODEL TERM SHEET

Key Provisions

Company	The Company
Security	Series A Convertible Preferred Stock
Aggregate Proceeds	$2,000,000.00
Price per Share	$0.50
New Investors	The New Investors are the purchasers of the Series A Preferred and include XYZ Partners and ABC Corporation. Each will purchase half of the shares offered.
Expected Closing Date	As soon as practical after all documentation has been completed (estimated Thursday, May 17th, 2001).

Capitalization Table

Founders' Common Stock	4,500,000	35.4%
Reserved for Options	4,200,000	33.1%
Pre-Money, Fully Diluted	8,700,000	68.5%
Series A Convertible Preferred	4,000,000	31.5%
Post-Money, Fully Diluted	12,700,000	100.0%

TIMING

Due Diligence. The New Investors will complete cursory due diligence including:

1 *References.* Detailed bios or résumés, as well as professional reference checks for each of the Founders.

2 *Legal.* Either verbal conversations or receipt of a summary statement from each of XYZ's legal counsel specializing in employment issues regarding their assessment of the legal issues surrounding the extraction, immediately prior to closing the Series A financing.

3 *Staffing.* Receipt and review of a list of individuals who would be desirable employees of XYZ. Such individuals may be employed currently at ABC or at another firm. The list should provide name (names excluded for ABC employees), current title or professional level, and estimated projected total annual compensation.

4 *Client Prospects.* Receipt and review of a list of client prospects. Such client prospects should include only those companies and individuals for whom ABC has not performed services within the past twelve months or with whom ABC has not had substantial professional contact within the past five years.

5 *Historical Operating Performance.* Receipt of summary historical financial information regarding the Founders' Real Estate practice at ABC. This may include estimates of the type of work performed, average job size, segmentation of clients (dot-coms, brick and mortar, etc.). It may also include summary financials from 1998 or 1999.

Events Prior to Close.

1 Signed term sheet by all three Founders (fax signatures acceptable) and a representative from each of XYZ Corporation and ABC Partners.

2 Due diligence as outlined above.

3 Selection of a new corporate name or temporary name.

4 The Founders will be the executive management team of the Company. NOTE THAT BASED ON OUR LIMITED CONTACT, IT IS NOT YET APPARENT TO THE NEW INVESTORS THAT ANY OF THE FOUNDERS IS PERFECTLY SUITED TO ACT AS CEO OF XYZ. Such evaluation will be made by the New Investors and the Founders, in conjunction with the investors in the next equity financing, and may result in appointing a non-Founder to the position of CEO.

5 Execution of Employment Agreements, in a form satisfactory to the New Investors by all Founders and employees.

6 Progress with ABC as it relates to the extraction.

Events Postclosing.

1 Purchase of Director and Officer Insurance for the Board and the Founders and Officers.

2 Purchase of Key Man Life Insurance Policies for the Founders.

3 Begin discussion with a lending institution regarding equipment financing. It is likely $1 million to $2 million may be made available for software and hardware purchases concurrent with closing the next equity financing. XYZ Partners suggests starting with:

TERMS OF THE SERIES A

Founders. Founder #1, Founder #2, etc.

Use of Proceeds. Working capital

Security. Series A Convertible Preferred Stock

Purchase Price and Initial Conversion Price. $0.50 per share.

Rights, Preferences, Privileges, and Restrictions of Preferred.

1 *Dividend Provisions.* No dividend will accrue or be paid on Preferred A unless declared by the Board of Directors. As long as the Preferred A is outstanding, no dividends shall be paid on the common stock of the Company (the "Common"), the Preferred A, or any other class of preferred stock of the Company without the approval of 66 percent of the outstanding shares of the Preferred A.

2 *Liquidation Preference.* In the event of liquidation, sale, merger, consolidation, or winding up of the Company, the holders of Preferred A will be entitled to receive in preference to holders of Common an amount ("Liquidation Amount") equal to the purchase price of the shares plus all accrued and unpaid dividends.

Following full payment of the liquidation preference for the Preferred A, any further distributions or payments shall be shared proportionately by the Preferred A and Common Stock (treating Preferred stock on an as-converted basis) subject to the Preferred A being capped at two times the original purchase price per share (in addition to the Liquidation Amount). The balance of the proceeds shall be paid to the Common Stock.

3 *Merger or Reorganization of the Company.* A merger, consolidation, or reorganization of the Company will be deemed to be a liquidation provided that 50 percent of the voting power is held by shareholders who were not shareholders prior to such event. The conversion of Preferred A into Common Stock of the Company shall be permitted at any time up to or simultaneously with consummation of such merger, consolidation, or reorganization of the Company.

4 *Conversion Price.* The total number of shares of Common into which Preferred A may be converted will be determined by dividing the original purchase price plus any declared and unpaid dividends by the conversion price per share. The initial conversion price will be the original purchase price per share. The conversion price will be subject to adjustment, as provided in paragraph (6) below.

5 *Conversion at IPO.* Upon the closing of an initial public offering of shares of the Common at a public offering price that is not less than four times the conversion price per share, with net proceeds to the Company of at least $30 million (the "IPO"), the Preferred A holders will automatically convert into Common at the then-applicable conversion price.

6 *Antidilution Provisions.* If the Company issues additional shares at a purchase price less than the applicable conversion price of the Preferred A (excluding shares issued to employees pursuant to the Stock Option Plan or any other incentive compensation plan or arrangement), the conversion price used to determine the number of shares of Common into which shares of Preferred A may be converted will be reduced on a broad-based weighted average formula basis. The conversion price will also be subject to other customary antidilution provisions, including for stock splits, stock combinations, stock dividends, merger, reorganization, and other similar events.

7 *Voting Rights.* Except with respect to election of directors and certain protective provisions or as required by law, the Preferred A will vote together with the Common, with the right to that number of votes equal to the number of shares of common issuable upon conversion of the Preferred A.

8 *Protective Provisions.* For so long as the Preferred A remain outstanding, consent of the holders of at least 66 percent of the Preferred A will be required for: (i) any sale by the Company of all or substantially all of its assets, (ii) any merger of the Company with another entity or (iii) any liquidation, dissolution, or winding up of the Company, (iv) any amendment of the Company's charter in a manner adverse to this class of stock, (v) the issuance of any security senior to or on a parity with the Preferred, (vi) borrowing in excess of $1 million, (vii) any increase in the number of shares issuable pursuant to the Stock Option Plan, or (viii) the payment of any dividend on or the purchase, redemption, or other acquisition of any security junior to the Preferred.

9 *Redemption.* Holders of at least 66 percent of the Preferred A may elect to cause the Company to redeem the Preferred A in two equal annual installments, commencing on the fifth anniversary of the issuance of the Preferred A, at a redemption price equal to the greater of the fair market value or purchase price plus all accrued and unpaid dividends.

Upon default in the payment of any required redemption installment, the unpaid balance shall accrue interest at the rate of 15 percent per annum, payable quarterly in arrears. Default in the payment of any required redemption installment that continues for more than ninety days after notice shall be a voting-right event permitting the Preferred A to elect a majority of the Board of Directors during the pendency of such default.

10 *Transferability.* Holders of Preferred A shall be subject to standard restrictions on transferability.

11 *Preemptive Rights.* Holders of Preferred A shall have the right to purchase a pro rata portion of any securities offered in the future by the Company.

12 *Qualified Small Business Stock.* The Preferred A will constitute "qualified small business stock" within the meaning of Section 1202 of the Internal Revenue Code. The Company will use best efforts to comply with any applicable reporting and record keeping requirements of Section 1202 and the related regulations.

Board of Directors. The Company's Board of Directors shall be adjusted to provide for a total of five representatives, of which two shall be representatives of the Preferred A (including one from XYZ Corporation and one from ABC Partners), and three shall be representatives of the Founders.

The two Preferred A representatives shall be elected by a majority of the Preferred A. The Company will reimburse all nonemployee directors for their reasonable expenses to attend Board meetings.

Information Rights. So long as any of the Preferred A are outstanding, the Company will deliver to each investor who owns at least 400,000 shares of Preferred A audited annual and unaudited quarterly and monthly financial statements, annual budgets, and other information reasonably requested by such investor.

Inspection Rights. The Company shall permit the New Investors, or their authorized representatives, to visit and inspect the properties of the Company, including its corporate and financial records, and to discuss its business and finances with officers of the Company, during normal business hours following reasonable notice and as often as may be reasonably requested.

Registration Rights.
1 *Demand Rights.* Commencing on the earlier of the date of the Company's IPO and five years from the Closing, the holders of 66 percent of the Preferred A, voting collectively (or Common Stock issued upon conversion of the Preferred A, or a combination of such Common Stock and Preferred A) may request at any time that the Company file a registration statement under the Securities Act of 1933, as amended, covering the Common Stock issued upon conversion of the Preferred A requested to be registered, and

the Company will use its best efforts to cause such shares to be so registered.

The Company will not be obligated to effect and consummate a demand registration within six months of its IPO or more than two demand registrations (other than on Form S-2 or Form S-3 or any equivalent successor form) under this provision. A registration will not count for this purpose unless it is closed or withdrawn at the request of the New Investors (other than as a result of a material adverse change to the Company).

All preferred stockholders, founders, and employees with stock or stock options and their equivalent will agree to a customary lock-up in connection with the Company's IPO, as determined by the Board of Directors and underwriters.

2 *Registration on Form S-2 or Form S-3.* Holders of the Preferred A will have the right to require the Company to file two additional Registration Statements on Form S-2 or Form S-3 (or any equivalent successor form).

3 *Piggyback Registration.* The New Investors will be entitled to unlimited "piggyback" registration rights subject to customary underwriter's cutback.

4 *Registration Expenses.* The Registration expenses (exclusive of underwriting discounts and commissions but including the fees of one counsel of the selling shareholders) of each of the registrations under paragraphs (1), (2), and (3) above will be borne by the Company.

5 *Transfer of Registration Rights.* The registration rights may be transferred to a transferee who acquires at least 10 percent of the Preferred A shares from an investor. Transfer of registration rights to a partner or shareholder of any Investor will be without restriction as to minimum shareholding.

Key Person Insurance. The Company will use best efforts to purchase and maintain at least a $1 million policy on each of the Founders, with proceeds payable to the Company.

Co-Sale and Right of First Refusal Agreement. The Founders and the Company's key employees will each execute a Co-Sale and

Right of First Refusal Agreement (the "Co-Sale Agreement") with the Investors and the Company pursuant to which the Company first and the Investors second will have a right of refusal with respect to any shares proposed to be sold by such persons. The Co-Sale Agreement will contain a right of co-sale in favor of the Investors providing that before any such person may sell any of his Common shares, he will give the New Investors an opportunity to participate in such sale on a basis proportionate to the amount of securities held by the seller and those held by the New Investors.

Noncompetition, Nonsolicitation, and Nondisclosure Agreement. The Company will cause each Founder and key employee to enter into a two-year noncompetition, nonsolicitation, and nondisclosure agreement to be in a form reasonably acceptable to the New Investors.

Founders' Stock. Founders' Stock shall vest over four years, beginning with 12 percent vesting immediately upon closing the Series A financing and the remaining 88 percent vesting 5.5 percent per quarter for the next sixteen quarters.

In the event the company is acquired, the vesting of Founders' Stock will accelerate by four quarters.

Employee Stock Options. Employee stock options will vest over four years, with the first 12 percent vesting after six months and the remaining 87.5 percent vesting 6.25 percent per quarter for the next fourteen quarters.

Certain key executive officers of the Company, such as the CEO and CFO, may be entitled to an accelerated vesting provision similar to that of the Founders in the event of an acquisition of the Company. This will be determined by the Compensation Committee.

Compensation Committee. The Compensation Committee will initially be the Board of Directors, however, no Founder will participate in the Board's approval of any Founder's compensation.

Shareholders' Agreement. To be drafted by the Company counsel.

Investors' Rights Agreement. To be drafted by the Company counsel.

Purchase Agreement. The purchase of the Preferred will be made pursuant to a Stock Purchase Agreement drafted by counsel to the Company. Such agreement shall contain, among other things, appropriate representations and warranties of the Company; covenants of the Company reflecting the provisions set forth herein and other typical covenants; and appropriate conditions of closing.

Binding Term Sheet. Upon execution, this term sheet shall constitute a binding commitment on the part of the parties hereto to proceed with the transactions provided for herein.

Conditions to Closing. The proposed transaction is subject to customary closing conditions, including without limitation satisfactory completion of due diligence by the New Investors.

Expenses. In the event of a successful closing of the Preferred A, the Company will pay the New Investors' reasonable and actual expenses of up to $25,000 in the aggregate.

Other Terms.

1 *Expenses Incurred Prior to Closing Series A.* Upon successful closing of the Series A financing, the Founders will begin drawing salaries and receiving benefits. All reasonable business expenses incurred by the Founders from the date this term sheet is signed until closing will be reimbursable by the Company.

2 *Salary Cap.* Until the Next Equity Financing of $5 million or more is closed, the Founders will each receive a salary of $125,000 per year. The Board of Directors will determine an appropriate salary for the Founders that will go into effect upon closing the Next Equity Financing of $5 million or more.

By signing this term sheet below, the Founders agree that, without the prior written consent of the New Investors, they will not solicit or engage in discussions with any other party regarding funding capital into the Company, until the earlier of (i) four weeks or (ii) until both ABC Partners and XYZ Corporation declare that they will not participate in this Series A financing. In the event either ABC Partners or XYZ Corporation declares that they will not participate in this Series A financing, the remaining New Investor and the Founders agree that the remaining New Investor shall be entitled to purchase $1.5 million of Preferred A under the terms provided herein.

Signed and Agreed to by:

Founder:
Date: May _____, 2001

Founder:
Date: May _____, 2001

Founder:
Date: May _____, 2001

Investor:
Title: CEO, XYZ Corporation
Date: May _____, 2001

Investor:
Title: Managing Partner, ABC Partners
Date: May _____, 2001

VALUATION CASE STUDY

Valuation Case Study

DEAR _____:

Enclosed per our discussion of last week is a brief analysis of a supportable valuation range for XYZ Company. I stress at the outset that this analysis and the conclusions drawn from it are very cursory and, of course, highly dependent on the 2001 projections you provided to me. Consequently, it should not be considered an appraisal or used as such, and I caution that if a full analysis were undertaken the estimated present value of XYZ Company could vary substantially. Specifically, this information is provided to assist you in your negotiations with prospective investors or purchasers of XYZ Company.

The enclosed material is divided into three elements and, given the limited scope of this assignment, each is presented in a summarized "talking point" format:

1 Summarized five-year projections and key assumptions

2 Considerations in selecting the discount rate

3 Valuation calculations using the Income Approach and the Venture Capital Model

I believe the data, discussions, and calculations are fairly straight-forward, but if you have any questions or need amplification of any aspect I will be happy to comply. However, a few brief comments are in order:

◆ **Projections.** I notice the XYZ projections for 2001 exclude any compensation for the owner or for administrative support, etc. When valuing an ongoing business it is important to do so on a strand-alone basis, which includes appropriate management costs, even if the owner is not taking a salary. I have arbitrarily allocated $100,000 in Year 1 for total salaries and benefits, increasing at 15 percent per year. This may be more than you had in mind, but it certainly adds an element of conservatism. Also, in keeping with the stand-alone concept, the projections assume XYZ Company is a C Corporation and pays taxes at the corporate level at a combined Federal and State rate of 40 percent.

◆ **Discount rate.** In any business valuation using a method dependent on the present value of future earnings or cash flows, selection of an appropriate discount rate or required rate of return is both pivotal and highly subjective. In fact, a full appraisal report would devote considerable space to justifying selection of this factor. Obviously, I have had to be fairly arbitrary in the rate chosen for the calculations, especially in addressing the particular strengths and vulnerabilities of XYZ's business. You may or may not agree with my brief list of these factors, but they are extremely important in pinning down a reasonable and supportable rate. Having said all that, I have used a base rate of 25 percent with a range of 20 percent to 30 percent. On the surface, and given XYZ's profitable history, I feel reasonably comfortable with this preliminary estimate.

◆ **Valuation methods.** Two calculation methodologies were employed in arriving at an XYZ present value estimate. The Income Approach is a well accepted and commonly used method by the professional business valuation community to value small and large companies alike. It is somewhat theoretical, but I believe the concept is easy to grasp, and the calculations are not overly complex. As a "sanity check" I have also used the Venture Capital Model, which you and I have talked about many times and which takes a more "real world" view of XYZ's potential value. The fact that both of these techniques result in a fairly tight valuation range adds a degree of confidence that the calculations are supportable.

The results of the two calculation methods are summarized below:

XYZ Present Value Estimate

Discount Rate	Income Approach	Venture Capital Model
30%	$610,000	$550,000
25%	$765,000	$668,000
20%	$1,038,000	$820,000

Based on the information supplied and applying the base case discount rate of 25 percent, it is my opinion that a negotiating range valuing XYZ Company between $650,000 and $750,000 is supportable. It should be understood, however, that this estimate is highly dependent on attainment of the 2001 (Year 1) earnings forecast.

I hope this information and my comments and opinions are useful in your current negotiations. Again, don't hesitate to contact me if you want to review any part of this analysis.

Sincerely,

Enclosures

XYZ Company: Preliminary Projections under Acquisition Scenario

KEY ASSUMPTIONS

◆ Year 1 begins the day the acquisition of XYZ is complete.

◆ Year 1 projection per XYZ 2001 "Financial Plan."

◆ Gross margin remains constant over projection period.

◆ Operating expenses increase from 15 percent in Year 1 to 20 percent in Year 5.

◆ The XYZ Financial Plan does not include salaries. In order to

XYZ Company: Preliminary Projections under Acquisition Scenario ($ thousands)

	Year 1	Year 2	Year 3	Year 4	Year 5
Recurring Revenues	$549	$659	$758	$833	$917
(% change)	—	+20%	+15%	+10%	+10%
Gross Margin	385	461	531	583	642
(% of revenues)	70%	70%	70%	70%	70%
Operating Expenses	84	112	137	158	184
(% of revenues)	15%	17%	18%	19%	20%
Operating Profit	301	349	394	425	458
(% of revenues)	55%	53%	52%	51%	50%
Salaries	100	115	132	152	175
Pretax Profit	201	234	262	273	283
Taxes @ 40%	80	94	105	109	113
Aftertax Profit	$121	$140	$157	$164	$170

value XYZ's business on a stand-alone basis, salaries are included for the owner and administrative support. Salaries and benefits begin arbitrarily at $100,000 in Year 1 and increase at 15 percent per year through Year 5.

◆ XYZ Company is valued as if it were a C Corporation and income taxes were payable at the corporate level. Consequently, a total tax burden, Federal and State, of 40 percent is applied.

◆ Aftertax profit is equivalent to free cash flow.

XYZ Company: Considerations in Selecting the Valuation Discount Rate

IN ANY VALUATION METHODOLOGY that focuses on the future performance of a business as an indicator of its present value, the discount rate is the key and a highly subjective variable. The discount rate is the rate of return required by investors in or acquirers of a business to compensate them for the perceived risk of the situation compared with similar opportunities. In practical terms, the discount rate is used to convert a benefit (earnings or cash flow) receivable in the future into a present value.

Typically, there are three approaches used to derive an appropriate discount rate: the Capital Asset Pricing Model, the Build-up Method, and the Venture Capital Rule of Thumb. Unlike the first two approaches, which are based on financial theory, the Venture Capital Rule of Thumb is based on a hierarchy of required rates of return connected to a company's stage of development. The other two methods, which are more widely used particularly with profitable businesses, develop a base required return factoring in the current risk-free Treasury rate, plus equity and small-company premiums. These rates are readily available from published valuation research sources. Once this generic required return is established, the risk characteristics of the specific company are considered and an additional amount is either added to or subtracted from the base rate. In a full valuation analysis, the determination of this "alpha" factor generally entails a full review of the company, including management, the market potential, the merits of the product or service offering, competition, etc.

Developing a full justification for the discount rate used in the following calculations, including the subjective but critical alpha factor for XYZ Company, is beyond the scope of this limited exercise. Nonetheless, it is useful to list some of the XYZ specific characteristics that could have a bearing on this important variable. Note: The following are only preliminary observations, and the list would most likely be expanded and possibly revised if a complete valuation analysis were undertaken.

STRENGTHS (REDUCE DISCOUNT RATE)

◆ Well-established business with six consecutive years of profitable operation

◆ Principal and current owner exposure and reputation

◆ Primarily a cash business

◆ Licensee network and investor and company databases—are there any "hidden" assets?

CONCERNS (INCREASE DISCOUNT RATE)

◆ Angel investing's sensitivity to economic conditions

◆ Few barriers to entry, established competition, threat from Internet players

◆ Business still highly dependent on Principals' involvement in the short term

In the absence of a thorough discount rate review, a *base rate of 25 percent,* with a range of 5 percentage points on either side, is used in the following calculations. Given the established nature of XYZ's business and its history of profitable operations, this rate seems reasonable and, at least on the surface, defensible. Again, it is cautioned that this rate could change under the scrutiny of a complete valuation analysis.

XYZ Company: Valuation Calculation Using the Income Approach

METHODOLOGY

THE INCOME APPROACH derives an enterprise valuation by applying a discount rate or required rate of return to a stream of future cash flows or earnings to arrive at the net present value of "all future benefits." In the classic application of the Income Approach, each annual projected earnings or free cash flow is discounted to present value until a stabilized growth rate in perpetuity is assumed. At this point, a capitalization rate, which by definition is the discount rate minus the assumed future growth rate, is used to discount all future flows to the present, and the two amounts are added.

◆ **Present Value of Discrete Projections.** The present value calculation is made under the assumption that cash flows are received evenly over the entire year. Thus the "midyear correction" is used in deriving the present value periods. For example, a factor of 0.5 is used for Year 1, 1.5 for Year 2, and so on. The Year 1 to Year 5 cash flow projections at a base case discount rate of 25 percent results in the following present value for the discrete projections ($ thousands).

Year	Net Cash Flow	PV Factor @25%	Present Value
1	$121	.8889	$108
2	140	.7111	100
3	157	.5689	89
4	164	.4551	75
5	170	.3641	62
	Total Present Value		**$434**

◆ **Present Value of the Terminal Value.** To calculate a terminal value, a sustainable growth rate or growth rate in perpetuity must be assumed. In the case of XYZ Company, a rate of 7 percent, or 70 percent of the Year 5 revenue growth rate, is used. The year following the last discrete projection year (Year 5) is used as the base year, and the sustainable cash flow becomes this year's amount times the growth rate, or Year 5 cash flow x 1.07. This amount is then divided by the capitalization rate to derive the value of all future benefits discounted back to the end of Year 5 ($ thousands):

$$\text{Terminal value} = \frac{n\,(1+g)}{\text{Discount rate} - g}$$

$$\frac{\$170\,(1 + .07)}{.25 - .07} \text{ Or } \frac{\$182}{.18} = \$1{,}011$$

Since the terminal value is "received" at the end of Year 5, it is discounted to the present at this point using the discount rate of 25 percent:

PV of $1,011 – Year 5 @ 25% = $331

◆ **Total Present Value.** The fair market value of XYZ Company under the base case 25 percent discount rate assumption is the sum of the discrete cash flows and the terminal value:

PV of discrete projections	$434,000
PV of the terminal value	331,000
Total	**$765,000**

VALUATION MATRIX

BRACKETING THE BASE CASE discount rate, which by definition is subjective in nature, by 5 percentage points results in the following valuation range for XYZ Company ($ thousands).

Liquidation P/E Ratio		Discount	
	30%	25%	20%
PV of discrete projections	$397	$434	$475
PV of terminal value	213	331	563
Total	**$610**	**$765**	**$1,038**

XYZ Company: Valuation Calculation Using the Venture Capital Model

METHODOLOGY

THIS VARIATION OF THE Income Approach has been employed in one form or another by the professional venture capital community as an effective means to screen business plan projections to determine if they meet the firm's hurdle rates. If the perceived risk/return ratio is positive, further due diligence and valuation refinement is undertaken. The Venture Capital Model is an income approach in that the projected future value of the company is discounted back to the present at a rate that compensates for the perceived inherent risk in the company and the probability of achieving the projections. However, rather than use the annual free cash flow stream out to perpetuity as the theoretical value of the company, the Venture Capital Model assumes a time-certain liquidity event (sale or initial public offering) and discounts the proceeds of that event to the present. In keeping with the "real world" concept of the Venture Capital Model, the two key variables in the calculation are based on experience and rules of thumb developed over thousands of transactions:

◆ **Required rate of return (discount rate).** Typically based on the stage of maturity of the company adjusted for an initial assessment of its strengths and weaknesses versus similar businesses.

◆ **Liquidation price/earnings multiple.** Typically a conservative multiple based on the company's industry and recent consummated transactions.

VALUATION MATRIX

THE MATRIX BELOW APPLIES the Venture Capital Model to XYZ Company's projections using the end of Year 5 as the date of liquidation (sale) and Year 5's net income after tax of $170,000 as the earnings base. While somewhat arbitrary given the absence of research in this preliminary analysis, a P/E range of 10X to 14X seems both reasonable and conservative. As in the Income Approach calculation, a discount rate range of 20 percent to 30 percent is used.

The table below shows the range of present values for XYZ Company employing the calculation model and variables described above ($ thousands).

Liquidation P/E Ratio	Discount 30%	25%	20%
10x	$458	$557	$683
12x	550	668	820
14x	641	780	956

HYPOTHETICAL VALUATION EXAMPLE

Venture Capital Model

THIS VARIATION OF THE CLASSIC income approach has been employed in one form or another by the professional venture capital community as an effective means of screening business plan projections to determine if they meet the firm's return hurdle rates. If the perceived risk/return ratio is positive, further due diligence and valuation refinement is undertaken. The venture capital model is an income approach, in that the projected future value of a company is discounted back to the present at a rate that compensates for the perceived risk inherent in the investment opportunity and the probability of achieving management's projections. However, rather than use an annual cash flow stream out to perpetuity as the theoretical value of the company, the venture capital model assumes a time-certain liquidity event (sale or initial public offering) and discounts the proceeds of that event to the present. In fact, most venture-capital-backed companies do not generate cash flow in the early years but are net users of cash up until the liquidity event occurs.

Like the income approach, the value estimate derived from the venture capital model is highly sensitive to a few key subjective factors. These include: the "reasonableness" of the projections and the probability of their realization; the required rate of return or discount rate of the particular investor (which in turn hinges on the perceived strengths and weaknesses of the company); additional investment that may be required; length of the holding period and the probability of achieving ultimate liquidity; and the price/earnings ratio realized on the sale or IPO.

The actual calculations employed to arrive at a company's current value are fairly straightforward and entail the following process:

1 It is assumed the company will undergo a "liquidity event" either by sale or IPO at some point in the future, generally three to seven years out.

2 A discount or "haircut" is applied to the net income after tax in the last projection year. The amount of the discount is based on a subjective feel for the reasonableness of the projections that will be verified by future due diligence.

3 An appropriate price-earnings multiple is applied to the discounted final projection year earnings to generate the assumed proceeds from the sale or IPO. The size of the P/E multiple depends on the company's industry and its anticipated future performance versus the industry in general. It should be noted that the ratio selected is usually on the conservative side and is not necessarily based on current stock market multiples.

4 The investor's initial capital contribution is compounded by the required rate of return or hurdle rate to determine the proceeds needed on liquidation to provide an appropriate return to compensate for the perceived risk.

5 The investor's required proceeds upon liquidation divided by the total company proceeds provides the required investor ownership position upon liquidation. A "dilution factor" is generally applied to this future ownership percentage to compensate for the probability of additional equity capital rounds, option grants, etc., which will reduce the investor's initial ownership position. In other words, the investor's initial ownership position generally needs to be higher than the calculated future ownership position.

6 The "post-money" valuation is determined by dividing the required initial ownership position into the initial investment. This must be converted into a "pre-money" valuation by subtracting the initial investment from the company's post-money valuation. The pre-money number represents the current value of the company before the investor's capital is contributed.

Given the highly subjective nature of the resulting valuation, the results are usually presented in the form of a matrix rather than a single value by varying the critical factors that influence the calculations. The most likely range of values is used as the decision point to either reject the proposed investment or to proceed with further due diligence.

ASSUMPTIONS
◆ $5 million equity investment
◆ Five-year holding period
◆ 30 percent dilution factor (see definition below)
◆ Projected net income after tax in Year 5 of $8 million
◆ Sale or IPO at multiple of Year 5 net income

DEFINITIONS
◆ **Required Internal Rate of Return (IRR).** Projected annualized return on investment over five-year period to compensate investor for perceived risk of the venture and loss of other opportunities for the capital.

◆ **Dilution Factor.** Occurs when additional stock is issued, which thereby reduces the percentage of ownership of those who already own stock.

◆ **Post-Money Valuation.** Value of the company *after* the investor has contributed capital.

◆ **Pre-Money Valuation.** Value of the company *before* the investor has contributed capital. This reflects the value of the founder's contribution (e.g., sweat equity).

Hypothetical Valuation Matrix

Required IRR

25%	Investor Ownership
	Pre-Money Value (MM)
30%	Investor Ownership
	Pre-Money Value (MM)
35%	Investor Ownership
	Pre-Money Value (MM)
40%	Investor Ownership
	Pre-Money Value (MM)
45%	Investor Ownership
	Pre-Money Value (MM)

Assumptions:
- ◆ $5 million equity investment
- ◆ 5-year holding period
- ◆ 30% dilution
- ◆ Year 5 net income after tax of $8,000,000

CALCULATION EXAMPLE

PREVIOUS ASSUMPTIONS PLUS:

- ◆ 35 percent required investor IRR
- ◆ Liquidation (sale or IPO) multiple of 12X

1 Investor's required proceeds at the end of Year 5:
$5 million @ 35 percent compounded for five years =
$22,420,000

2 Value of the total company at the end of Year 5:
$8 million earnings @ 12x multiple = $96 million

	Liquidation Multiple		
20%	**15X**	**12X**	**10X**
13.6%	18.2%	22.7%	27.2%
$31.8	$22.5	$17.0	$13.4
16.6%	22.1%	27.6%	33.1%
$25.1	$17.6	$13.1	$10.1
20.0%	26.7%	33.4%	40.0%
$20.0	$13.7	$10.0	$7.5
24.0%	32.0%	40.0%	48.0%
$15.8	$10.6	$7.5	$5.4
28.6%	38.1%	47.7%	57.2%
$12.5	$8.1	$5.5	$3.7

3 Investor's required ownership at the end of Year 5:
$22,420,000/$96 million = 23.3 percent
**4 Investor's required ownership today, assuming 30 percent dilu-
tion:** 23.3 percent/.70 = 33.4 percent
5 Post-Money Valuation: $5 million/.334 = $15 million
6 Pre-Money Valuation: $15 million - $5 million = $10 million

FREQUENTLY ASKED QUESTIONS

Q: How much do angel investors typically invest?

A: There are approximately 10,000 investors in ICR's proprietary database. Approximately 20 percent of the investors invest less than $25,000. Approximately 40 percent invest anywhere from $25,000 to $99,999. Twenty-five percent invest between $100,000 and $250,000, and approximately 15 percent invest more than $250,000 per investment.

Q: What is the typical amount of equity that angel investors look for in the first round of investment?

A: Once family, friends, acquaintances, and resources basically investing in the integrity and the vision of the individual without extensive due diligence have been exhausted, and the entrepreneur turns to sophisticated angel investors he has either just met or with whom he has just developed relationships, these investors typically will obtain anywhere from 20 percent to 30 percent of the equity in the company in exchange for their investment in the first round after family and friends. This is the typical amount of equity obtained when, in fact, entrepreneurs are raising only the amount of money necessary to get them to the next critical milestone that reduces the actual or perceived risk in the deal, plus provides them some monies to raise further capital after that round. If entrepreneurs are raising more money than they need to reach the next critical milestone, that could affect the amount of equity surrendered.

Q: Is it true that angel investors like to invest in companies close to where they live?

A: Based on our research at International Capital Resources, we have found that 65 percent of the almost 10,000 investors in our database do have a preference for investing reasonably close to where they live, which is typically around 300 to 400 miles maximum distance. However, 35 percent are willing to coinvest when a lead investor is geographically close to the investee company. A lead angel investor must be sophisticated, accredited, and experienced, and must garner the respect of the coinvestment angels.

Q: To what extent do you see coinvestment in deals?

A: We have seen some level of coinvestment in almost every single deal that exceeds $500,000. If you review the typology of investors that we developed in *Finding Your Wings* and *Angel Financing* you will see that a number of investors gravitate to a lead role while others, for reasons such as time commitment and net worth liquidity for investing, tend to gravitate to a coinvestment position.

Q: How many investors do you typically see in a deal?

A: Again, this is directly related to the capitalization strategy of the entrepreneur and the size of angel investment made by the individual investors that the entrepreneur has targeted. If the entrepreneur is targeting accredited investors who have the ability to invest at the $50,000 to $100,000 level and they are trying to raise $1 million, it's a simple calculation to estimate how many investors will be involved in a deal. What typically happens is that the lead investor will be able to come forward and, in a more significant way, put in a little larger investment and secure a lead position for himself. Then coinvestors will invest smaller amounts following that lead investor. So your average number of investors, for example in a million-dollar transaction, could be as small as four or five or as large as seven to ten.

Q: Do angel investors only invest in private companies? Or do they also invest in the public market, real estate, bonds, and so on?
A: The majority of investors who have invested in transactions that we've had the opportunity to study are those who have invested in privately held ventures before and are, or were, very active in the public market. Rarely do we see individual investors investing *only* in the private arena. They are diversifying their portfolio, taking a small percentage—perhaps 5 percent or 10 percent—of their equity portfolio and diversifying it into the private equity arena.

Q: What is the main reason that angel investors either don't make an investment or perhaps don't expand the number of investments they make?
A: For the majority of investors with whom ICR has developed relationships, money is not the issue. These are individuals who have the discretionary net worth to invest. The first issue is the quality of the deals and, specifically, the experience, believability, confidence, and trust that can be developed in the management team. Second is the venture itself and its potential. Third is the vision of the management and how well they capture that vision in their documentation, in their telephone pitches, and in their road show presentations. And last, their preparation and ability to weather the due diligence process.

For the most part, the majority of entrepreneurs with whom we work enter the process with reasonable pricing, reasonable valuations, and reasonable expectations on the equity and control that they're going to give up; they have excellent legal counsel with regard to structuring the transactions and realistic expectations of how the structuring will unfold. I think the real lack of liquidity in this market and, of course, based on our research, the long time an individual would need to hold these investments suggest approximately eight years before liquidity.

If the venture does not have some real promise and if its goals cannot be achieved within a reasonable time following the due diligence process, the risk/reward ratio in the mind of the investor begins to pale, and then he or she won't go forward. What contributes to that, again, is the quality of the management team, the depth to which the technology has been developed, and the degree to which they have studied the market. Perhaps most important is the compelling way they've captured their vision in their documentation and presentations.

Q: Is the government playing, or could it play, a more significant role in bringing angel investors and entrepreneurs together?

A: We admit to a strong bias against the government's role in the venture capital process. The government's "contributions" have served only to divert the attention of entrepreneurs from their real task: to get out there and find investors who themselves find a match in your deal. Actions by the government have simply not succeeded: its tax incentive through the reduction of capital gains tax under strict conditions; its crippling of the market by the regulations it imposed on SBICs; or its public relations effort, ACENet, the failed Internet matching service. None of these interventions have helped.

Individuals do not make these kinds of investments for tax incentive. Individuals in start-up companies cannot raise money from institutions that borrow the money to make these investments, because start-ups cannot pay the dividends so that the investors can service their debt. Last, you cannot find money on the Internet. In 1999, $44 million was raised, in a $30 billion market, on the Internet. That's it! It's a drop in the bucket. And all it serves to do is divert angels from the grueling task of building deal flow; evaluating ventures; and enduring the grinding, time-consuming process of due diligence. Individuals have to build a deal-flow network as we describe in this book; they have to learn the skills to do the critical prescreening and evaluation and then incur the cost and time of due diligence, valuation, and deal structuring. And only by doing those things do angels position themselves to take advantage of exit and liquidity.

Q: What else could be done to facilitate opening up this market and closing the capital gap?

A: First is the development of fund structures that will make the risks associated with early-stage and expansion-stage investing more palatable to a large segment of the investor market, a segment interested in diversifying their portfolios but without the time or the experience to individually, company by company, direct investing.

We believe that funds that package a number of private placements into one investment—but in different industries and in different stages of development and perhaps even in different economic regions—may provide a diversification tool to mediate some of the risk. In addition, as long as the funds remain closed funds (funds in which people can invest only in companies specifically defined), the angel investor is still able to closely monitor the prescreening-evaluation due-diligence process and closely examine the evaluations and deal structures. And last, a top fund manager—not just a money manager but an entrepreneurial fund manager who can monitor the companies, move in if any problems develop, apportion the investments, make the investments, and harvest the investments over the term of the fund—will make it a much more palatable vehicle.

The second thing is that we must make more professional the financial intermediary arena—not only the individual financial intermediaries and finders but also these vast computerized networks and other entities, such as venture forums, Internet-linking mechanisms, and all publications. We must develop a new level of regulation that will accredit, regulate, and license individuals or entities that wish to enter the "matchmaking" market. It doesn't have to be onerous and compliance-restrictive.

Q: How old is the typical angel investor?
A: The typical age for the angel investors in ICR's database is forty-eight to fifty-six years old. That accounts for about 80 percent of the investors in the database. Many of the novice investors are younger. There are older investors, but typically the late fifties is the oldest.

Q: Do you see a trend or a preference for different industry segments among the angel investors that you've worked with?
A: The angel market in some ways is different from the more traditional venture capital money management market and in some ways is similar. The unique thing about angel investors is that they tend to invest in what they know. Since 90 percent of angel investors are self-made millionaires who own their own businesses, obviously almost every SIC code of any substance is probably represented. So we see interest in the full range of industries, from

health care and medical, software, hardware, and communications, all the way through manufacturing of consumer products, commercial/industrial products, and high technology. We see interest in computer peripherals and electronics; even services businesses, financial services, publishing, education, recreation, and media— all of these areas and others.

Clearly, the angel market is not monolithic, and it is extremely diverse in its orientation and interests. In comparison, if you tally up the numbers of expressions of interest, clear trends emerge. Right now software is hot, as are communications, telecommunications, wireless, and to some extent, health care services and medical devices. E-commerce infrastructure remains attractive. But we're seeing less interest now in nontechnology-based services, less interest in retail, and less interest in biotechnology, because of its burdensome capital intensity and regulatory issues.

Benjamin, Gerald A., and Margulis, Joel. (2000). *Angel Financing: How to Find and Invest in Private Equity.* New York: John Wiley & Sons, Inc. In this updated edition of the highly successful *Finding Your Wings* (1996), Benjamin and Margulis offer relevant, practical information to investors, entrepreneurs, and intermediaries. They provide the groundbreaking typology of angel investors: who they are, and why they do and don't invest in the pre-IPO market.

Coveney, Patrick, and Moore, Karl. (1998). *Business Angels: Securing Start Up Finance.* New York: John Wiley & Sons. From their study of the informal venture capital market, Coveney and Moore have categorized the types of private investors, offering advice on identifying angel investors, creating business plans, and managing risk and valuation.

Gladstone, David. (1988). *Venture Capital Investing: The Complete Handbook for Investing in Small Private Businesses for Outstanding Profits.* New Jersey: Prentice Hall. Gladstone provides investors with the knowledge necessary to invest wisely in small private businesses with potentially high rates of return. He steers his readers through the stages of venture capital investing.

Lipper, Arthur III. (1996). *The Guide to Venture Investing Angels: Financing and Investing in Private Capital.* Missouri: Missouri Innovation Center. Lipper offers a guide to angels investing in private companies and to entrepreneurs seeking the necessary backing from those angels, who provide what financial institutions and professional investors do not.

Rappaport, Stephen P. (1990). *The Guide to Venture Investing Angels: Financing and Investing in Private Capital.* Rappaport's analysis distinguishes the affluent from other investors, particularly in their way of buying and selling securities. The book's focus is on financial stock portfolios, fixed-income securities or bonds, short-term investments, and cash vehicles.

Van Osnabrugge, Mark, and Robinson, Robert J. (2000). *Angel Investing: Matching Start-Up Funds with Start-Up Companies.* San Francisco: Jossey-Bass. Van Osnabrugge and Robinson offer a guide to helping entrepreneurs, individual investors, and venture capitalists connect. They offer a studied account of who angel investors are, how they operate, and the large part they play in the country's economy.

APPENDIX H

SUPPLEMENTARY READING

Aernoudt, R. 1999, April-June. Business angels: should they fly? *Venture Capital,* 187–195.

An angel flexes wings. 1997, October 20. *Electronic Times,* 23.

Angels advance. 1995, November 20. *The Daily Telegraph,* 33.

Angels are no fools but they do rush in. 1998, July 20. *The Daily Telegraph,* 31.

Angels aren't afraid to tread. 1997, February 20. *Commerce Business Magazine.*

Angels fly in with financial support. 1999, February 18. *The Herald* (Glasgow), 29.

Angels have deeper pockets than ever before. 1998, November 2. *The Daily Telegraph* (London), 30.

Angels ... invisible, naturally. 1998, August 8. *The Daily Telegraph,* 29.

Applegate, J. 1997, February 20. Try online angle to meet an "angel." *Chicago Sun-Times,* 42.

Avery, R. B., Bostic, R. W., and K. A. Samolyk. 1998. The evolution of small business finance: the role of personal wealth. *Journal of Banking and Finance* 22: 1019–1061.

Baxter, A. 1999, November 25. Tax cut inspires business angels enterprise zone. *Financial Times* (London), 147.

Becket, M. 2000, February 7. Study shows growth of investment by angels. *The Daily Telegraph* (London), 31.

———. 1996, November 11. Angels rush in but small firms fear to borrow. *The Daily Telegraph* (London), 31.

Bernstein, M. C., and L. Wolosoff. 1999. *Raising capital: the Grant Thornton LLP guide for entrepreneurs.* Chicago: Irwin.

Blakely, S. 1997, April. Finding angels on the Internet. *Nation's Business,* 78.

Brav, A., and P. A. Gompers. 1997. Myth or reality?: Long-run underperformance of initial public offerings; evidence from venture capital and non-venture-capital-backed IPOs. *Journal of Finance,* 52: 1791–1821.

Business angel report. 1997, December 15. *Electronic Times,* 12.

Business angel toy story. 1996, November 22. *Commerce Business Magazine.*

Campbell, K. 1999, September 16. Angels operating a high-risk business. *Financial Times* (London), 16.

———. 1998, July 23. Venturing out with the angels and venture capitalists. *Financial Times* (London), 21.

Carey, M., S. Prowse, J. Rea, and G. F. Udell. 1993. The economics of private placements: A new look. *Financial Markets.*

Casecentral.com secures six million dollars in initial round of funding. 1999, November 1. *PR Newswire.*

Chan, Y. S., D. Siegal, and A. V. Thakor. 1990. Learning, corporate control and performance requirements in venture capital contracts. *International Economic Review* 31: 365–381.

Chen, D. W. 1997, July 2. Now in New York: Angels that rescue new companies. *New York Times,* B5.

Coghlan, A. 1996, August 24. Pennies from heaven. *New Scientist,* 14.

Cornelli, F., and O. Yosha. 1997. Stage financing and the role of convertible debt. Institute of Financing and Accounting WP253. London Business School.

Cullen, L. R. 1996, September 8. When you invest with angels, the portfolio is never boring. *New York Times,* 3,3.

Digital tempest raises $5.7 million for starters. 2000, March 2. *Los Angeles Times,* 4.

Directors and angels invest in future of e-services for small business. 2000, January 25. *Business Wire.*

Dugdale, J. 2000, January 30. *Sunday Times* (London).

Enslin, S. 1999, October 8. Angels play crucial role in rescuing small firms. *Business Day* (South Africa), 17.

Entrepreneurs forgo due diligence on investors in rush to find funding.... 2000, April 3. *M2 Presswire.*

Farleigh, R. 1999, October 7. A fast-thinking angel: Investor profile. *Financial Times* (London), 19.

Fenn, G. W., and N. Liang. 1998, August. New resources and new ideas: Private equity for small businesses. *Journal of Banking and Finance,* 22 (6-8): 1077–1084.

Financial advisors' plans include offroad capital to get clients into private emerging growth companies. 1999, December 16. *Business Wire.*

Flynn, L. J. 1998, July 27. Angels invest in sendmail. *New York Times,* 4.

Forgrieve, J. 2000, March 2. Angels with deep pockets. *Tampa Tribune,* 1.

Freear, J., and W. E. Wetzel Jr. 1990. Who bankrolls high-tech entrepreneurs? *Journal of Business Venturing,* 5, 77–89.

Freear, J., J. E. Sohl, and W. E. Wetzel Jr. 1994. Angels and nonangels. *Journal of Business Venturing,* 9, 109–123.

Freear, J., J. E. Sohl, and W. E. Wetzel Jr. 1994. The private investor market for venture capital. *The Financier* 1, 7–19.

Fried, V. H., and R. D. Hisrich. 1994. Toward a model of venture investment decision making. *Financial Management* 23, 28–37.

Goff, L. 1997, March. Angel investors breed success. *Home Office Computing,* 26.

Gompers, P. 1999. *The venture capital cycle.* Cambridge, MA: MIT Press.

———. 1995. Optimal investment, monitoring, and the staging of venture capital. *Journal of Finance,* 50: 1461–1489.

Gompers, P., and J. Lerner. 1997. The valuation of private equity investments. Working paper. Cambridge, MA: Harvard Business School.

Gompers, P., and J. Lerner. 1996. The use of covenants: An empirical analysis of venture partnership agreements. *Journal of Law and Economics* 39: 463–498.

Gracie, S. 1999, May 9. Private investors help with more than cash. *Sunday Times* (London).

Gupta, A. K., and J. J. Sapienza. 1992. Determinants of capital firms' preference regarding the industry diversity and geographic scope of their investments. *Journal of Business Venturing* 7, 347–362.

Harmon, S. 1999. *Zero gravity: Riding venture capital from high-tech start-up to breakout IPO.* Princeton, NJ: Bloomberg Press.

Harrington, P. 1999, October 19. Where venture capitalists fear to tread. *Seattle Times,* B1.

Hobson, R. 1998, March 3. Financial backers keep a low profile on deals. *The Times.*

Houlder, V. 1996, December 14. On the wings of angels. *Financial Times* (London), 1.

Hovey, J. 2000, January 12. Work the Web for that elusive angel investor. *Los Angeles Times,* 6.

How corporate venture capitalists build bridges with venture capitalists. 2000, April 6. *PR Newswire.*

Kelly, G. 1999, November 14. The angels have landed, investors in start-up companies 'realizing the power they have.' *Denver Rocky Mountain News,* 12G.

Kennickell, A. B., M. Starr-McCluer, and A. E. Sunden. 1997. Family finances in the U.S.: Recent evidence from the survey of consumer finances. *Federal Reserve Bulletin* 83, 1–24.

King, R. 1999. Angels unite. *Tech Capital Venture Financing Special Issue,* Vol. 3, No. 8: 22–31.

Kirlin Holding Corp. raises $7.65 million for start-up subsidiary. 1999, December 8. *PR Newswire.*

Korn, D. J. 1999, November 1. Private equity turns inside out: OffRoad Capital's online private equity marketplace is democratizing the clubby world of venture capital. *Financial Planning.*

Largest U.S. business angel finance publications merge and

relaunch. 1999, June 3. *Business Wire.*

Larson, J. 1998, September 30. Angel financing gains popularity among private investors. *Arizona Republic.*

Lerner, J. 1998, August. "Angel" financing and public policy: An overview. *Journal of Banking and Finance* 22 (6-8): 773–83.

———. 1995. Venture capitalists and the oversight of private firms. *Journal of Finance* 50, 301–318.

———. 1994. The syndication of venture capital investments. *Financial Management* 23: 16–27.

———. 1994. Venture capitalists and the decision to go public. *Journal of Financial Economics,* 293–316.

Levin, J. S. 1998. *Structuring venture capital, private, and entrepreneurial transactions.* New York: Aspen Law & Business.

Liang, N., and S. Prowse. 1997. The private equity market: An overview. *Financial Management, Institutions, and Instruments* 6: 1–106.

Lien, J. 1999, December 16. Angel investor. *Business Times* (Singapore), 30.

Logan, T. M. 1995. Cross-section analysis of the pricing of private equity placements. The Ohio State University.

Loizos, C. 1999, October 25. Know a good thing, put up big bucks in e-launches: Exclusive club hits up angels in the tech field. *Investment News,* 1.

McConnell, I. 1996, November 7. Business angels flock to plug equity gap for Scottish start-ups. *The Herald* (Glasgow), 22.

McCraw, T. K., and J. L. Cruikshank. 1999. *The intellectual venture capitalist: John H. Arthur and the work of the Harvard Business School, 1980–1995.* Boston, MA: Harvard Business School Press.

McNally, Kevin. 1997. *Corporate venture capital: Bridging the equity gap in the small business sector.* London, New York: Routledge.

Mikkelson, W., and M. Partch. 1986. Valuation effects of securities offerings and the issuance process. *Journal of Financial Economics* 15, 31–60.

Mooney, E. V. 1999, June 14. Offroad seeks to partner angel investors and companies via Internet. *RCR Radio Communications Report,* 6.

Mowbray, R. 2000, January 26. Start-up 'angels' taking wing here.

3 Star Edition, Business, 1.

Myers, S. C., and N. C. Majluf. 1984. Corporate financing and investment decisions when firms have information that investors do not have. *Journal of Financial Economics* 13, 187–221.

NetClerk raises $10 million in second round financing. 2000, January 21. *Business Wire.*

News: Venture Capital–Chase teams up with Murdoch and Tahta. 2000, March 1. *European Venture Capital Journal.*

Norton, E., and B. H. Tenenbaum. 1993. Specialization versus diversification as a venture capital investment strategy. *Journal of Business Venturing* 8, 431–442.

NVST technology releases ASP product for angel investor groups. 2000, February 14. *Business Wire.*

NVST.com acquires world's largest angel investor network. 1999, September 14. *Business Wire.*

Off-Road vehicle for private equity. 1999, September. *U.S. Banker*

Ong, C. 1999, November 26. An Internet Age angel who helps start-ups fly. *Business Times,* 8.

———. 1999, November 26. Silicon Valley here? Get market savvy first. *Business Times,* 2.

Onorato, N. R. 1997. *Trends in venture capital funding in the 1990s.* Washington, D.C.: U.S. Small Business Administration, Office of Advocacy.

Poole, S. 1996, October 13. Start-up firm finds salvation from an "angel." *Atlanta Journal and Constitution.*

Price, C. 1996, January 8. Angels may be answers to your prayers. *Denver Rocky Mountain News,* 34A.

Prowse, S. 1998, August. Angel investors and the market for angel investments. *Journal of Banking and Finance* 22 (6-8), 785–92.

RiskWatch grabs angel funding. 2000, February 22. *Newsbytes News Network.*

Rudnick, D. 1996, October 26. Angels tread carefully. *The Times.*

———. 1996, July 7. Under the wings of angels. *The Times.*

Ruhnka, J. C., and J. E. Young. 1991. Some hypotheses about risk in venture capital investing. *Journal of Business Venturing* 6, 115–133.

Sahlman, W. A. 1998. Aspects of financial contracting in venture-capital investment. *Journal of Applied Corporate Finance* 1, 23–26.

Schwab, R. 1999, October 31. Angel investors look out for small start-ups. *Denver Post,* N-04.

Seglin, J. L. 1998, May 19. What angels want. *Inc.,* 43–44.

Sherrid, P. 1997, October 13. Angels of capitalism. *U.S. News and World Report,* 43.

Sing the praises of business angels. 1998, August 9. *Sunday Telegraph,* 4.

Sohl, J. E. 1999, April-June. The early-stage market in the U.S. *Venture Capital,* 101–20.

Soundbreak.com raises $19 million in equity financing. 200, March 8. *PR Newswire.*

Spirrison, J. B. 2000, January 10. Investors serve OpenTable.com with $10M first round financing. *Private Equity Week.*

Star, M. G. 1997, January 6. Private equity's popularity drives up prices. *Pensions and Investments,* 3.

Stewart, C. 1996, February 24. Returns free of tax for angels with big wallets. *The Times.*

Strier, L., and R. Greenwood. 1999, April-June. Newly created firms and informal angel investors: A four-stage model of network development. *Venture Capital,* 147–67.

Surgery breakthrough wins business angel's backing. 1996, November 8. *Commerce Business Magazine.*

Sykes, D. 1999, May. Do angels have wings? *Business Development.*

Temple, P. 1999, September 17. Backers help fledglings try out their wings: early stage investment. *Financial Times* (London), 4.

Texas investors, MoneyHunt pick favorites at the Capital Network's NewMedia. 2000, April 3. *PR Newswire.*

Trapp, R. 1997, November 3. Angels double their investments in start-ups. *The Independent* (London), 19.

———. 1996, November 10. Angels answer the prayers of small business. *The Independent* (London), 8.

Venture capital: Angel at twelve o'clock high. 1999, April 15. *Accounting Age,* 32.

Weisul, K. 1996, November 4. Heavy hitters match equity investors with entrepreneurs. *Investment Dealers' Digest,* 9.

Wetzel Jr., W. E. 1983. Angels and informal risk capital. *Sloan Management Review* 24: 23–24.

Where angels fear not to tread. 1997, October 20. *Electronic Times,* 22.

Wright, M. 2000, January 15. Money-go-round: How Charlotte 'the angel' should invest her fortune. *Daily Telegraph* (London), 3.

Wruck, K. H. 1998. *Private Equity Financing.* (Dissertation) The University of Rochester.

Yu, R. 2000, January 10. Internet catalyst: People with big ideas given chance to stand out in crowd. *Star Tribune* (Minneapolis), 1D.

Zuckerman, S. 2000, February 22. Getting in before the IPO: Web companies make it easier for individuals to invest in private firms, but buyers should be cautious. *San Francisco Chronicle,* E1.

GLOSSARY

Accounts payable. The amount of money owed by a business or service to its creditors.

Accounts receivable. The amount of credit a business or service has extended to its customers.

Accumulated amortization. Accumulated write-off of an intangible asset, such as goodwill or a covenant not to compete.

Acquisition/merger. A venture that is in need of capital to finance an acquisition or merger.

Antidilution. The action investors must take to put in additional money to maintain the percentage of ownership they had when they first invested in the deal.

Automatic conversion. Accomplished at the time of underwriting rather than at the time of an IPO; occurs when an investor's priority shares are immediately converted to ordinary shares.

Board. A corporation's board of directors; persons who for the good of a corporation's shareholders follow—or refuse to follow—the recommendations of management.

Board rights. Allows an investor to become a member of a company's board of directors.

Boilerplate. Standard wording in standard paragraphs contained in business documents.

Breakeven. When the money earned from a business equals the money invested.

Bridge financing. A venture that requires short-term capital to reach stability and the next round of funding.

Burn rate. The rate at which cash is flowing out of the business on a monthly basis.

Business angel. Private individual investors who often add their knowledge and experience to companies they invest in.

Buyback. The exit route whereby the investor expects to cash out by selling securities back to the founders.

Buyout. Investors, management, employees, or any other company personnel buy shares in the company in order to buy or retain ownership.

Capital gains. The profit derived from selling a capital asset.

Capital loss. The loss incurred from selling a capital asset.

Cash flow. The money that comes in and goes out of a business. Cash flow determines the continued survival of a company and is tied closely to cash management.

Collateral. Assets used to guarantee payment to a creditor for money lent.

Controlability. Ownership of enough equity in a company to control the decisions of the management.

Convertible. Bonds that can be exchanged for stock at some previously set rate; convertibles can be a source of cash for a company under financial pressure.

Current ratio. The ratio of current assets to current liabilities. This ratio appears on a balance sheet and specifies a company's liquidity, that is, its ability to meet its short-term obligations. This ratio often helps determine the company's credit rating.

Current return. The agreement struck between entrepreneurs and an investor.

Deal flow. The number of transactions an investor is able to peruse that may be worth further consideration.

Debenture. A corporate bond backed not by a specific asset but by the issuer's credit.

Debt to equity ratio. Ratio of long-term liabilities to net worth. This measures debt financing to equity financing, that is, the degree to which a company is leveraged.

Default. Failure of a borrower to repay a lender in full; or when a provision in a written agreement with an investor is violated by an entrepreneur.

Dilution. Occurs when additional stock is issued, which thereby reduces the percentage of ownership of those who already own stock.

Discount rate. Face value minus discount charge; what banks and other lending institutions charge for money loaned.

Downside. The amount of risk taken by an investor in an enterprise.

Due diligence. The absolutely critical investigation by the investor of the entrepreneur (and by the entrepreneur of the investor) on every aspect of the other party's history, character, and dealings past and present—and of the soundness of the pending deal.

EBIT. Earnings before interest and taxes, or what the company has earned before having to pay interest and taxes.

Equity. The amount of ownership someone has in a company.

Exit. The strategy by which investors realize returns or otherwise free themselves from involvement in a transaction.

Fully diluted ownership. When a company issues all of its shares, their dilutive impact can be measured.

Gross margin percentage. The ratio of gross profit to sales.

Gross margin ratio. The ratio of gross profit to net sales. This assesses the efficiency in cost and pricing strategy.

Holding period. The period of time an investor's investment remains illiquid.

Hurdle. In the investor's judgment, the point at which anticipated compensation exceeds risk in an investment.

Income statement. Probably better known as a profit and loss statement, a report that summarizes a company's income and costs for a specific time period.

Initial public offering (IPO). A company's attempt to sustain growth by raising money on an exchange, such as the New York Stock Exchange.

Intellectual property. The ideas on which a company has been built, which receive only limited protection from patents, trademarks, etc.

Internal rate of return (IRR). Also called the "time-adjusted rate of return"; the rate of interest that equates the value of cash inflows with the value of cash outflows.

Inventory turnover. Costs of sales divided by average inventory. This specifies the company's average inventory cycle, that is, how many times a company's inventory is sold and replenished during a set period.

Investee firm. The firm into which investors have invested their money and the added value of their knowledge, expertise, and experience.

Junior securities. When a firm is liquidated, investors holding junior securities will not have their claims considered until after those holding senior securities have had their claims met.

Lead investor. The investor who takes the lead in inducting other investors into a venture.

Leveraged buyout (LBO). A group of investors that usually includes management acquires the stock/assets of a private company largely through debt financing.

Liquidation. Going out of business; when creditors (including shareholders) take over the assets of a company.

Liquidation preferences. Allows investors on their own to liquidate the company.

Living dead. Financial purgatory, when an investor is stuck in a venture with little or no liquidity.

Mezzanine. A venture that has increasing sales volume and is breaking even or is profitable; additional funds are to be used for further expansion, marketing, or working capital.

Net present value. The measure of assets (in the investment base) based on the discounted cash flow (DFC); future cash flows are discounted to their value now.

Options. Seen as a hedge by some and as a risk by others, the right given to the investor to buy or sell stock in the future at a preset price.

Payback period. How many years it takes for an investor to recoup an initial investment.

Post-money valuation. The dollars invested divided by the percentage of ownership, or the valuation of a company after the investment has been made.

Pre-money valuation. The valuation of a company before investments in it have been made.

Prepaid expenses. Expenses incurred in advance, such as rent or insurance.

Price-earnings ratio. The "P/E ratio" or "multiple": the ratio of current price per share to earnings per share. This is the relationship between the current-market share price of a stock and its earnings; used to determine a share's fair price.

Pricing. The cost a company sets for the customer or client for its product or service.

Profit margin percentage. Net income before taxes divided by net sales. Measures the percentage of sales dollars that result in net income.

Public offering. The extremely complicated act of "going public"; usually used to sustain a company's long-term expansion.

Receivables turnover. Year-end accounts receivable divided by credit sales. This is divided, in turn, by the number of days in the year, used to measure collection problems.

Redeemable shares. Shares that a company can repurchase in the future for an agreed-upon price.

Representations. What the entrepreneur vouches is true about the venture to the investor.

Restricted stock. Stocks that an investor can purchase directly from a company.

Return on equity ratio. The ratio of net income to total shareholder equity, used to measure management's effectiveness.

Return on investment (ROI). The amount of return plus the time an investor deems acceptable in realizing that return on the investment.

Screening. The process by which investors weed out the deals that fail to meet their criteria as they look for those they consider worthy of further investigation.

Second-round financing. The round of financing that follows the initial or start-up round.

Seed stage. A venture in the idea stage or in the process of being organized.

Staging. Rather than an investor handing over the entire investment in the beginning, he or she invests in increments as specified milestones are met by the entrepreneur.

Start-up stage. A venture that is completing product development and initial marketing and has been in business less than two years.

Structure. The way in which a company's financing will be accomplished.

Sweat equity. The time and effort entrepreneurs have previously invested in building a venture.

Syndication. A major hedging strategy by which individual investors form a group and pool the money they invest in a deal, thereby ameliorating financial risk.

Third-round financing. Follows the second round of financing for a start-up.

Treasury stock. Repurchased stock previously owned by shareholders and now held in the company's treasury.

Turnaround. A venture that is in need of capital to effect a change from unprofitability to profitability.

Upside. The potential and often anticipated amount of money investors think they can make on a particular deal.

Valuation. An investor's assessment of the viability and financeability of a venture.

Venture capital. The money raised from investors for equity in early-stage enterprises.

Warranties. Implied or stated in writing that what an entrepreneur tells an investor about a product or service is true.

Warrants. A "right" owned by an investor; a guarantee bought by investors when they think a stock will rise; allow investors to buy stock during a fixed period at a fixed price.

Working capital. Current assets minus current liabilities equals working capital, the net assets used to continue the company's operations.

Workout. A company's rather urgent need for getting itself out of financial difficulty through an additional round of financing, reorganization, or possibly both.

Database systems, 110, 112–113

Datamerge, 113

Dataquest, 113

Deal-flow development strategies

advertising, 112–120

approaches to avoid, 128–129

clubs, 119–120

communicating your preferences, 110–112

computer matching networks, 115–116

elements of, 102–104

forums, networking through, 114–115

goals and objectives, developing, 97–100

historical methods, 95–96

Internet networks, 117

investor identity materials, organizing, 108–110

newsletters, subscribing to, 117–119

public relations strategies, 121–126

referral-based networking, 126–128

shifting from informal to formal, 100–102

targeting, positioning, and defining investment size, 104–107

tracking systems, 108–110

traditional techniques, 95–97

Deal generation, 34–35

Deal-mart meeting, 114–115

Deals, negotiating and structuring, 35

definition of negotiation, 197–198

guidelines for, 201–202

legal documentation, 206–211

market inefficiencies and, 198–199

mistakes made by investors, 199–200

private placements, 202–204, 208

term sheet document for structuring, 211–218

the transaction, 199

valuation and, 227

DEC (Digital Equipment Corp.), 7

Dell Computer Corp., 83

Demographics of angel investors, investment strategies and, 70–72

Dilution

factor, 234–235

term sheet for, 214–215

valuation and, 228–229, 234–235

Dinner Club, 120

Direct investment, 60–63

Directories, use of, 112–113

Discounting projections, valuation and, 231–232

Documentation. *See* Legal documentation

Due diligence, 35, 41, 67

business plan, use of, 146–149

case examples where invest-

About the Authors

Gerald A. Benjamin, M.S., founded the largest nationwide angel investor network, which links almost 10,000 accredited investors with prescreened ventures from across the United States. He is the senior managing partner of International Capital Resources, a capital sourcing firm in San Francisco matching ventures with investors throughout the United States, Canada, and Mexico; chairman of the Northern California Venture Forum; and executive director of the Private Equity Research Institute. Mr. Benjamin has coauthored several books, including two on angel investing, *Finding Your Wings* and *Angel Financing,* and has worked as an entrepreneurial financial adviser for more than twenty-five years.

Joel Margulis is the author of *An Awareness of Language* and has coauthored two books with Gerald Benjamin on angel financing for the entrepreneur. He teaches writing at San Francisco State University.

About Bloomberg

Bloomberg L.P., founded in 1981, is a global information services, news, and media company. Headquartered in New York, the company has nine sales offices, two data centers, and 79 news bureaus worldwide.

Bloomberg, serving customers in 100 countries around the world, holds a unique position within the financial services industry by providing an unparalleled range of features in a single package known as the BLOOMBERG PROFESSIONAL™ service. By addressing the demand for investment performance and efficiency through an exceptional combination of information, analytic, electronic trading, and Straight Through Processing tools, Bloomberg has built a worldwide customer base of corporations, issuers, financial intermediaries, and institutional investors.

BLOOMBERG NEWSˢᴹ, founded in 1990, provides stories and columns on business, general news, politics, and sports to leading newspapers and magazines throughout the world. BLOOMBERG TELEVISION®, a 24-hour business and financial news network, is produced and distributed globally in seven different languages. BLOOMBERG RADIO™ is an international radio network anchored by flagship station BLOOMBERG® WBBR 1130 in New York.

In addition to the BLOOMBERG PRESS® line of books, Bloomberg publishes *BLOOMBERG® MARKETS, BLOOMBERG PERSONAL FINANCE™*, and *BLOOMBERG® WEALTH MANAGER*. To learn more about Bloomberg, call a sales representative:

Frankfurt	49-69-92041-200	São Paulo	5511-3048-4530
Hong Kong	85-2-2977-6600	Singapore	65-212-1200
London	44-20-7330-7500	Sydney	61-2-9777-8601
New York	1-212-318-2200	Tokyo	81-3-3201-8950
San Francisco	1-415-912-2980		

FOR IN-DEPTH MARKET INFORMATION and news, visit BLOOMBERG.COM®, which draws from the news and power of the BLOOMBERG PROFESSIONAL™ service and Bloomberg's host of media products to provide high-quality news and information in multiple languages on stocks, bonds, currencies, and commodities, at **www.bloomberg.com.**